C++ Primer
Answer Book

Clovis L. Tondo

T&T TechWorks, Inc.
Coral Springs, FL

Bruce P. Leung

Connected Components Corporation
Boston, MA

ADDISON–WESLEY

An Imprint of Addison Wesley Longman, Inc.

Reading, Massachusetts • Harlow, England • Menlo Park, California
Berkeley, California • Don Mills, Ontario • Sydney
Bonn • Amsterdam • Tokyo • Mexico City

Exercises from *C++ Primer*, Third Edition, by S. Lippman and J. Lajoie. © 1998 from AT&T, Objectwrite, Inc., and Josée Lajoie. Reprinted by permission of Addison Wesley Longman, Inc.

Many of the designations used by manufacturers and sellers to distinguish their products are claimed as trademarks. Where those designations appear in this book, and Addison Wesley Longman, Inc. was aware of a trademark claim, the designations have been printed in initial capital letters or all capital letters.

The publisher offers discounts on this book when ordered in quantity for special sales. For more information, please contact:

Computer and Engineering Publishing Group
Addison Wesley Longman, Inc.
One Jacob Way
Reading, Massachusetts 01867

Library of Congress Cataloging-in-Publication Data
Tondo, Clovis L.
    C++ primer answer book / Clovis L. Tondo, Bruce P. Leung.
    p.   cm.
  Includes index.
  ISBN 0-201-30993-9
    1. C++ (Computer program language)—Problems, exercises, etc.   I.
Leung, Bruce P.   II. Title.
  QA76.73.C153   T66   1999
  005.13'3—ddc21   98-48504
                                                          CIP

Text printed on recycled paper.

ISBN 0-201-30993-9
1 2 3 4 5 6 7 8 9—MA—0201009998
First printing, December 1998

Contents

Foreword

For more than a decade, readers of *C++ Primer* pursued Stan down conference halls, cornering him in elevators, surrounding him at book signings, and inundating him with e-mail asking where, when, why, and — well then — why aren't the answers to the exercises available?

Well. Hmm. Eyes fixed on his shoelaces. "It's a tradition," he finally answered. "Within Bell Laboratories, I mean. No answers to the exercises. At least, not within the text." Silence. He knew what many people were thinking: yep, Kernighan and Ritchie (K&R) had an answer book. So did Bjarne. "Well. Hey." (Diffident shrug.) Stan never dreamed he'd ever see an independent answer book for the *Primer*.

Well, that was then. Now with great satisfaction — voilà — we introduce *C++ Primer Answer Book*!

The involvement of Clovis Tondo is something of a tradition for both *C++ Primer* and *Inside the Object Model*. He first reviewed the *Primer* in 1986 during an early draft of the first edition; his comments were both helpful and encouraging. (The value of encouragement for a newbie author should not be underestimated!) He followed that up with an excellent critique of the second edition as well as many helpful comments and encouragement on *Inside the Object Model*. (Hey, the value of encouragement for a veteran author should not be underestimated!) Finally, as a reviewer of the third edition, he provided an exceptionally in-depth reading.

When it was suggested to us that Dr. Tondo, together with Bruce Leung, might author an answer book for the third edition, it felt like a perfect fit, as if he had been preparing for just this book these past ten years. Of course, he had done *The C Answer Book* for the K&R text as well, so this makes for a second tradition. It's one that we are thrilled to be a part of.

The exercises within *C++ Primer* are intended (a) to reinforce the key elements of the material presented within the preceding section, (b) to provide a concrete set of design and programming tasks to allow the reader to exercise his or her new-won expertise, and in some few occasions (c) to provoke consideration of C++ as a language invention in which theoretical concerns at times take a back seat to practical considerations. These latter exercises do not call so much for an answer as a more or less well-articulated position.

Are all the exercises we presented in the *Primer* absolutely the best we could have done? Reading through the answers presented here, it is clear that a small number of the exercises could have undergone some revision. And so we appreciate the forbearance of the authors.

In one case, we accidentally requested that an OrQuery binary operator be derived from an abstract UnaryOperator class. Sorry! Stan was sure he wrote NotQuery! That was certainly the class he intended to have revised.

C++ Primer Answer Book, then, can be grouped into two primary categories. The first is answers to the exercises in which an item is either correct or incorrect. This material provides a useful summary of the salient points of each section in addition to providing the solutions. The second category covers solutions to the design and programming tasks. These are our favorites, in general, perhaps because they offer the most surprises. After all, we know category 1 pretty well. This latter category allowed the authors to exercise their expertise. The programs in Chapters 6, 12, and 17 are particularly impressive.

We think you'll both enjoy and learn from *C++ Primer Answer Book.* And we extend a warm thanks to the two authors for their work.

Stanley B. Lippman
Josée Lajoie

Preface

C++ has proven to be a popular programming language, and *C++ Primer* has proven to be just as popular among those wishing to learn the language. Learning a programming language, however, requires more than just reading about the language constructs. You must program, write your own code, and study code written by those who are more experienced with the use of the language.

To this end, Lippman and Lajoie (L&L) have provided exercises throughout *C++ Primer* to encourage their readers to test their understanding of the material. Our book provides the solutions to those exercises.

C++ Primer Answer Book is intended to be used in conjunction with *C++ Primer*. We assume that you have read the material in L&L preceding each exercise. We present our solution along with an explanation, but we do not repeat the material found in L&L. Only those concepts and constructs that have already been introduced are used in the solutions.

When the solution involves a complete program, we generally include the entire source code so that each solution stands on its own. All programs have been compiled using Microsoft Visual C++ Version 5.0. In some instances when the compiler did not meet the standard, a workaround was used and an explanation given.

We recommend that you use L&L to learn C++, work the exercises, and study the solutions presented here. We hope *C++ Answer Book* will aid you in understanding C++ while eliminating the frustration of being stuck without an answer to a problem.

Acknowledgments

Special thanks go to Stan Lippman and Josée Lajoie for having the faith to allow us to write this answer book and for their careful review of the text.

Sean Davey, Steve Edwards, S. Rollins Guild, Cay Horstmann, and Jeffrey Oldham provided many helpful comments on the manuscript.

Clovis thanks George Edmunds, Sam Hsu, Mohammad Ilyas, Mahesh Neelakanta, and Cyril Párkányi for their continued support; Sean Davey for the C++ review, for the LaTeX macros, and for his technical support; Andrew Nathanson for his friendship and software/hardware support; S. Rollins Guild for the C++ review and his friendship; A. Carlos

Tondo, Julia Mistrello, and Luiz and Elizabete T. Biavatti for helping our company succeed; and Caren E. Tondo for her love, patience, and sense of humor.

Bruce thanks Andrew Bellezza, Jodi Solomon, and Mary Walstrom for their friendship and encouragement; Zahira Ammarguellat, Luddy Harrison, Sandra Loosemore, and Cotton Seed — one couldn't ask for better co-workers; and Misty and Buddy for their boundless patience.

Last, but certainly not least, we thank the staff at Addison-Wesley. We are especially grateful to our associate editor, Debbie Lafferty, for her patience and knowing when and how hard to push; the production editor, Maureen Willard, for guiding us through the editing, proofs, and final pages; the production manager, John Fuller, for getting the macros approved and improved early in the process; and the freelancer, Diane Freed, for assisting with the production of this book. We appreciate your kind help.

Clovis L. Tondo
Bruce P. Leung

chapter one

Getting Started

Chapter 1 of the C++ *Primer* does not contain any exercises.

chapter two

A Tour of C++

Exercise 2.1

Why do you think the built-in array does not support the assignment of one array with another? What information is required to support this operation?

The name of a built-in array is a synonym for an address, so assigning one array to another is similar to assigning the constant 5 to the constant 3. This is syntactically correct but semantically generates an error message.

The language was not designed to handle array assignments. The compiler would have to know the length of the arrays at run-time to generate code to support the assignment of one array with another.

Exercise 2.2

What operations should a first class array support?

"Although C++ provides built-in support for an array type, that support is limited to the mechanics required to read and write individual elements. C++ does not support the *abstraction* of an array; there is no support for the operations one might wish to perform on an array, such as the assignment of one array to another, the comparison of two arrays for equality, or asking an array its size" (L&L, page 26). That is, a first class array support should allow us to treat the array as a unit as well as allow us to access the individual elements of the array.

The operations that a first class array should support include

- Array initialization

- Array assignment

- Comparison of arrays

- Array size

- Index range check

Exercise 2.3

Explain the difference between the four objects defined below.
```
(a) int ival = 1024;   (c) int *pi2 = new int( 1024 );
(b) int *pi = &ival;   (d) int *pi3 = new int[ 1024 ];
```

(a) `int ival = 1024;`

   The object `ival` has static or automatic memory allocation. The declaration "instructs the compiler to allocate sufficient storage to hold any value of type `int`, associate the name `ival` with that storage, and then place an initial value of 1024 in that storage" (L&L, page 27).

(b) `int *pi = &ival;`

   The object `pi` has a pointer type that may hold the memory address of an `int`. The *address-of* operator (`&`) returns the address of the `int` object `ival`. So `pi` is a pointer to an `int`, and it has been initialized with the address of the `int` object `ival`.

(c) `int *pi2 = new int( 1024 );`

   The object `pi2` has a pointer type that may hold the memory address of an `int`. The `new` expression allocates a single unnamed object of type `int`, initializes that object to a value of 1024, and then returns the address of the object in memory, and `pi2` is initialized with that address.

(d) `int *pi3 = new int[ 1024 ];`

   The object `pi3` has a pointer type that may hold the memory address of an `int`. The `new` expression allocates an array of 1024 integer elements (it does not initialize the elements of the array) and then returns the address of the first element of the array in memory, and `pi3` is initialized with that address.

   The object `ival` is of type `int` and may hold any positive or negative integer value that can be contained in the underlying machine support of an `int`. So (a) holds a value, whereas the others ((b), (c), and (d)) are pointers that hold addresses.

Exercise 2.4

What does the following code fragment do? What is its significant error? (Note that the use of the subscript operator with the pointer `pia`, below, is correct; the reason we can do this is explained in Section 3.9.2.)
```
int *pi = new int( 10 );
int *pia = new int[ 10 ];
```

```
while ( *pi < 10 ) {
    pia[ *pi ] = *pi;
    *pi = *pi + 1;
}
delete pi;
delete [] pia;
```

The preceding code fragment attempts to initialize the array of ints that pia points to. pi points to an unnamed int object initially set to 10. The test expression in the while loop compares the object that pi points to against 10 and executes the body of the loop as long as the object has a value less than 10. The problem is that the test will fail the first time, and the body of the loop will not be executed at all. One possible way to fix the initialization of the array that pia points to is

```
int *pi = new int( 10 );
int *pia = new int[ 10 ];
int i = 0;

while ( i < 10 ) {
    pia[ i ] = *pi;
    i++;
}
```

The remainder of the code fragment correctly deallocates the unnamed int object that pi points to and then deallocates the array of ints that pia points to.

Exercise 2.5

The key feature of a C++ class is the separation of interface and implementation. The interface is the set of operations that users can apply to objects of the class. It consists of three parts: the name of the operations, their return values, and their parameter lists. Generally, that is all the user of the class is required to know. The private implementation consists of the algorithms and data necessary to support the public interface. Ideally, even though the class interface may grow, it does not change in ways incompatible with earlier versions during the lifetime of the class. The implementation, on the other hand, is free to evolve over the lifetime of the class. Choose one of the following abstractions and write the public interface for that class:

```
(a) Matrix      (c) Person      (e) Pointer
(b) Boolean     (d) Date        (f) Point
```

(a) Matrix

```
class Matrix {
   public:
```

```
                                    // default constructor
        Matrix( int = defaultRowSize,
                int = defaultColumnSize );
        Matrix( const Matrix & );      // copy constructor
        ~Matrix();                     // destructor
                                       // copy assignment operator
        Matrix &operator=( const Matrix & );
                                       // equality operator
        bool operator==( const Matrix & ) const;
                                       // inequality operator
        bool operator!=( const Matrix & ) const;
                                       // indexing operators
        int &operator()( int, int );
        int operator()( int, int ) const;
        int getRowSize() const;        // number of rows
        int getColumnSize() const;     // number of columns
                                       // iostream output operator
        friend ostream &operator<<( ostream &, const Matrix & );
                                       // iostream input operator
        friend istream &operator>>( istream &, Matrix & );
    private:
        int **im;                      // implementation...
        int rows;                      // how many rows
        int cols;                      // how many columns
        static const int defaultRowSize = 5;
        static const int defaultColumnSize = 5;
    };
```

For the class Matrix we provided two constructors:

1.   The default constructor Matrix() (see L&L, page 698)

2.   A copy constructor that expects another Matrix object as its argument (see L&L, page 700)

Destructors, unlike constructors, cannot take any argument. So we can create a single destructor for Matrix.

We provided a copy assignment operator

```
    Matrix &operator=( const Matrix & );
```

and equality and inequality operators

```
    bool operator==( const Matrix & ) const;
    bool operator!=( const Matrix & ) const;
```

(see L&L, page 738). We also provided Fortran-style index operators

```
    int &operator()( int, int );
    int operator()( int, int ) const;
```
and iostream output and input operators:
```
    friend ostream &operator<<( ostream &, const Matrix & );
    friend ostream &operator>>( ostream &, Matrix & );
```
   L&L have not yet discussed `friend` functions, but we included the `<<` and `>>` operators to obtain a reasonably complete interface. See Section 13.5 in L&L.

Exercise 2.6

The words *constructor* and *destructor* are somewhat misleading in that these programmer-supplied functions neither construct nor destroy the objects of the class to which they are applied by the compiler automatically. When we write
```
    int main() {
        IntArray myArray( 1024 );
        // ...
        return 0;
    }
```
the memory necessary to maintain the data members of `myArray` is allocated prior to application of the constructor. The compiler, in effect, internally transforms our program as follows (note that this is not legal C++ code):
```
    int main() {
        IntArray myArray;

        // Pseudo C++ Code -- apply constructor
        myArray.IntArray::IntArray( 1024 );
        // ...
        // Pseudo C++ Code -- apply destructor
        myArray.IntArray::~IntArray();

        return 0;
    }
```
The constructors of a class serve primarily to initialize the data members of the class object. The destructor primarily frees any resources acquired by the class object during its lifetime. Define the set of constructors needed by the class you chose in Exercise 2.5. Does your class require a destructor?

   The constructors are
```
    Matrix( int = defaultRowSize, // default constructor
            int = defaultColumnSize );
    Matrix( int, int, int * );    // constructor
    Matrix( const Matrix & );     // copy constructor
```

See L&L, page 698, for a discussion of default constructors. On page 700, L&L address copy constructors. We added the other constructor to be able to initialize a Matrix with an array of ints (see Exercise 2.7).

We have a destructor because Matrix has a data member that is a pointer. Remember that if a class needs a copy constructor, a copy assignment operator, or a destructor, the class needs them all. And a class needs them all if the class has at least one pointer that addresses heap memory allocated within the class constructor and that must be freed by the destructor.

Exercise 2.7

In Exercises 2.5 and 2.6, you have specified nearly the complete public interface necessary for use of the class. (We may still need to define a copy assignment operator, but we'll ignore that fact for now — C++ provides default support for the assignment of one class object with another. The problem is that this default behavior is often inadequate. See Section 14.6 for a discussion.) Write a program to exercise the public interface of the class you defined in the two previous exercises. Is it easy or awkward to use? Do you wish to revise the specification? Can you do that and maintain compatibility?

When we implemented the class we added two private init() functions.

```
class Matrix {
  public:
                                 // default constructor
    Matrix(int = defaultRowSize,
           int = defaultColumnSize);
    Matrix(int, int, int *);     // constructor
    Matrix(const Matrix &);      // copy constructor
    ~Matrix();                   // destructor
                                 // assignment operator
    Matrix &operator =(const Matrix &);
    int &operator()(int, int);
    const int &operator()(int, int) const;
    friend ostream &operator <<(ostream &, const Matrix &);
  private:
    int **im;                    // implementation...
    int rows;                    // how many rows
    int cols;                    // how many columns
    static const int defaultRowSize;
    static const int defaultColumnSize;
    void initMatrix(int *);      // init with a row
    void initMatrix(int **);     // init with a matrix
    void initData(int r, int c);
};
```

Here is the default constructor:

```
Matrix::Matrix(int r, int c)
{
    initData(r, c);
    initMatrix(static_cast<int *>(0));
}
```

See L&L, page 181, for a discussion of static_cast<>.
   Here is the second constructor:

```
Matrix::Matrix(int r, int c, int *array)
{
    initData(r, c);
    initMatrix(array);
}
```

Here is the copy constructor:

```
Matrix::Matrix(const Matrix &rhs)
{
    initData(rhs.rows, rhs.cols);
    initMatrix(rhs.im);
}
```

The two private member functions initMatrix() are similar:

```
void Matrix::initMatrix(int *array)
{
    for (int i = 0; i < rows; ++i)
        for (int j = 0; j < cols; ++j)
            if (array)
                im[i][j] = *array++;
            else
                im[i][j] = 0;
}
```

```
void Matrix::initMatrix(int **matrix)
{
    for (int i = 0; i < rows; ++i)
        for (int j = 0; j < cols; ++j)
            im[i][j] = matrix[i][j];
}
```

The private member function initData() is called from the constructors:

```
void Matrix::initData(int r, int c)
{
    rows = r;
    cols = c;
```

```
        im = new int *[rows];
        for (int i = 0; i < rows; ++i)
            im[i] = new int[cols];
    }
```

Here is the destructor:

```
    Matrix::~Matrix()
    {
        for (int i = 0; i < rows; ++i)
            delete [] im[i];
        delete [] im;
    }
```

Here is the copy assignment operator:

```
    Matrix &Matrix::operator =(const Matrix &rhs)
    {
        if (this != &rhs) {
            if (rows != rhs.rows || cols != rhs.cols) {
                Matrix::~Matrix();  // deallocate old matrix
                initData(rhs.rows, rhs.cols);
            }
            initMatrix(rhs.im);
        }
        return *this;
    }
```

We provided a Fortran-like indexed access to Matrix:

```
    int &Matrix::operator ()(int r, int c)
    {
        assert(r >= 0 && r < rows && c >= 0 && c < cols);
        return im[r][c];
    }

    const int &Matrix::operator ()(int r, int c) const
    {
        assert(r >= 0 && r < rows && c >= 0 && c < cols);
        return im[r][c];
    }
```

Exercise 2.8

A type/subtype inheritance relationship in general reflects an *is-a* relationship: a range-checking ArrayRC **is a kind of** Array, a Book **is a kind of** LibraryRentalMaterial, an AudioBook **is a kind of** Book, **and so on. Which of the following pairs reflect an is-a relationship?**

(a) member function isA_kindOf function
(b) member function isA_kindOf class
(c) constructor isA_kindOf member function
(d) airplane isA_kindOf vehicle
(e) motor isA_kindOf truck
(f) circle isA_kindOf geometry
(g) square isA_kindOf rectangle
(h) automobile isA_kindOf airplane
(i) borrower isA_kindOf library

Pairs that reflect an is-a relationship: (a), (c), (d), and (g).

Exercise 2.9

Identify which of the following operations are likely to be type-dependent and therefore candidates to be made virtual functions, and which can either be shared among all classes or are likely unique to a single base or derived class.

(a) rotate();   (b) print();
(c) size();   (d) dateBorrowed();
(e) rewind();   (f) borrower();
(g) is_late();   (h) is_on_loan();

Possible virtual functions: (a), (b), and (e).
Possible functions that can be shared among all classes: (c).
Possible functions that are likely to be unique to a single class: (d), (f), (g), and (h).

Items (d), (f), (g), and (h) refer to materials that are lent by a library. (g) may be a virtual function if each material lent has a different algorithm. (d), (f), and (h) can be factored into an abstract class (the parent class for lent materials). Items (a), (b), (c), and (e) may refer to geometric shapes. Because each geometric shape may be rotated, printed, and rewound differently, (a), (b), and (e) were selected as virtual functions.

Exercise 2.10

There has been some controversy as to the use of the protected access level. Some people argue that the use of the protected access level to allow derived classes direct access to base class members violates the notion of encapsulation and therefore that all base class implementation details should be private. Others argue that without direct access to the base class members, the implementation of the derived class cannot be made sufficiently efficient to be of use and without the `protected` keyword the class designer would be forced to make the base class members public. What do you think?

The protected access level provides access to protected information in the base class. Yes, it violates encapsulation because the information in the base class is not hidden from derived classes, although it is hidden from the rest of the program. It is a matter of efficiency. We do not want the data members in the base class to be `public`, and we do not want the derived classes to access `private` data members through `get()` and `set()` kinds of functions. So the protected access level provides a good compromise between pure encapsulation and efficiency.

Exercise 2.11

A second controversy has to do with the need to explicitly declare a member function virtual. Some people argue that this means that if a class designer fails to recognize a function as needing to be virtual, the derived class designer is helpless to override the necessary function. They recommend making all member functions virtual. On the other hand, virtual functions are less efficient than nonvirtual functions. Because they cannot be inlined (inlining occurs at compile-time, virtual functions are resolved at run-time), they can be a source of run-time program inefficiency, particularly for small, frequently invoked type-independent functions such as the size of our `Array`. Again, what do you think?

Presumably, class designers can anticipate which functions will have different behavior and will be overridden in derived classes. If a class designer fails to recognize such a need, the designer of the derived class is up the proverbial creek without a paddle and without a virtual function. If a class has at least one virtual function, each object of that class type will have a virtual pointer (`vptr`) to a virtual table (`vtbl`) that contains the addresses of the virtual functions for the class (one `vptr` per object and one `vtbl` per class). To make all the member functions virtual can be inefficient because of the dynamic dispatch costs for all the methods. Another point is that virtual functions are not inlined. It brings us back to efficiency: we declare virtual only those functions that must be virtual and, consequently, can be overridden in derived classes.

Exercise 2.12

Each of the following abstractions implicitly consists of a family of abstract subtypes. For example, a `LibraryRentalMaterial` abstraction implicitly contains `Books`, `Puppets`, `Videos`, and so on. Choose one of the following and (1) identify a hierarchy of subtypes for that abstraction, (2) specify a small public interface for that hierarchy, including constructors, (3) identify which, if any, functions are virtual, and (4) write a small pseudocode program to exercise the public interface.

(a) `Points`	(b) `Employees`
(c) `Shapes`	(d) `TelephoneNumbers`
(e) `BankAccounts`	(f) `CourseOfferings`

Let's use Shapes.

(1)   Identify a hierarchy of subtypes for that abstraction.

-   Shapes is the base class.

-   Derived classes could include Rectangle, Circle, and Square.

-   The class Square is a subtype derived from Rectangle because a square is a special kind of rectangle.

(2)   Specify a small public interface for that hierarchy, including constructors.

-   Public interface for Shapes:
```
class Shapes {
  public:
    Shapes();
    virtual ~Shapes();
    virtual void draw();
    virtual void rotate( float );
  protected:
    // ...
};
```

-   Public interface for Rectangle:
```
class Rectangle::public Shapes {
  public:
    Rectangle( float width, float height );
    Rectangle( const Rectangle & );
    virtual ~Rectangle();
    Rectangle &operator=( const Rectangle & );
    virtual void draw();
    virtual void rotate( float );
  protected:
    // ...
};
```

-   Public interface for Circle:
```
class Circle::public Shapes {
  public:
    Circle( float radius );
    Circle( const Circle & );
    virtual ~Circle();
    Circle &operator=( const Circle & );
    virtual void draw();
    virtual void rotate( float );
  protected:
    // ...
};
```

- Public interface for Square:

```
class Square::public Rectangle {
  public:
    Square( float side );
    Square( const Square & );
    virtual ~Square();
    Square &operator=( const Square & );
    virtual void draw();
    virtual void rotate( float );
  protected:
    // ...
};
```

(3) Identify which, if any, functions are virtual.

- The virtual functions are preceded by the keyword `virtual`.

- `virtual` functions, such as `draw()` and `rotate()` in the class Shapes, are virtual for the rest of the inheritance tree; consequently, `draw()` and `rotate()` do not have to be declared virtual in the derived classes, but it helps to repeat the keyword `virtual` in the derived classes — it makes things clear for somebody looking only at the derived classes.

- See Chapter 17 in L&L for an explanation of virtual destructors.

(4) Write a small pseudocode program to exercise the public interface.

```
Shapes *ps;                    // pointer to Shapes
ps = new Rectangle;            // point to a Rectangle
ps->draw();                    // draw the Rectangle
ps->rotate(90.);               // rotate 90 degrees
Shapes *qs = new Rectangle;
*qs = *ps;                     // copy the Rectangle
qs->draw();                    // draw the copy
delete ps;                     // delete Rectangle
delete qs;                     // delete the copy
```

Exercise 2.13

Given the following type declarations

```
template <class elemType> class Array;
enum Status { ... };
typedef string *Pstring;
```

which, if any, of the following object definitions are in error?

```
(a) Array< int*& > pri( 1024 );
(b) Array< Array< int > > aai( 1024 );
(c) Array< complex< double > > acd( 1024 );
(d) Array< Status > as( 1024 );
(e) Array< Pstring > aps( 1024);
```

(a) `Array< int*& > pri( 1024 );`

The type `int *&` is a reference to a pointer. References must be initialized when they are defined. The `Array` template does not provide a way to initialize the elements that `pri` points to, so the object definition is in error.

(b) `Array< Array< int > > aai( 1024 );`

The object `aai` is an `Array` of `Array`s of `int`s.

(c) `Array< complex< double > > acd( 1024 );`

The object `acd` is an `Array` of `complex` numbers in which the members are of type `double`.

(d) `Array< Status > as( 1024 );`

The object `as` is an `Array` of enumerators of type `Status`.

(e) `Array< Pstring > aps( 1024);`

The object `aps` is an `Array` of pointers to `string`.

Exercise 2.14

Rewrite the following class definition to make it a class template:

```
class example1 {
  public:
    example1(double min, double max);
    example1(const double *array, int size);

    double &operator[](int index);
    bool operator ==(const example1 &) const;

    bool insert(const double *, int);
    bool insert(double);

    double min() const { return _min; }
    double max() const { return _max; }

    void min(double);
    void max(double);

    int count(double value) const;
```

```
    private:
      int size;
      double *parray;
      double _min;
      double _max;
  };
```

Here's the class template:

```
    template <class elemType >
    class example1 {
      public:
        example1(const elemType &min,
                   const elemType &max);
        example1(const elemType *array, int size);

        elemType &operator [](int index);
        bool operator ==(const example1 &) const;

        bool insert(const elemType *, int);
        bool insert(const elemType &);

        elemType min() const { return _min; }
        elemType max() const { return _max; }

        void min(const elemType &);
        void max(const elemType &);

        int count(const elemType &value) const;

      private:
        int size;
        elemType *parray;
        elemType _min;
        elemType _max;
  };
```

  The constructors

```
    example1( double min, double max );
    example1( const double *array, int size );
```

change to

```
    example1( const elemType &min,
               const elemType &max );
    example1( const elemType *array, int size );
```

or

```
example1< elemType >( const elemType &min,
                      const elemType &max );
example1< elemType >( const elemType *array, int size );
```

because the incoming arguments change from double to elemType. The name of the constructors become example1< elemType > to allow the compiler to create a constructor specific for type elemType.

The operator

```
double &operator[]( int index );
```

has a return type of elemType instead of double.

```
elemType &operator[]( int index );
```

The other member functions change similarly.

The data members of type double change to elemType. size remains int.

Note that the original method

```
void min( double );
```

became

```
void min( const elemType & );
```

Why not change it to

```
void min( elemType );
```

instead? Because it is common and acceptable to pass built-in types by value, but we should avoid passing objects by value. If we passed an elemType object by value, the compiler would invoke a copy constructor to make a copy of the object and then pass the copy by value (L&L, page 37). Consequently, we pass the argument by const reference (L&L, pages 38 and 105).

Exercise 2.15

Given the following class template

```
template < class elemType >
class Example2 {
  public:
    Example2(elemType val = 0)
         : _val(val) { }
    boolean min(elemType value) {
         return _val < value ? True : False; }
    void value(elemType new_val) { _val = new_val; }
    void print(ostream &os) const { os << _val; }
```

```
    private:
        elemType _val;
    };
    template < class elemType >
    ostream &operator <<(ostream &os, const Example2<elemType> &x)
                { x.print(os); return os; }
```

what happens when we write the following?

  (a) Example2< Array< int >* > ex1;
  (b) ex1.min(&ex1);
  (c) Example2< int > sa(1024), sb;
  (d) sa = sb;
  (e) Example2< string > exs("Walden");
  (f) cout << "exs: " << exs << endl;

(a) Example2< Array< int >* > ex1;
    ex1 is an Example2 object that manages a pointer to an Array of ints.

(b) ex1.min(&ex1);
    It will not compile because we do not have a mechanism to convert Example2 < Array < int >* > to Array< int > *, which is the type of the second argument to min().

(c) Example2< int > sa(1024), sb;
    sa and sb are Example2 objects of type int. sa is initialized with 1024, and sb is initialized with the default value of zero.

(d) sa = sb;
    sa gets a copy of sb.

(e) Example2< string > exs("Walden");
    exs is an Example2 object of type string that has been initialized to "Walden".

(f) cout << "exs: " << exs << endl;
  This prints

```
    exs: Walden
```

Exercise 2.16

In our definition of Example2, **we write**

```
    explicit Example2( elemType val = 0 )
            : _val( val ) { }
```

The intention is to specify a default value so that a user can write either

```
Example2< Type > ex1( value );
Example2< Type > ex2;
```

However, our implementation constrains Type to be the subset of Types that can legally be initialized with a value of 0. (For example, initializing a string object with a value of 0 is an error.) In a similar manner, if Type does not support the output operator, an invocation of print() (and therefore of the Example2 output operator) fails. If Type does not support the less-than operator, an invocation of min() fails.

The language provides no means of indicating implicit constraints on the Type that a template can be instantiated with. The programmer discovers these constraints, in the worst case, when a program fails to compile. Do you think the language should support a Type-constraint syntax? If so, indicate the syntax, and rewrite the Example2 definition to use it. If you do not, explain why.

The language should not support a Type-constraint syntax. There are three reasons.

- It would complicate templates.

- The user can always verify that the Type provides the methods necessary to instantiate the template; if they are missing, the compiler produces an error message with the instantiation of a particular method that contains an implicit constraint (instead of producing an error message at the instantiation of the template).

- See the idiom that appears as a footnote to Exercise 2.16 in L&L.

Exercise 2.17

In the previous exercise, we say that if Type does not support either the output or the less-than operator, an attempt to invoke either print() or min() generates an error. In Standard C++, the errors are generated not when the class template is created but rather when (and therefore if) the print() or min() function is invoked. Do you think this is the correct language semantics? Should the error be flagged at the point of template definition? Why or why not?

This is the correct language semantics. The alternative is to have the language check all possible uses of a template when the class template is created, a practice that could become expensive at compilation time. The drawback of this semantics is that the instantiation of the template with one type might work in one program but fail in another depending on which functions are invoked.

Exercise 2.18

The following function provides absolutely no checking of either possible bad data or the possible failure of an operation. Identify all the things that might possibly go wrong

within the function (in this exercise, we don't yet want to worry about possible exception raised).

```
int *alloc_and_init(string file_name)
{
    ifstream infile(file_name.c_str());
    int elem_cnt;
    infile >> elem_cnt;

    int *pi = allocate_array(elem_cnt);

    int elem;
    int index = 0;
    while (cin >> elem)
        pi[ index++ ] = elem;

    sort_array(pi, elem_cnt);
    register_data(pi);

    return pi;
}
```

The following things might possibly go wrong within the function.

- `file_name` could be an empty `string`.

- The `ifstream` constructor may not be able to open the file even if `file_name` is a valid `string`.

- The file may not contain an `int` value at its beginning.

- `elem_cnt` receives an incorrect value: too large, zero, or a negative value.

- `allocate_array()` fails to allocate space for `elem_cnt` elements.

- The `while` loop reads too many elements; the loop depends on encountering EOF (or failing to read an `int`) to terminate the loop, and it does not take into account the size of the array that `pi` points to.

- `sort_array()` will sort the array that `pi` points to that supposedly contains `elem_cnt` items; the `while` loop may have terminated before `elem_cnt` items were read because the number of `int`s in the input was insufficient, and the remainder of the array will be uninitialized.

- `sort_array()` may receive an invalid pointer `pi` because there was no check against the return value from `allocate_array()`; this error may cause the program to crash in the `while` loop.

Exercise 2.19

The following functions invoked in `alloc_and_init()` raise the following exception types if they should fail:

```
allocate_array()      noMem
sort_array()          int
register_data()       string
```

Insert one or more `try` blocks and associated `catch` clauses where appropriate to handle these exceptions. Simply print the occurrence of the error within the `catch` clause.

```cpp
int *alloc_and_init(string file_name)
{
    ifstream infile(file_name.c_str());
    int elem_cnt;
    infile >> elem_cnt;

    try {
        int *pi = allocate_array(elem_cnt);

        int elem;
        int index = 0;
        while (cin >> elem)
            pi[ index++ ] = elem;

        sort_array(pi, elem_cnt);
        register_data(pi);
        return pi;
    }
    catch(const noMem &n) {
        cout << "allocate_array() error " << n << endl;
    }
    catch(int i) {
        cout << "sort_array() error " << i << endl;
    }
    catch(const string &s) {
        cout << "register_data() error " << s << endl;
    }
}
```

Exercise 2.20

Go through the set of conditions identified as potential program failures within `alloc_and_init()` in Exercise 2.18, identifying those serious enough to warrant throwing an exception. Revise the function (either the Exercise 2.18 version or preferably the

Exercise 2.19 version if you did that one) to throw the identified exceptions (throwing literal strings for now is good enough).

```cpp
int *alloc_and_init(string file_name)
{
    try {
        ifstream infile(file_name.c_str());
        if (!infile)
            throw "cannot open file";
        int elem_cnt;
        infile >> elem_cnt;
        if (!infile || elem_cnt <= 0)
            throw "invalid elem_cnt";

        int *pi = allocate_array(elem_cnt);

        int elem;
        int index = 0;
        while (cin >> elem) {
            if (index >= elem_cnt)
                throw "too many input elements";
            pi[ index++ ] = elem;
        }

        sort_array(pi, index);
        register_data(pi);
        return pi;
    }

    catch(const noMem &n) {
        cout << "allocate_array() error " << n << endl;
        throw;  // rethrow the exception to notify user
    }
    catch(int i) {
        cout << "sort_array() error " << i << endl;
        throw;
    }
    catch(const string &s) {
        cout << "register_data() error " << s << endl;
        throw;
    }
    catch(const char *s) {
        cout << "error: " << s << endl;
        throw;
    }
}
```

Exercise 2.21

Given the following namespace definition

```
namespace Exercise {
    template <class elemType>
        class Array { ... };

    template <class Etype>
        void print( Array< Etype > );

    class String;
    template <class listType>
        class List { ... };
}
```

and the following program

```
int main()
{
    const int size = 1024;
    Array< String > as( size );
    List< int > il( size );

    // ...

    Array< String > *pas = new Array< String >( as );
    List< int > *pil = new List< int >( il );

    print( *pas );
}
```

the current program implementation fails to compile because the type names are all encapsulated within the namespace. Modify the program to

    a.   Use the qualified name notation to access the type definitions within the Exercise namespace.

    b.   Use the using declaration to access the type definitions.

    c.   Use the namespace alias mechanism.

    d.   Use the using directive.

    a.   Use the qualified name notation to access the type definitions within the Exercise namespace.

```
int main()
{
    // using the 'qualified name notation'

    const int size = 1024;
    Exercise::Array< Exercise::String > as(size);
    Exercise::List< int > il(size);

    // ...

    Exercise::Array< Exercise::String > *pas =
        new Exercise::Array< Exercise::String >(as);
    Exercise::List< int > *pil = new Exercise::List< int >(il);

    Exercise::print(*pas);
}
```

b.   Use the using declaration to access the type definitions.

```
int main()
{
    // using the 'using declaration'

    using Exercise::String;
    using Exercise::Array;
    using Exercise::print;
    using Exercise::List;

    const int size = 1024;
    Array< String > as(size);
    List< int > il(size);

    // ...

    Array< String > *pas = new Array< String >(as);
    List< int > *pil = new List< int >(il);

    print(*pas);
}
```

c.   Use the namespace alias mechanism.

```
int main()
{
    // using namespace alias
```

```
        namespace E = Exercise;

        const int size = 1024;
        E::Array< E::String > as(size);
        E::List< int > il(size);

        // ...

        E::Array< E::String > *pas = new E::Array< E::String >(as);
        E::List< int > *pil = new E::List< int >(il);

        E::print(*pas);
    }
```

d.   Use the using directive.

```
    int main()
    {
        // using the 'using directive'

        using namespace Exercise;

        const int size = 1024;
        Array< String > as(size);
        List< int > il(size);

        // ...

        Array< String > *pas = new Array< String >(as);
        List< int > *pil = new List< int >(il);

        print(*pas);
    }
```

Exercise 2.22

Explain the results of each vector definition:

```
    string pals[] = { "pooh", "tigger", "piglet",
                      "eeyore", "kanga" };

    (a) vector< string > svec1( pals, pals+5 );
    (b) vector< int > ivec1( 10 );
    (c) vector< int > ivec2( 10, 10 );
    (d) vector< string > svec2( svec1 );
    (e) vector< double > dvec;
```

(a) vector< string > svec1(pals, pals+5);
   svec1 is a vector of strings that has been initialized with a copy of the array of strings pals.

(b) vector< int > ivec1(10);
   ivec1 is a vector of 10 ints, each initialized with the value 0.

(c) vector< int > ivec2(10, 10);
   ivec2 is a vector of 10 ints, each initialized with the value 10.

(d) vector< string > svec2(svec1);
   svec2 is a vector that is a copy of the vector svec1.

(e) vector< double > dvec;
   dvec is an empty vector of doubles.

Exercise 2.23

Given the following function declaration, implement the body of min() to find and return the smallest element of vec using a for loop indexing into vec and then a for loop using an iterator to traverse vec:

```
template <class elemType>
elemType min( const vector< elemType > &vec );
```

Here is the complete program:

```
#include      <iostream>
#include      <vector>

using namespace std;

template <class elemType>
elemType min1(const vector< elemType > &vec)
{
    elemType minimum;
    if (vec.size() >= 1)
        minimum = vec[0];
    else
        throw "Empty vector - index";
    for (int i = 1; i < vec.size(); i++)
        if (vec[i] < minimum)
            minimum = vec[i];
    return minimum;
}
```

```
template <class elemType>
elemType min2(const vector< elemType > &vec)
{
    vector< elemType >::const_iterator iter = vec.begin();
    elemType minimum;
    if (iter < vec.end())
        minimum = *iter;
    else
        throw "Empty vector - iterator";
    for (++iter; iter < vec.end(); ++iter)
        if (*iter < minimum)
            minimum = *iter;
    return minimum;
}

int main()
{
    int array[] = { 9, 4, 5, 6, 1, 3, 7, 8, 2, 0 };
    vector< int > a(array, array+10);

    cout << "should be 0: " << min1(a) << endl;
    cout << "should be 0: " << min2(a) << endl;

    vector< int > b(array, array+9);

    cout << "should be 1: " << min1(b) << endl;
    cout << "should be 1: " << min2(b) << endl;

    vector< int > c;

    try {
        cout << "should be 1: " << min1(c) << endl;
        cout << "should be 1: " << min2(c) << endl;
    }
    catch (char *s) {
        cerr << "Exception: " << s << endl;
    }

    return 0;
}
```

The functions min1() and min2() are similar. Both use a for loop, and they throw an exception when the vector is empty. min1() uses an index

```
for (int i = 1; i < vec.size(); i++)
    if (vec[i] < minimum)
        minimum = vec[i];
```

and min2() uses an iterator. The incoming argument is a const vector < elemType > &vec, so we cannot use the regular iterator that we have seen so far. Instead, we must use a const_iterator (see L&L, Section 12.4):

```
for (++iter; iter < vec.end(); ++iter)
        if (*iter < minimum)
            minimum = *iter;
```

We use the dereference operator * to access the data in the vector.

The main program initializes the vector a with the array array:

```
int array[] = { 9, 4, 5, 6, 1, 3, 7, 8, 2, 0 };
vector< int > a( array, array+10 );
```

Then it invokes the functions min1() and min2(), obtaining the same result in both cases. We also tried a vector b with the first nine elements of array, and we exercised the exception handling mechanism with an empty vector c.

chapter three

The C++ Data Types

Exercise 3.1

Explain the difference between the following sets of literal constants:

```
(a) 'a', L'a', "a", L"a"
(b) 10, 10u, 10L, 10uL, 012, 0xA
(c) 3.14, 3.14f, 3.14L
```

(a) 'a', L'a', "a", L"a"

The literal constant 'a' represents the single character a and has type char. L'a' + also represents the single character a but has type wchar_t because the leading L designates a wide-character literal.

The literals "a" and L"a" are strings that represent the single character a followed by the null character or null wide character, respectively. "a" is of type *array of const characters* and L"a" is of type *array of const wide characters*.

(b) 10, 10u, 10L, 10uL, 012, 0xA

All these represent integer constants with a decimal value of 10. The constants 10, 012, and 0xA all have type int because they have no modifiers. The leading 0 of 012 tells us that the literal is an octal constant, whereas the leading 0x of 0xA indicates a hexadecimal constant.

10u has type unsigned int, 10L has type long, and 10uL has type unsigned long.

(c) 3.14, 3.14f, 3.14L

These are floating point literal constants that differ in type. The unmodified constant 3.14 has type double by default. 3.14f indicates a single-precision float, and 3.14L designates an extended precision value.

Exercise 3.2

Which, if any, of the following are illegal?

    (a) `"Who goes with F\144rgus?\014"`
    (b) `3.14e1L`
    (c) `"two" L"some"`
    (d) `1024f`
    (e) `3.14UL`
    (f) `"multiple line`
         `comment"`

(c) is not illegal, but the result is undefined because "there is no standard behavior defined for concatenating the two different types" (L&L, page 78).

(e) and (f) are illegal. `3.14UL` is illegal because of the `U` (unsigned) designation on a floating point literal. The string constant in (f) requires a backslash at the end of the first line to allow continuation to the next line.

    (f) `"multiple line \`
         `comment"`

Or the strings can be made adjacent strings.

    (f) `"multiple line "`
         `"comment"`

Exercise 3.3

Which, if any, of the following are illegal definitions? Correct any that are identified as illegal.

    (a) `int car = 1024, auto = 2048;`
    (b) `int ival = ival;`
    (c) `int ival( int() );`
    (d) `double salary = wage = 9999.99;`
    (e) `cin >> int input_value;`

    (d) and (e) are illegal.

(d) `double salary = wage = 9999.99;`
   Here, `wage` is used but not defined. One possible fix is to define and initialize the two variables separately.
   `double salary = 9999.99, wage = 9999.99;`

(e) `cin >> int input_value;`
   This use of `cin` is not allowed as a form of initialization in a variable definition. The correct way is to define the variable and then read a value into it:
     `int input_value;`
     `cin >> input_value;`

Exercise 3.4

Distinguish between an lvalue and rvalue. Provide examples of both.

A variable's lvalue is its address value or the expression referring to the object's location in memory. A variable's rvalue is its data value. See L&L, Section 3.2.1.

A variable's identifier on the left-hand side of an assignment operator is an example of an lvalue. An identifier or literal constant on the right-hand side of an assignment is an rvalue, as in the following statement:

```
ivar = val + 2;
```

Here, ivar is an lvalue, and val and 2 are examples of rvalues.

Exercise 3.5

Explain the difference between the following two instances of students **and** name**:**

```
(a) extern string name;
    string name( "exercise 3.5a" );
```

```
(b) extern vector<string> students;
    vector<string> students;
```

Here are the answers:

```
(a) extern string name;
    string name( "exercise 3.5a" );
```

The first instance, extern string name;, is a *declaration* of name and makes known the type (string) of the object referred to by the identifier name. There is no allocation of storage.

The second instance, string name("exercise 3.5a");, is a *definition* and makes known the type (string) of the object referred to by name and causes storage to be allocated and initialized to the given string constant.

```
(b) extern vector<string> students;
    vector<string> students;
```

The first instance is a declaration of students and makes known the type (vector of strings) but does not allocate any storage.

The second instance is a definition and makes known the type (vector of strings) of the object referred to by students. It causes storage to be allocated and initialized by the default constructor for vector. The default constructor for string is not called because the vector is empty.

Exercise 3.6

Which, if any, of the following names are invalid? Correct each identified invalid name.

```
(a) int double = 3.14159;       (b) vector< int > _;
(c) string namespace;           (d) string catch-22;
(e) char 1_or_2 = '1';          (f) float Float = 3.14f;
```

See the rules for a legal identifier in L&L, page 83.

(a), (c), (d), and (e) are invalid.

(a) and (c) are invalid because they attempt to use reserved keywords (`double` and `namespace`) as identifiers.

(d) contains an invalid hyphen, and (e)'s identifier starts with a numeral.

Possible corrections:

```
(a) double pi = 3.14159;
(c) string namespace_string;
(d) string catch_22;
(e) char one_or_two = '1';
(e) char _1_or_2 = '1';    // another alternative
```

Exercise 3.7

What are the differences, if any, between the following global and local object definitions?

```
    string global_class;
    int global_int;

    int main() {
        int local_int;
        string local_class;

        // ...
    }
```

Both of the `string` objects will be initialized via the default constructor for the `string` class.

`global_int` will be initialized to zero, whereas `local_int` will be left uninitialized with an undefined value.

Global variables and objects can be accessed by other functions; local ones are visible only in the block where they are defined. See L&L, Section 3.2.3.

Exercise 3.8

Given the following definitions

```
int ival = 1024, ival2 = 2048;
int *pi1 = &ival, *pi2 = &ival2, **pi3 = 0;
```

explain what is occurring in the following assignments. Identify which, if any, are in error.

```
(a) ival = *pi3;      (e) pi1 = *pi3;
(b) *pi2 = *pi3;      (f) ival = *pi1;
(c) ival = pi2;       (g) pi1 = ival;
(d) pi2 = *pi1;       (h) pi3 = &pi2;
```

(a) ival = *pi3;

   This statement is an error because it attempts to assign an int * value to an int object. Another error: pi3 is a pointer to a pointer that is set to zero. It is a run-time error to dereference a null pointer.

(b) *pi2 = *pi3;

   This statement is also an error for the same reason as (a).

(c) ival = pi2;

   Again, an attempt to assign an int * value to an int object is an error.

(d) pi2 = *pi1;

   This statement is an error because it assigns an int value to an int * object.

(e) pi1 = *pi3;

   Here, pi1 is assigned the contents of pi3. The assignment is legal. If pi3 were not assigned to point to a valid address, the run-time behavior would be undefined.

(f) ival = *pi1;

   Because (e) will fail at run-time, pi1 will not be properly initialized. It is an error to dereference a pointer that has not been correctly initialized.

   If we assume that the original definitions hold prior to this statement, this assignment sets ival to itself. pi1 is initialized to the address of ival, so the dereference yields the contents of ival, which are then assigned to ival.

(g) pi1 = ival;

   This is an error because pi1 is type int * and ival is type int.

(h) pi3 = &pi2;

   This is correct because pi3 is type int **, pi2 is type int *, and thus &pi2 is type int **.

Exercise 3.9

Pointers are an important aspect of C and C++ programming and yet are a common source of program error. For example,

```
pi = &ival2;
pi = pi + 1024;
```

is almost guaranteed to leave `pi` addressing a random area of memory. What is the assignment doing, and when would it not be an error?

   The assignment is advancing the pointer pi by 1,024 positions. If pi is a pointer to int, this is 4,096 bytes with 32-bit ints. This would not be an error if pi initially pointed into an array of suitable size and ival2 were a reference into such an array.

Exercise 3.10

Similarly, the behavior of the following small program is undefined and likely to fail at run-time:

```
int foobar( int *pi ) {
    *pi = 1024;
    return *pi;
}

int main()
{
    int *pi2 = 0;
    int ival = foobar( pi2 );
    return 0;
}
```

What is going on here that is a problem? How might you fix it?

   The problem here is that the definition of pi2 does not point to allocated storage, but foobar() attempts to write into memory pointed to by its argument. In this case, pi2 is initialized to zero, so foobar() will try to write the value 1024 into memory location zero. Unless a pointer is assigned an actual value, the run-time behavior is undefined.

   Here is a possible fix.

```
int foobar( int *pi ) {
    if (pi) {
        *pi = 1024;
        return *pi;
```

```
        } else {
            return 0;
        }
    }

    int main()
    {
        int ival2 = 0;
        int ival = foobar( &ival2 );
        return 0;
    }
```

Instead of defining a pointer to int, we define an integer object ival2 and pass its address to foobar(). The real fix to the problem is the test of pi in foobar(). One cannot presume that the pointer is set but rather must test it.

Exercise 3.11

In the previous two exercises, errors occur because of an absence of run-time checking of the use of a pointer. If pointers play such a prominent part in C++ programming, why do you think there is not more safety built into the use of pointers? Can you think of any general guidelines for making the use of pointers safer?

Because pointers play such a prominent role, any run-time checking of pointers could create an unacceptable performance penalty. Compile-time checking of pointers is very difficult, because it is often impossible to determine what values they will have at run-time.

Some guidelines for pointer use include always initializing pointers and not subverting compiler errors or warnings with explicit casts to pointer variables.

Exercise 3.12

Which, if any, of the following are in error?

```
    (a) char ch = "The long, winding road";
    (b) int ival = &ch;
    (c) char *pc = &ival;
    (d) string st( &ch );
```

```
    (e) pc = 0;          (i) pc = '0';
    (f) st = pc;         (j) st = &ival;
    (g) ch = pc[0];      (k) ch = *pc;
    (h) pc = st;         (l) *pc = ival;
```

(a) char ch = "The long, winding road";
This is incorrect because ch is a single char but is initialized to a string.

(b) int ival = &ch;
(c) char *pc = &ival;

Both of these are incorrect because they attempt to initialize variables with incompatible values: int with char *, and char * with int *, respectively.

(d) string st(&ch);
This is syntactically correct. If ch is not correctly initialized, st may yield unexpected results. Another point: the string(const char *) constructor expects a null-terminated char array.

(e) pc = 0;
OK.

(f) st = pc;
This statement is syntactically correct. The run-time result depends on the value of pc.

(g) ch = pc[0];
This statement is syntactically correct. The run-time result depends on the value of pc.

(h) pc = st;
(i) pc = '0';

Both of these are incorrect because there are no implicit conversions from either string or const char to char *.

(j) st = &ival;
This too is incorrect because there is not an acceptable conversion from int * to string.

(k) ch = *pc;
This statement is syntactically correct. The run-time result depends on the value of pc.

(l) *pc = ival;
This assignment assigns an int value to a char. Overflow is possible in the assignment. The run-time result depends on the values of ival and pc.

Exercise 3.13

Explain the difference between the following two while loops:

```
while ( st++ )
    ++cnt;

while ( *st++ )
    ++cnt;
```

The first while loop will continue to increment cnt until the value of st is zero. Assuming that st does not start at zero, this will not occur until the value of st overflows the size of st.

The second while loop will increment cnt until the value pointed to by st is zero. Assuming that st points to a C-style string, this will occur at the end of the string.

Exercise 3.14

Consider the following two semantically equivalent programs, one using C-style character strings and the other using the string type.

```
// ***** C-style character string implementation *****

#include <iostream.h>
#include <string.h>

int main()
{
    int errors = 0;
    const char *pc = "a very long literal string";

    for (int ix = 0; ix < 1000000; ++ix)
    {
        int len = strlen(pc);
        char *pc2 = new char[len+1];
        strcpy( pc2, pc );

        if (strcmp(pc2, pc))
            ++errors;

        delete [] pc2;
    }
    cout << "C-style character strings: "
        << errors << " errors occurred.\n";
    return 0;
}

// ***** string implementation *****

#include <iostream>
#include <string>

using namespace std;
```

```
int main()
{
    int errors = 0;
    string str("a very long literal string");

    for (int ix = 0; ix < 1000000; ++ix)
    {
        int len = str.size();
        string str2 = str;

        if (str != str2)
            ++errors;
    }
    cout << "string class: "
         << errors << " errors occurred.\n";
    return 0;
}
```

(a) Explain what the programs do.
(b) As it happens, on average, the string class implementation executes twice as fast as
the C-style string class. The relative execution times under the UNIX `timex` command
are as follows:

```
    user        0.96    # string class
    user        1.98    # C-style character string
```

Did you expect that? How would you account for it?

  These programs loop 1,000,000 times, allocating, copying, comparing, and deallocating
a string. First, a base string is initialized outside the loop. Inside the loop, the program
determines the length of the base string. In the C-style version this value is used to allocate
a new array of char, and the base string is copied into this array. The class version defines
and initializes a new string in one statement. Next, the base string is compared with the new
string. If they differ, an error counter is incremented. Finally, the C-style version explicitly
frees the storage for the new string whereas the class version relies on the class destructor.
  The primary reason the class implementation takes less time is that the length of the string
is stored as a member of the class. When the C-style version calls `strlen`, the entire string
must be traversed to find the length. (Note: On our system the class implementation is
slower than the C-style version. In other systems `string` uses reference counting, and it is
therefore faster.)

Exercise 3.15

The C++ string type is an example of an object-based class abstraction. Is there anything
you would change about its use or set of operations as presented in this section? Are
there any additional operations you believe necessary? Useful? Explain.

Some additional operations that might be useful are those that operate on substrings. The ability to search for substrings within a string, replace occurrences of substrings or patterns, and copy, compare, or concatenate portions of a string would all be useful.

Other operations could include changing to upper/lowercase, atoi(), and atof().

Exercise 3.16

Explain the meaning of the following five definitions. Identify any illegal definitions.

(a) `int i;`
(b) `const int ic;`
(c) `const int *pic;`
(d) `int *const cpi;`
(e) `const int *const cpic;`

(a) `int i;`
An object of type `int` that can be modified.

(b) `const int ic;`
A constant object of type `int` that cannot be modified.

(c) `const int *pic;`
`pic` is a pointer to an object of type `int` defined as `const`. `pic` can be modified, but the object it points to cannot be modified.

(d) `int *const cpi;`
`cpi` is a constant pointer to an object of type `int`. `cpi` cannot be modified, but the object it points to can be modified.

(e) `const int *const cpic;`
`cpic` is a constant pointer to an object of type `int` defined as `const`. Neither `cpic` nor the object it points to can be modified.

(b), (d), and (e) are illegal definitions because constant objects must be initialized when they are defined. Any attempts to modify a constant object in a later statement will cause an error.

Exercise 3.17

Which of the following initializations are legal? Explain why.

(a) `int i = -1;`
(b) `const int ic = i;`
(c) `const int *pic = &ic;`
(d) `int *const cpi = &ic;`
(e) `const int *const cpic = &ic;`

(a) `int i = -1;`
   Legal. `i` is not constant and is initialized to the integer value −1.

(b) `const int ic = i;`
   Legal. `ic` is constant and is initialized to the value of `i`. It cannot be modified after this initial definition.

(c) `const int *pic = &ic;`
   Legal. `pic` is a pointer to an `int` defined as `const`. `pic` can be modified, but the object it points to must be `const int`. Because `ic` is so defined, this initialization is legal.

(d) `int *const cpi = &ic;`
   Illegal. `cpi` is a constant pointer to `int`, but `ic` is a `const int`.

(e) `const int *const cpic = &ic;`
   Legal. Here, `cpic` is a constant pointer to `const int` and `ic` is of type `const int`. Neither `cpic` nor the object it points to, `ic`, can be modified.

Exercise 3.18

Based on the definitions in the previous exercise, which of the following assignments are legal? Explain why.

(a) `i = ic;`	(d) `pic = cpic;`
(b) `pic = &ic;`	(e) `cpic = &ic;`
(c) `cpi = pic;`	(f) `ic = *cpic;`

(a) `i = ic;`
   Legal. `i` is not constant, so it can be modified.

(b) `pic = &ic;`
   Legal. `pic` is not constant, so it can be modified but the object it points to must be of type `const int`.

(c) `cpi = pic;`
   Illegal. `cpi` is constant, so it cannot be modified.

(d) `pic = cpic;`
   Legal. `pic` is not constant, so it can be modified but the object it points to must be of type `const int`.

(e) `cpic = &ic;`
   Illegal. `cpic` is constant, so it cannot be modified.

(f) `ic = *cpic;`
   Illegal. `ic` is constant, so it cannot be modified.

Exercise 3.19

Which of the following definitions, if any, are invalid? Why? How would you correct them?

```
(a) int ival = 1.01;          (b) int &rval1 = 1.01;
(c) int &rval2 = ival;        (d) int &rval3 = &ival;
(e) int *pi = &ival;          (f) int &rval4 = pi;
(g) int &rval5 = *pi;         (h) int &*prval1 = pi;
(i) const int &ival = 1;      (j) const int &*prval2 = &ival;
```

```
(b) int &rval1 = 1.01;
```
Invalid. A const reference is required for a literal constant. A possible correction is
```
    const int &rval1 = 1.01;
```

```
(d) int &rval3 = &ival;
```
Invalid. rval3 is of type int and not int *. Two possible corrections are
```
    int &rval3 = ival;
```
or
```
    int *const &rval3 = &ival;
```

```
(f) int &rval4 = pi;
```
Invalid. rval4 is of type int and not int *. A possible correction is
```
    int *const &rval4 = pi;
```

```
(h) int &*prval1 = pi;
```
Invalid. A pointer to reference is illegal. A possible correction is
```
    int *&prval1 = pi;
```

```
(j) const int &*prval2 = &ival;
```
Invalid. A pointer to reference is illegal. A possible correction is
```
    int *const &prval2 = &ival;
```

Exercise 3.20

Given the definitions above, which, if any, of the following assignments are invalid?

```
(a) rval1 = 3.14159;
(b) prval1 = prval2;
(c) prval2 = rval1;
(d) *prval2 = ival2;
```

All the assignments are invalid.

(a) rval1 = 3.14159;

Invalid because a const reference is required for a literal constant.

(b) prval1 = prval2;

Invalid because both prval1 and prval2 are pointers to references. That is illegal.

(c) prval2 = rval1;

Invalid because prval2 is a pointer to a reference. That is illegal.

(d) *prval2 = ival2;

Invalid because prval2 is a pointer to a reference. That is illegal.

Exercise 3.21

What are the differences among the definitions in (a) and between the assignments in (b)? Which, if any, are illegal?

```
(a) int ival = 1024;
    const int *pi = 0;
    const int &ri = 0;

(b) pi = &ival;
    ri = &ival;
    pi = &rval;
```

The first statement is correct: it assigns the address of ival to the pointer pi.

The second statement is incorrect because we cannot convert int * (the address of ival) to const int (the reference ri is of type const int).

The last statement is incorrect because rval is not defined.

Exercise 3.22

Which of the following array definitions are illegal? Explain why.

```
    int get_size();
    int buf_size = 1024;

(a) int ia[ buf_size ];
(b) int ia[ get_size() ];
(c) int ia[ 4 * 7 - 14 ];
(d) int ia[ 2 * 7 - 14 ];
(e) char st[ 11 ] = "fundamental";
```

(a) `int ia[ buf_size ];`
Illegal because buf_size is not a const.

(b) `int ia[ get_size() ];`
Illegal. get_size() is not a constant expression.

(d) `int ia[ 2 * 7 - 14 ];`
Illegal. It is an error to allocate an array of size 0.

(e) `char st[ 11 ] = "fundamental";`
Illegal. Not enough space was allowed for the initialization string. One more element is needed to store the end of string character '\0'.

Exercise 3.23

This code fragment intends to initialize each array element with the value of its index. It contains a number of indexing errors. Identify them.

```
int main() {
    const int array_size = 10;
    int ia[ array_size ];

    for (int ix = 1; ix <= array_size; ++ix )
        ia[ ix ] = ix;

    // ...
}
```

Arrays are indexed starting from zero. Thus, the elements in ia are indexed from 0 to 9. In this code fragment the for loop runs from 1 to 10. Here is a corrected version:

```
int main() {
    const int array_size = 10;
    int ia[ array_size ];

    for (int ix = 0; ix < array_size; ++ix )
        ia[ ix ] = ix;

    // ...
}
```

Exercise 3.24

Which, if any, of the following vector definitions are in error?

```
int ia[ 7 ] = { 0, 1, 1, 2, 3, 5, 8 };

    (a) vector< vector< int > > ivec;
    (b) vector< int > ivec = { 0, 1, 1, 2, 3, 5, 8 };
    (c) vector< int > ivec( ia, ia+7 );
    (d) vector< string > svec = ivec;
    (e) vector< string > svec( 10, string("null") );
```

(a) vector< vector< int > > ivec;
  Correct.

(b) vector< int > ivec = { 0, 1, 1, 2, 3, 5, 8 };
  Incorrect. This form of initialization cannot be used with a vector object.

(c) vector< int > ivec(ia, ia+7);
  Correct.

(d) vector< string > svec = ivec;
  Incorrect. There is no conversion from a vector of int to a vector of string.

(e) vector< string > svec(10, string("null"));
  Correct.

Exercise 3.25

Given the following function declaration
```
    bool is_equal( const int* ia, int ia_size, const vector<int> &ivec);
```
implement the following behavior: if the two containers are of different sizes, compare only the elements of the size common to both. As soon as an element is not equal, return false. **If all the elements compared are equal, then, of course, return** true. **Iterate across the vector using an iterator — follow the example in this section as a model. Write a** main() **function to exercise** is_equal().

We keep an index, i, into the array as well as using an iterator for the vector. If we reach the end of the vector, the for loop will end and we return true. If the end of the array is reached, we break out of the loop early. (We could also return true; instead of using break;.) If an inequality is found, we return false immediately and do not complete the loop.

```
    bool is_equal(const int* ia, int ia_size, const vector<int> &ivec)
    {
        int i = 0;

        for (vector<int>::const_iterator it = ivec.begin();
                it != ivec.end(); ++it) {
```

```
        // if we reach the end of the array, don't go on
        if (i == ia_size)
            break;

        // if we find an inequality return immediately
        if (ia[i++] != *it)
            return false;
    }
    return true;
}
```

Here is our test program.

```
int main()
{
    const int asize = 7;

    int ia6eq[6] = { 0, 1, 1, 2, 3, 5 };
    int ia6ne[6] = { 0, 1, 1, 3, 3, 5 };
    int ia8eq[8] = { 0, 1, 1, 2, 3, 5, 8, 13 };
    int ia8ne[8] = { 0, 1, 1, 2, 3, 5, 9, 13 };
    int iane[asize] = { 1, 1, 1, 2, 3, 5, 8 };
    int ia[asize] = { 0, 1, 1, 2, 3, 5, 8 };

    vector<int> ivec(ia, ia+asize);

    cout << "is_equal(ia6eq, 6, ivec): ";
    if (is_equal(ia6eq, 6, ivec))
        cout << "equal\n";
    else
        cout << "not equal\n";

    cout << "is_equal(ia6ne, 6, ivec): ";
    if (is_equal(ia6ne, 6, ivec))
        cout << "equal\n";
    else
        cout << "not equal\n";

    cout << "is_equal(ia8eq, 8, ivec): ";
    if (is_equal(ia8eq, 8, ivec))
        cout << "equal\n";
    else
        cout << "not equal\n";
```

```
    cout << "is_equal(ia8ne, 8, ivec): ";
    if (is_equal(ia8ne, 8, ivec))
        cout << "equal\n";
    else
        cout << "not equal\n";

    cout << "is_equal(ia, asize, ivec): ";
    if (is_equal(ia, asize, ivec))
        cout << "equal\n";
    else
        cout << "not equal\n";

    cout << "is_equal(iane, asize, ivec): ";
    if (is_equal(iane, asize, ivec))
        cout << "equal\n";
    else
        cout << "not equal\n";

    return 0;
}
```

Exercise 3.26

There is a great deal of duplicated code in the implementation of the constructors and assignment operators of the String class. Using the model presented in Section 2.3, try to factor the common code into a separate private member function. Reimplement the constructors and assignment operators to make use of it. Rerun the program to make sure it still works.

We see that the duplicated code involves the initialization of _size and _string. We factor this code into two private overloaded member functions init() and place the appropriate calls in the constructors and assignment operators.

First, we add declarations for the new functions in the private section of the String class.

```
    private:
        int  _size;
        char *_string;

        void init(const char*);
        void init(const String&);
```

The common initialization code is placed in the two new functions.

```
inline void
String::init(const char *s)
{
    if (!s) {
        _size = 0;
        _string = 0;
    } else {
        _size = strlen(s);
        _string = new char[_size+1];
        strcpy(_string, s);
    }
}

inline void
String::init(const String &rhs)
{
    _size = rhs._size;
    if (!rhs._string)
        _string = 0;
    else {
        _string = new char[_size+1];
        strcpy(_string, rhs._string);
    }
}
```

We modify the constructors to call init().

```
inline String::String()
{
    init(0);
}

inline String::String(const char *s)
{
    init(s);
}

inline String::String(const String &rhs)
{
    init(rhs);
}
```

The assignment operators are similarly modified.

```
inline String&
String::operator=(const char *s)
{
    delete [] _string;
    init(s);

    return *this;
}

inline String&
String::operator=(const String &rhs)
{
    if (this != &rhs) {
        delete [] _string;
        init(rhs);
    }
    return *this;
}
```

Exercise 3.27

Modify the program to count the consonants b,d,f,s, **and** t **as well.**

The changes are straightforward. We add counters for the new letters.

```
bCnt = 0, dCnt = 0, fCnt = 0, sCnt = 0, tCnt = 0
```

Inside the switch statement we add new cases for the consonants we want to count. We still need to increment notVowel for each of the consonants.

```
case 'b': case 'B': ++bCnt; ++notVowel; break;
case 'd': case 'D': ++dCnt; ++notVowel; break;
case 'f': case 'F': ++fCnt; ++notVowel; break;
case 's': case 'S': ++sCnt; ++notVowel; break;
case 't': case 'T': ++tCnt; ++notVowel; break;
```

Finally, we modify the output to display the counts for the consonants we counted. Here is the complete program.

```
#include "string.h"

int main()
{
    int aCnt = 0, eCnt = 0, iCnt = 0, oCnt = 0, uCnt = 0,
        bCnt = 0, dCnt = 0, fCnt = 0, sCnt = 0, tCnt = 0,
        theCnt = 0, itCnt = 0, wdCnt = 0, notVowel = 0;
    String buf, the("the"), it("it");
```

```
        while (cin >> buf) {
            ++wdCnt;
            cout << buf << ' ';
            if (wdCnt % 12 == 0)
                cout << endl;
            if (buf == the || buf == "The")
                ++theCnt;
            else if (buf == it || buf == "It")
                ++itCnt;
            for (int ix = 0; ix < buf.size(); ++ix) {
                switch (buf[ix]) {
                case 'a': case 'A': ++aCnt; break;
                case 'e': case 'E': ++eCnt; break;
                case 'i': case 'I': ++iCnt; break;
                case 'o': case 'O': ++oCnt; break;
                case 'u': case 'U': ++uCnt; break;
                case 'b': case 'B': ++bCnt; ++notVowel; break;
                case 'd': case 'D': ++dCnt; ++notVowel; break;
                case 'f': case 'F': ++fCnt; ++notVowel; break;
                case 's': case 'S': ++sCnt; ++notVowel; break;
                case 't': case 'T': ++tCnt; ++notVowel; break;
                default: ++notVowel; break;
                }
            }
        }
        cout << "\n\n"
            << "Words read: " << wdCnt << "\n\n"
            << "the/The: " << theCnt << "\n"
            << "it/It: " << itCnt << "\n\n"
            << "non-vowels read: " << notVowel << "\n\n"
            << "a: " << aCnt << "\n"
            << "e: " << eCnt << "\n"
            << "i: " << iCnt << "\n"
            << "o: " << oCnt << "\n"
            << "u: " << uCnt << "\n\n"
            << "b: " << bCnt << "\n"
            << "d: " << dCnt << "\n"
            << "f: " << fCnt << "\n"
            << "s: " << sCnt << "\n"
            << "t: " << tCnt << endl;
        return 0;
    }
```

Exercise 3.28

Implement a member function to count the occurrence of a character in a String. Its declaration is as follows:

```
class String {
public:
    // ...
    int count( char ch ) const;
    // ...
};
```

Here is the implementation:

```
inline int
String::count(char ch) const
{
    int chCnt = 0;

    for (int ix = 0; ix < _size; ++ix)
        if (_string[ix] == ch) ++chCnt;

    return chCnt;
}
```

We modified our original program to test the new routine. This is a very inefficient way to count vowels, but it does allow us to compare the results with the original results.

```
#include "string.h"

int main()
{
    int aCnt = 0, eCnt = 0, iCnt = 0, oCnt = 0, uCnt = 0,
        theCnt = 0, itCnt = 0, wdCnt = 0;

    String buf, the("the"), it("it");

    while (cin >> buf) {
        ++wdCnt;

        cout << buf << ' ';

        if (wdCnt % 12 == 0)
            cout << endl;
```

```
            if (buf == the || buf == "The")
                ++theCnt;
            else if (buf == it || buf == "It")
                ++itCnt;


            aCnt += buf.count('a');
            aCnt += buf.count('A');
            eCnt += buf.count('e');
            eCnt += buf.count('E');
            iCnt += buf.count('i');
            iCnt += buf.count('I');
            oCnt += buf.count('o');
            oCnt += buf.count('O');
            uCnt += buf.count('u');
            uCnt += buf.count('U');
        }


        cout << "\n\n"
            << "Words read: " << wdCnt << "\n\n"
            << "the/The: " << theCnt << "\n"
            << "it/It: " << itCnt << "\n\n"
            << "a: " << aCnt << "\n"
            << "e: " << eCnt << "\n"
            << "i: " << iCnt << "\n"
            << "o: " << oCnt << "\n"
            << "u: " << uCnt << endl;


        return 0;
    }
```

Exercise 3.29

Implement a member operator function to concatenate one String with another, returning
a new String. Its declaration is as follows:

```
class String {
public:
    // ...
    String operator+( const String &rhs ) const;
    // ...
};
```

Here is our new function:

```
inline String
String::operator+(const String &rhs) const
{
    String newString;

    if (!rhs._string)
        newString = *this;
    else if (!_string)
        newString = rhs;
    else {
        newString._size = _size + rhs._size;
        newString._string = new char[newString._size+1];
        strcpy(newString._string, _string);
        strcat(newString._string, rhs._string);
    }

    return newString;
}
```

We first check whether either string is the empty string. If it is, we return a copy of the non-empty string. If both are empty we return a new copy of an empty string.

If both operands are non-empty strings, we calculate the new size

```
    newString._size = _size + rhs._size;
```

and allocate memory for the new string.

```
    newString._string = new char[newString._size+1];
```

Using the C Standard library functions, we copy the first string

```
    strcpy(newString._string, _string);
```

and then concatenate the second.

```
    strcat(newString._string, rhs._string);
```

Finally, the new string is returned.

Here is a small test program.

```
    #include "string.h"

    int main()
    {
        String empty;
        String str1("The cow ");
        String str2("jumped over the moon.");
        String str3 = str1 + str2;
```

```
        cout << "String 1: |" << str1 << "|\n";
        cout << "String 2: |" << str2 << "|\n";

        // test concatenation of empty string
        str3 = str3 + empty;
        str3 = empty + str3;

        cout << "String 1 + String 2: |" << str3 << "|\n";

        return 0;
}
```

chapter four

Expressions

Exercise 4.1

What is the primary difference between the following two division expressions?

```
double dval1 = 10.0, dval2 = 3.0;
int ival1 = 10, ival2 = 3;

dval1 / dval2;
ival1 / ival2;
```

The expression

```
dval1 / dval2;
```

is a floating point division because the operands are of type `double`. The result is the `double` value 3.33333. . . .

The expression

```
ival1 / ival2;
```

is an integer division because the operands are of type `int`. The result is the `int` value 3.

Exercise 4.2

Given an integral object, what operator might we use to determine whether it is even or odd? Write the expression.

```
i % 2 == 0
```

We use %, the remainder operator, to divide the integral `i` by 2. If the remainder is 0, then `i` is even.

Exercise 4.3

Locate and examine the Standard C++ header file `limits` and the Standard C header files `climits` and `cfloat` on your system.

In MS Visual C++, the include files usually appear under .../DevStudio/VC/include; in UNIX and Linux, the include files usually appear under /usr/include. In our system, limits indirectly includes both limits.h and float.h and has a number of template definitions.

Exercise 4.4

Which, if any, of the following are likely to be incorrect or not portable? Why? How might each be corrected? (Note that the type of object(s) is not significant in these examples.)

```
(a) ptr->ival != 0                (b) ival != jval < kval
(c) ptr != 0 && *ptr++            (d) ival++ && ival
(e) vec[ ival++ ] <= vec[ ival ]
```

(a) ptr->ival != 0
    Correct.

(b) ival != jval < kval
    It may be correct. The right-hand side of the expression checks whether jval is less than kval and returns true (1) if that is the case; otherwise, it returns false (0). Then ival is compared to make sure it is not equal to the result of the earlier evaluation. So the expression is correct if that is what the programmer had in mind.
    It may be nonportable if jval is an int and if kval is an unsigned int.

(c) ptr != 0 && *ptr++
    Correct. The expression first checks that ptr is not zero. If the expression is false, the evaluation terminates with the result false. If the expression is true, the right-hand side checks whether the object that ptr points to is not zero and increments the pointer ptr. The result will be true if ptr is not zero *and* if the object that ptr points to is not zero. Otherwise, the result will be false.

(d) ival++ && ival
    The language guarantees that the expressions in && (logical and) and in || (logical or) are evaluated left to right. So ival++ will be evaluated first; if ival is not zero, then ival will be evaluated again (on the right-hand side of &&) after ival has been incremented. Here are some possible results:

```
    ival = -1      result is false:   -1  &&  0
    ival =  0      result is false:    0
    ival =  1      result is true:     1  &&  2
```

The variable `ival` will be incremented regardless of the outcome.

```
(e) vec[ ival++ ] <= vec[ ival ]
```

Nonportable. There is no guarantee that the left-hand side of the expression will be evaluated first. If it works on your system, it may not work on the next system that the code will be ported to.

Exercise 4.5

The order of evaluation of the binary operators is left undefined to permit the compiler freedom to provide an optimal implementation. The trade-off is between an efficient implementation and a potential pitfall in the use of the language by the programmer. Do you consider that an acceptable trade-off? Why or why not?

It is an acceptable trade-off because the benefits of efficient implementation and optimization potentially outweigh the risks. Once we become aware that the order of the evaluation of the operands when binary operators are involved is not defined, that knowledge becomes second nature.

Exercise 4.6

The following is illegal. Why? How would you correct it?

```
int main() {
    float fval;
    int    ival;
    int  *pi;

    fval = ival = pi = 0;
}
```

The assignment is incorrect because the language does not provide an automatic conversion from "pointer to int" to int. We could rewrite the assignment as

```
fval = ival = 0;
pi = 0;
```

or any other variation that does not mix a pointer with any other nonpointer type.

Exercise 4.7

Although the following are not illegal, they do not behave as the programmer expects. Why? How would you reimplement them to reflect the programmer's likely intention?

```
(a) if ( ptr = retrieve_pointer() != 0 )
(b) if ( ival = 1024 )
(c) ival += ival + 1;
```

(a) if (ptr = retrieve_pointer() != 0)

Because the inequality operator != has higher precedence than the assignment operator =, the value returned by retrieve_pointer() will be compared to zero, and the result (true or false) will be assigned to ptr.

Here is the reimplemented version:

```
if ( ( ptr = retrieve_pointer() ) != 0 )
```

(b) if (ival = 1024)

The assignment operator = assigns the result of the expression on the right-hand side to the lvalue on the left. It is likely that the expression should be a comparison instead of an assignment.

The reimplemented version:

```
if ( ival == 1024 )
```

(c) ival += ival + 1;

The compound assignment operator

```
a op= expression
```

is defined to mean

```
a = a op ( expression )
```

So the original expression means

```
ival = ival + ( ival + 1 );
```

Presumably the programmer's intention was to increment ival by 1.

The reimplemented version:

```
ival += 1;
```

Or, as discussed in Section 4.5 of L&L:

```
ival++;
```

Exercise 4.8

Why do you think C++ wasn't named ++C?

The reason is that C was incremented (improved) after it had been in use for a while.

Exercise 4.9

In the Rogue Wave implementation of the standard library available to us at the time of this writing, the four compound assignment operators support only a right-hand operand of type complex. For example, an attempt to write

```
complex_obj += 1;
```

results in a compile-time error, although Standard C++ specifies that the assignment is legal. (It is not uncommon to find implementations at this point still lagging behind the Standard.) We can fix this lapse by providing our own instance of the compound operators. For example, here is a nontemplate instance of compound addition assignment operator for complex< double >:

```
#include    <complex>
inline complex< double >&
operator+=( complex< double > &cval, double dval)
{
    return cval += complex< double >( dval );
}
```

When we include this instance in our program, the compound assignment of 1, above, executes correctly. (This is an example of providing an overloaded operator for a class type. Operator overloading is discussed in detail in Chapter 15.)

Using the preceding definition as a model, provide implementations of the other three compound operators for complex< double >. Add them to the following small program and execute it.

```
#include    <iostream>
#include    <complex>

using namespace std;

// compound operator definitions go here

int main()
{
    complex< double > cval(4.0, 1.0);

    cout << cval << "\n";
    cval += 1;
    cout << cval << endl;
    cval -= 1;
    cout << cval << endl;
    cval *= 2;
    cout << cval << endl;
    cval /= 2;
    cout << cval << endl;

    return 0;
}
```

Here is operator -=:

```
inline complex< double > &
operator -=(complex< double > &cval, double dval)
{
    return cval -= complex< double >(dval);
}
```

Here is operator *=:

```
inline complex< double > &
operator *=(complex< double > &cval, double dval)
{
    return cval *= complex< double >(dval);
}
```

Here is operator /=:

```
inline complex< double > &
operator /=(complex< double > &cval, double dval)
{
    return cval /= complex< double >(dval);
}
```

Exercise 4.10

The Standard C++ complex number type does not provide an increment operator, although its absence is not intrinsic to the nature of complex numbers — after all,

```
cval += 1;
```

in effect increments cval's real part by 1. Provide a definition of the increment operator, add it to the following program, and then compile and execute:

```
#include    <iostream>
#include    <complex>

using namespace std;

// increment operator definitions go here

int main()
{
    complex< double > cval(4.0, 1.0);

    cout << cval << "\n";
    ++cval;
    cout << cval << endl;
```

```
        return 0;
    }
```

Here is the pre-increment operator ++:

```
    inline complex< double > &
    operator ++(complex< double > &cval)
    {
        return cval += complex< double >(1);
    }
```

The post-increment operator ++ is similar, but it returns the old complex number by value instead of returning a reference. It has an extra int parameter to differentiate it from a call to the pre-increment version.

```
    inline complex< double >
    operator ++(complex< double > &cval, int)
    {
        complex< double > oldcval = cval;
        cval += complex< double >(1);
        return oldcval;
    }
```

Here's a modified version of main() that invokes both pre- and post-increment operators:

```
    int main()
    {
        complex< double > cval(4.0, 1.0);

        cout << cval << "\n";
        ++cval;
        cout << cval << endl;
        cout << cval++ << endl;
        cout << cval << endl;

        return 0;
    }
```

Exercise 4.11

Which of the following, if any, are illegal or in error?

```
    (a) vector< string > svec( 10 );
    (b) vector< string > *pvec1 = new vector< string > ( 10 );
    (c) vector< string > **pvec2 = new vector< string > [ 10 ];
    (d) vector< string > *pv1 = &svec;
    (e) vector< string > *pv2 = pvec1;
```

```
(f) delete svec;
(g) delete pvec1;
(h) delete [] pvec2;
(i) delete pv1;
(j) delete pv2;
```

(a) `vector< string > svec( 10 );`
   Correct. svec is a vector of 10 strings.

(b) `vector< string > *pvec1 = new vector< string > ( 10 );`
   Correct. pvec1 is a pointer to a vector of 10 strings.

(c) `vector< string > **pvec2 = new vector< string > [ 10 ];`
   Error. The expression on the right-hand side produces a pointer to a vector of `strings` that is not compatible with a pointer to a pointer to a vector of `strings` on the left-hand side.

(d) `vector< string > *pv1 = &svec;`
   Correct. pv1 points to the object svec that is a vector of `strings`.

(e) `vector< string > *pv2 = pvec1;`
   Correct. pv2 is a pointer to a vector of `strings`. After the initialization, pv2 points to the same object that pvec1 points to.
   Both pv2 and pvec1 have the same type.

(f) `delete svec;`
   Illegal. We cannot issue a `delete` on an object.

(g) `delete pvec1;`
   Correct. It deallocates the space that pvec1 points to.

(h) `delete [] pvec2;`
   Syntactically correct. The run-time behavior depends on the value of pvec2.

(i) `delete pv1;`
   This is legal because the compiler cannot catch the error. It is an error because we cannot issue a `delete` on a pointer to an object that was not created with `new`.

(j) `delete pv2;`
   Both correct and incorrect.
   It is correct because pv2 points to the same object that pvec1 points to and the object was created with `new`.
   It is incorrect because the object that pv2 is pointing to was already deallocated in (g). It is illegal to deallocate the same object more than once. It will produce an undefined behavior at run-time that neither one of us wants to track down.

Exercise 4.12

Assume the following two definitions:

```
unsigned int ui1 = 3, ui2 = 7;
```

What is the result of each of the following expressions?

(a) ui1 & ui2   (c) ui1 | ui2
(b) ui1 && ui2   (d) ui1 || ui2

The following numbers represent binary values although they look like octal numbers.

(a) ui1 & ui2
    0101 & 0111 = 0101

We used a binary representation for ui1 and ui2. The value 5 in binary (base 2), using only four bits to represent the value, is 0101, and 7 is 0111. Because the bitwise AND operator & returns 1 only when both corresponding bits are 1, the result is 0101.

(b) ui1 && ui2
    true && true = true

The result is true because the logical AND operator && returns true when both operands are nonzero (or true). The logical AND operator guarantees left-to-right evaluation, and the evaluation ceases as soon as the result is known.

(c) ui1 | ui2
    0101 | 0111 = 0111

The bitwise OR operator | returns 1 when either of the corresponding bits is 1. The result is 0111.

(d) ui1 || ui2
    true || true = true

The result is true because the logical OR operator || returns true when either operand is nonzero (or true). The logical OR operator guarantees left-to-right evaluation, and the evaluation ceases as soon as the result is known.

Exercise 4.13

Using the model of the bit_on() **inline function, provide a** bit_turn_on() **(turns on a specified bit), a** bit_turn_off() **(turns off a specified bit), a** flip_bit() **(reverses the value of a specified bit), and a** bit_off() **(tests whether the specified bit is off) collection of inline functions operating on a bitvector represented as an** unsigned int. **Then write a small program to exercise the functions.**

```cpp
inline void bit_turn_on(unsigned int &ui, int pos)
{
    ui |= (1 << pos);
}


inline void bit_turn_off(unsigned int &ui, int pos)
{
    ui &= ~ (1 << pos);
}


inline void flip_bit(unsigned int &ui, int pos)
{
    ui ^= (1 << pos);
}


inline bool bit_off(unsigned int ui, int pos)
{
    return !bit_on(ui, pos);
}
```

Here is a program that exercises the functions:

```cpp
int main()
{
    unsigned int ui = 0xd3;        // 1101 0011 in binary
                                   // bits are numbered from the right
                                   // starting at position 0
    cout << "ui in hex: "
         << hex << ui << '\n';
    // turn on the 4th bit from the right
    bit_turn_on(ui, 3);
    cout << "result should be 'db', it is "
         << hex << ui << '\n';
    // turn off the 4th bit from the right
    bit_turn_off(ui, 3);
    cout << "result should be 'd3', it is "
         << hex << ui << '\n';
    // flip the 4th bit from the right
    flip_bit(ui, 3);
    cout << "result should be 'db', it is "
         << hex << ui << '\n';
    // flip the 4th bit from the right
    flip_bit(ui, 3);
```

```
        cout << "result should be 'd3', it is "
             << hex << ui << '\n';
        cout << "4th bit should be 0, it is "
             << bit_on(ui, 3) << '\n';
        cout << "1st bit should be 1, it is "
             << bit_on(ui, 0) << '\n';


        return 0;
    }
```

Exercise 4.14

What is the weakness of explicitly coding the functions of Exercise 4.13 to operate on an unsigned int**? One alternative is the use of a** typedef**. A second alternative is the use of the template mechanism introduced back in Section 2.5. Rewrite the** bit_on() **inline function defined above using a** typedef **and then using the function template mechanism.**

Here is the typedef version of bit_on():

```
    typedef unsigned int bitvec;


    inline void bit_turn_on_typedef(bitvec &ui, int pos)
    {
        ui |= (1 << pos);
    }
```

One drawback of the typedef version is that after the typedef has been defined, it cannot be changed for the same compilation. Another drawback is that we cannot flip the bits of an unsigned char — for example, because we cannot convert an unsigned char & into unsigned &.

Here is the template version of bit_on():

```
    template < class Type >
    inline void bit_turn_on(Type &ui, int pos)
    {
        ui |= (1 << pos);
    }
```

The advantage of the template version is that we can create objects of different types for the same compilation.

Here is the program that exercises the functions. It is a variation of the program in Exercise 4.13.

```cpp
int main()
{
    unsigned int ui = 0xd3;      // 1101 0011 in binary
                                 // bits are numbered from the right
                                 // starting at position 0
    cout << "ui in hex: "
         << hex << ui << '\n';
    // turn on the 4th bit from the right
    bit_turn_on_typedef(ui, 3);
    cout << "result should be 'db', it is "
         << hex << ui << '\n';
    // turn off the 4th bit from the right
    bit_turn_off(ui, 3);
    cout << "result should be 'd3', it is "
         << hex << ui << '\n';
    // turn on the 4th bit from the right
    bit_turn_on(ui, 3);
    cout << "result should be 'db', it is "
         << hex << ui << '\n';
    // turn off the 4th bit from the right
    bit_turn_off(ui, 3);
    cout << "result should be 'd3', it is "
         << hex << ui << '\n';
    // flip the 4th bit from the right
    flip_bit(ui, 3);
    cout << "result should be 'db', it is "
         << hex << ui << '\n';
    // flip the 4th bit from the right
    flip_bit(ui, 3);
    cout << "result should be 'd3', it is "
         << hex << ui << '\n';
    cout << "4th bit should be 0, it is "
         << bit_off(ui, 3) << '\n';
    cout << "1st bit should be 1, it is "
         << bit_off(ui, 0) << '\n';


    return 0;
}
```

Exercise 4.15

Which of the following declarations of a bitset object, if any, are in error?

```
(a) bitset<64> bitvec(32);
(b) bitset<32> bv( 1010101 );
(c) string bstr;   cin >> bstr;   bitset<8> bv( bstr );
(d) bitset<32> bv;   bitset<16> bv16( bv );
```

(a) bitset<64> bitvec(32);

Correct. The bitset template takes a size_t type of argument. 64 is a valid value for a size_t. bitvec will use 32 of the 64 bits.

(b) bitset<32> bv(1010101);

Incorrect. bv is not initialized with the bits 1010101 because that argument to the constructor is taken as an unsigned long decimal value, which in a bit representation means something different.

To initialize bv with the bits 1010101 we could use

```
bitset<32> bv( "1010101" );
```

because bitset has a constructor that takes a string argument.

(c) string bstr;   cin >> bstr;   bitset<8> bv(bstr);

Correct. The string bstr is the argument to the constructor.

(d) bitset<32> bv;   bitset<16> bv16(bv);

Incorrect. bv is the argument to the constructor to build bv16. The argument is expected to be an unsigned long. But bitset does not provide a conversion operator to go from a bitset object to an unsigned long.

Exercise 4.16

Which, if any, of the following uses of a bitset object are in error?

```
    extern void bitstring( const char * );
    bool bit_on( unsigned long, int );
    bitset<32> bitvec;
```

```
(a) bitstring( bitvec.to_string().c_str() );
(b) if ( bit_on( bitvec.to_ulong(), 64 ) ) ...
(c) bitvec.flip( bitvec.count() );
```

(a) bitstring(bitvec.to_string().c_str());

Correct. bitset provides conversion to string with the method to_string(). The method c_str() from the class string produces a C-style string.

(b) if (bit_on(bitvec.to_ulong(), 64)) ...

Correct. `bitset` provides a conversion method to unsigned long: `to_ulong()`.

(c) bitvec.flip(bitvec.count());

Correct. The result may not be exactly what we had in mind: `count()` returns the number of bits that are on, let's say 3; `flip()` will flip bit 3 and not the three bits that were on.

Exercise 4.17

Consider the sequence 1, 2, 3, 5, 8, 13, 21. How might we initialize a `bitset<32>` to represent this sequence? Alternatively, given an empty `bitset`, write a small program to turn on each of the appropriate bits.

Because the sequence of numbers represents a Fibonacci sequence, we could write a function to initialize a `bitset` with the first seven members of the sequence.

```
void buildFibonacci(int fib[], int n)
{
    fib[0] = 1;
    fib[1] = 2;
    for (int i = 2; i < n; i++)
        fib[i] = fib[i - 1] + fib[i - 2];
}
void initFibonacci(bitset<32> &bv, int n)
{
    assert(n > 0 && n <= 32);

    int fib[32];
    buildFibonacci(fib, n);
    for (int i = 0; i < n; i++) {
        bv.set(fib[i]);
    }
}
```

Here is the program that tests `initFibonacci()`:

```
// output: 1, 2, 3, 5, 8, 13, 21
int main()
{
    bitset<32> bv;

    initFibonacci(bv, 7);
    for (int i = 0; i < bv.size(); i++) {
        if (bv.test(i))
            cout << "bit " << setw(2) << i << " on\n";
    }
```

```
        return 0;
    }
```

Exercise 4.18

Using Table 4.4, identify the order of evaluation of the following compound expressions:

```
(a) ! ptr == ptr->next
(b) ~ uc ^ 0377 & ui << 4
(c) ch = buf[ bp++ ] != '\e'
```

(a) ! ptr == ptr->next

1.   ptr->next

2.   ! ptr

3.   ! ptr == ptr->next

(b) ~ uc ^ 0377 & ui << 4

1.   ~ uc

2.   ui << 4

3.   0377 & ui << 4

4.   ~ uc ^ 0377 & ui << 4

(c) ch = buf[bp++] != '\e'

1.   buf[bp]

2.   bp++

3.   buf[bp] != '\e'

4.   ch = buf[bp] != '\e'

Exercise 4.19

The three expressions in Exercise 4.18 all evaluate in an order contrary to the intentions of the programmer. Parenthesize them to evaluate in an order you imagine to be the intention of the programmer.

(a) ! ptr == ptr->next
       ! (ptr == ptr->next)

(b) ~ uc ^ 0377 & ui << 4
       ~ (uc ^ 0377) & (ui << 4)

(c) ch = buf[bp++] != '\e'
       (ch = buf[bp++]) != '\e'

Exercise 4.20

The following two expressions fail to compile due to operator precedence. Explain why using Table 4.4. How would you fix them?
  (a) int i = doSomething(), 0;
  (b) cout << ival % 2 ? "odd" : "even";

(a) int i = doSomething(), 0;

The definition

int i = doSomething();

is OK. The syntax error comes up when the compiler detects a constant following the definition of i. The problem is the low precedence of the comma operator. One possible solution uses parentheses:

int i = (doSomething(), 0);

This forces the evaluation of doSomething(), followed by 0. The result of the expressions separated by the comma operator is the value of the last expression (keep in mind that all the expressions separated by commas are evaluated, left to right); in this case, it is the constant 0. So 0 is assigned to i.

(b) cout << ival % 2 ? "odd" : "even";
  Because << and % have higher priority than the ?:, the compiler understands that we mean

      cout << ival % 2

which would print the remainder when we divide ival by 2. The expression then becomes

      cout ? "odd" : "even"

which converts cout to void * and so evaluates to "odd" and throws it away.
  To obtain the intended result of displaying either odd or even, we force the evaluation of the ?: operator before <<:

      cout << (ival % 2 ? "odd" : "even");

Caution: (b), without the parentheses compiles just fine.

Exercise 4.21

Given the following set of definitions

```
char cval; int ival;
float fval; double dval;
unsigned int ui;
```

identify the implicit type conversions, if any, taking place:

```
(a) cval = 'a' + 3;
(b) fval = ui - ival * 1.0;
(c) dval = ui * fval;
(d) cval = ival + fval + dval;
```

(a) cval = 'a' + 3;

1. 'a' is converted to int.

2. The result of the addition is int.

3. The int is converted to char for the assignment.

(b) fval = ui - ival * 1.0;

1. ival is converted to double before the multiplication.

2. The result of the multiplication is double.

3. ui is converted to double before the subtraction.

4. The result of the subtraction is double.

5. The double is converted to float for the assignment.

(c) dval = ui * fval;

1. ui is converted to float before the multiplication.

2. The result of the multiplication is float.

3. The float is converted to double for the assignment.

(d) cval = ival + fval + dval;

   1.   ival is converted to `float` before the addition to `fval`.

   2.   The result of the addition is `float`, and it is converted to `double` before the addition to `dval`.

   3.   The result of the addition is `double`.

   4.   The `double` is converted to char for the assignment.

Exercise 4.22

Given the following set of definitions
```
void *pv; int ival;
char *pc; double dval;
const string *ps;
```
rewrite each of the following using the named cast notation:
```
(a) pv = (void *) ps;
(b) ival = int( *pc );
(c) pv = &dval;
(d) pc = (char *) pv;
```

(a) pv = (void *) ps;
  ps is a pointer to a const string. We cannot use the `static_cast` to remove const-ness. Consequently, we first used the `const_cast` to convert const string * into string *, and then we used `static_cast` to convert string * into void *.
  Here is the new expression:
```
pv = static_cast< void * >( const_cast< string * >( ps ) );
```

(b) ival = int(*pc);
  pc is a pointer to a char. int(*pc) gets the char that pc points to and converts it to int. We accomplish that with `static_cast`:
```
ival = static_cast< int >( *pc );
```

(c) pv = &dval;
  It is not necessary to change this expression because pv is a pointer to void.
  We could explicitly indicate the conversion from double * to void * with `static_cast`:
```
pv = static_cast< void * >( &dval );
```

(d) pc = (char *) pv;
  pv is a pointer of type void that really points to a double because of the expression in (c). (char *) converts the pointer to a pointer to a different type. This is a case for `reinterpret_cast`:

```
pc = reinterpret_cast< char * >( pv );
```
So we must be careful how we use pc because it really points to an object of type double, allowing us to treat the individual bytes of the double object as chars. There is no explicit '\0' end of string marker in the double value, of course.

Exercise 4.23

Some of our users have requested a peek() **operation.** peek() **reads the top value without removing it from the stack, provided that the stack is not empty, of course. Provide an implementation of** peek() **and then augment our** main() **program to exercise it.**

Here is peek():
```
bool iStack::peek(int &top_value)
{
    if (empty())
        return false;

    top_value = _stack[ _top - 1 ];
    cout << "iStack::peek(): " << top_value << endl;
    return true;
}
```

We peeked at the top of the stack at every fifth iteration of the loop:
```
if (ix % 5 == 0) {
    int dummy;
    stack.display();
    stack.peek(dummy);
}
```

Exercise 4.24

What are the two primary weaknesses of our iStack **design? How might they be corrected?**

1. Fixed-type int. As the name of the class implies, iStack can handle only ints. A template implementation would help solve the problem.

2. Fixed-size stack. This limitation could be corrected by avoiding the restriction on the stack size. vectors do not have a small fixed size — that is, they can grow and shrink during execution and iStack already uses a vector of ints.

Another solution is to use the stack container available in Standard C++.

chapter five

Statements

Exercise 5.1

Imagine that you have just been made lead of a small programming project and wish all the code to follow a uniform declaration policy. Clearly define and justify the declaration rules you wish the project to follow.

Declaration rules are largely a matter of personal preference, but there are various factors to consider on a programming project. Multiple programmers are working on the same project, and the interaction among the code they write must be clearly defined. More than one programmer may work on the same section of code at different times during the project. Efficiency may sometimes be sacrificed for ease of maintainability.

The following are some examples of possible declaration rules.

- Avoid the use of global declarations. Use a namespace if appropriate.

- Group all declarations at the beginning of blocks so that it is easy to see all the objects that are defined and used.

- Declarations that involve modifiers should be placed one per line so as to avoid any confusion about which objects are modified.

- Initialize all variables.

Exercise 5.2

Imagine that you have just been assigned to the project group of Exercise 5.1. You completely disagree not only with the stated declaration policy but also with any declaration policy at all. Clearly define and justify your reasons.

Some arguments against a declaration policy are as follows.

- Declarations should be placed to maximize program efficiency.

- Declarations should be placed as close to their first use as possible so that the type and initialization (if any) of an object are easy to find.

Exercise 5.3

Correct each of the following:

```
(a) if (ival1 != ival2)
        ival1 ival2
    else ival1 = ival2 = 0;

(b) if (ival < minval)
        minval = ival;
        occurs = 1;

(c) if (int ival = get_value())
        cout << "ival = "
            << ival << endl;
    if (!ival)
        cout << "ival = 0\n";

(d) if (ival = 0)
        ival = get_value();

(e) if (ival == 0)
    else ival = 0;
```

The correct forms are as follows:

```
(a) if (ival1 != ival2)
        ival1 ival2
    else ival1 = ival2 = 0;
```

The *then* clause of the if is invalid.

```
    if (ival1 != ival2)
        ival1 = ival2;
    else
        ival1 = ival2 = 0;

(b) if (ival < minval)
        minval = ival;
        occurs = 1;
```

occurs will always be set to 1 unless a compound statement is used.

```
if (ival < minval) {
    minval = ival;
    occurs = 1;
}
```

(c)
```
if (int ival = get_value())
    cout << "ival = "
        << ival << endl;
if (!ival)
    cout << "ival = 0\n";
```

The scope of `ival` is limited to the first `if` statement.

```
int ival;

if (ival = get_value())
    cout << "ival = "
        << ival << endl;
if (!ival)
    cout << "ival = 0\n";
```

or

```
if (int ival = get_value())
    cout << "ival = "
        << ival << endl;
else
    cout << "ival = 0\n";
```

(d)
```
if (ival = 0)
    ival = get_value();
```

The condition clause contains an *assignment* and not a conditional expression.

```
if (ival == 0)
    ival = get_value();
```

(e)
```
if (ival == 0)
    else ival = 0;
```

The *then* clause is missing.

```
if (ival == 0)
    ;
else
    ival = 0;
```

or

```
if (ival != 0)
    ival = 0;
```

Exercise 5.4

Change the declaration of `occurs` **in the argument list of** `min()` **to be a nonreference argument type and rerun the program. How does the behavior of the program change?**

If we change

```
int min(const vector<int> &ivec, int &occurs)
```

to

```
int min(const vector<int> &ivec, int occurs)
```

any modifications to `occurs` within `min()` remain local to `min()`. Because this becomes call-by-value, the initial value of `occurs` in `main()` is unchanged by the call to `min()`, and the program produces the following output:

```
Minimum value: 1 occurs: 0 times.
```

Exercise 5.5

Modify our vowel count program so that it also counts the number of blank spaces, tabs, and newlines read.

Our first change is to add three new counters and initialize them to zero.

```
blankCnt = 0, tabCnt = 0, newlineCnt = 0,
```

Skipping the `while` loop for the moment, we must modify the output to display the three new counters.

```
<< "Number of blanks: \t" << blankCnt << "\n"
<< "Number of tabs: \t" << tabCnt << "\n"
<< "Number of newlines: \t" << newlineCnt << "\n";
```

Operator `>>` skips over white space, so we cannot use it if we expect to count the white space characters. Instead, we use the member function `get()`.

```
while (cin.get(ch))
```

Finally, we add three new cases to the `switch` statement.

```
case ' ':
    ++blankCnt;
    break;
case '\t':
    ++tabCnt;
    break;
case '\n':
    ++newlineCnt;
    break;
```

Exercise 5.5

Here is the complete program:

```
#include <iostream>
#include <cctype>
using namespace std;

int main()
{
    char ch;
    int aCnt = 0, eCnt = 0, iCnt = 0, oCnt = 0, uCnt = 0,
        blankCnt = 0, tabCnt = 0, newlineCnt = 0,
        consonantCnt = 0;

    while (cin.get(ch))
        switch (ch) {
        case 'a': case 'A':
            ++aCnt;
            break;
        case 'e': case 'E':
            ++eCnt;
            break;
        case 'i': case 'I':
            ++iCnt;
            break;
        case 'o': case 'O':
            ++oCnt;
            break;
        case 'u': case 'U':
            ++uCnt;
            break;
        case ' ':
            ++blankCnt;
            break;
        case '\t':
            ++tabCnt;
            break;
        case '\n':
            ++newlineCnt;
            break;
        default:
            if (isalpha(ch))
                ++consonantCnt;
            break;
        }
```

```
cout << "Number of vowel a: \t" << aCnt << "\n"
     << "Number of vowel e: \t" << eCnt << "\n"
     << "Number of vowel i: \t" << iCnt << "\n"
     << "Number of vowel o: \t" << oCnt << "\n"
     << "Number of vowel u: \t" << uCnt << "\n"
     << "Number of consonants: \t" << consonantCnt << "\n"
     << "Number of blanks: \t" << blankCnt << "\n"
     << "Number of tabs: \t" << tabCnt << "\n"
     << "Number of newlines: \t" << newlineCnt << "\n";

    return 0;
}
```

Exercise 5.6

Modify our vowel count program so that it counts the number of occurrences of the following two-character sequences: ff, fl, and fi.

Once again we add new counters and modify the output to display their values. The more interesting change involves counting the two-character sequences.

First, we add a new case for 'f', count it as a consonant, and fetch the next character from input.

```
case 'f':
    ++consonantCnt; // count the f
    cin.get(ch);
```

Next, we check whether the new character is one of the three needed to complete a sequence and, if it is, increment the appropriate counters.

```
switch (ch) {
case 'f':
    ++consonantCnt;
    ++ffCnt;
    break;
case 'i':
    ++iCnt;
    ++fiCnt;
    break;
case 'l':
    ++consonantCnt;
    ++flCnt;
    break;
```

If the new character is not one that completes a sequence, we return it to t̶
so that it is handled by the next iteration of the `while` loop.

```
        default:
            cin.putback(ch);
            break;
    }
```

Here is the complete program:

```
#include <iostream.h>
#include <ctype.h>

int main()
{
    char ch;
    int aCnt = 0, eCnt = 0, iCnt = 0, oCnt = 0, uCnt = 0,
        blankCnt = 0, tabCnt = 0, newlineCnt = 0,
        ffCnt = 0, flCnt = 0, fiCnt = 0,
        consonantCnt = 0;

    while (cin.get(ch))
        switch (ch) {
        case 'a': case 'A':
            ++aCnt;
            break;
        case 'e': case 'E':
            ++eCnt;
            break;
        case 'i': case 'I':
            ++iCnt;
            break;
        case 'o': case 'O':
            ++oCnt;
            break;
        case 'u': case 'U':
            ++uCnt;
            break;
        case ' ':
            ++blankCnt;
            break;
        case '\t':
            ++tabCnt;
            break;
```

```
        case '\n':
            ++newlineCnt;
            break;
        case 'f':
            ++consonantCnt; // count the f
            cin.get(ch);
            switch (ch) {
            case 'f':
                ++consonantCnt;
                ++ffCnt;
                break;
            case 'i':
                ++iCnt;
                ++fiCnt;
                break;
            case 'l':
                ++consonantCnt;
                ++flCnt;
                break;
            default:
                cin.putback(ch);
                break;
            }
            break;
        default:
            if (isalpha(ch))
                ++consonantCnt;
            break;
        }
    cout << "Number of vowel a: \t" << aCnt << "\n"
         << "Number of vowel e: \t" << eCnt << "\n"
         << "Number of vowel i: \t" << iCnt << "\n"
         << "Number of vowel o: \t" << oCnt << "\n"
         << "Number of vowel u: \t" << uCnt << "\n"
         << "Number of consonants: \t" << consonantCnt << "\n"
         << "Number of ff sequences: \t" << ffCnt << "\n"
         << "Number of fl sequences: \t" << flCnt << "\n"
         << "Number of fi sequences: \t" << fiCnt << "\n"
         << "Number of blanks: \t" << blankCnt << "\n"
         << "Number of tabs: \t" << tabCnt << "\n"
         << "Number of newlines: \t" << newlineCnt << "\n";
    return 0;
}
```

Exercise 5.7

Each of the following exhibits a common programming error in the use of the switch statement. Identify and correct each error.

(a)

```
switch (ival) {
case 'a': aCnt++;
case 'e': eCnt++;
default: iouCnt++;
}
```

(b)

```
switch (ival) {
case 1:
    int ix = get_value();
    ivec[ix] = ival;
    break;
default:
    ix = ivec.size()-1;
    ivec[ix] = ival;
}
```

(c)

```
switch (ival) {
case 1, 3, 5, 7, 9:
    oddcnt++;
    break;
case 2, 4, 6, 8, 10:
    evencnt++;
    break;
}
```

(d)

```
int ival = 512, jval = 1024, kval = 4096;
int chunksize;
// ...
switch (swt) {
case ival:
    chunksize = ival * sizeof(int);
    break;
case jval:
    chunksize = jval * sizeof(int);
```

```
        break;
    case kval:
        chunksize = kval * sizeof(int);
        break;
    }
```

(e)

```
    enum { illustrator = 1, photoshop, photostyler = 2 };

    switch (ival) {
    case illustrator:
        --illus_license;
        break;
    case photoshop:
        --pshop_license;
        break;
    case photostyler:
        --pstyler_license;
        break;
    }
```

The corrections are as follows.

(a)

```
    switch (ival) {
    case 'a': aCnt++;
    case 'e': eCnt++;
    default: iouCnt++;
    }
```

The break statements are missing, so iouCnt will always be incremented and eCnt will be incremented for 'a' as well as 'e'.

```
    switch (ival) {
    case 'a': aCnt++; break;
    case 'e': eCnt++; break;
    default: iouCnt++;
    }
```

(b)

```
    switch (ival) {
    case 1:
        int ix = get_value();
        ivec[ix] = ival;
```

```
        break;
    default:
        ix = ivec.size()-1;
        ivec[ix] = ival;
    }
```

ix is not defined in the default branch.

```
    switch (ival) {
    case 1:
        int ix = get_value();
        ivec[ix] = ival;
        break;
    default:
        int ix = ivec.size()-1;
        ivec[ix] = ival;
    }
```

(c)

```
    switch (ival) {
    case 1, 3, 5, 7, 9:
        oddcnt++;
        break;
    case 2, 4, 6, 8, 10:
        evencnt++;
        break;
    }
```

(c) does not compile because a case label cannot be a list. It should read as follows:

```
    switch (ival) {
    case 1: case 3: case 5: case 7: case 9:
        oddcnt++;
        break;
    case 2: case 4: case 6: case 8: case 10:
        evencnt++;
        break;
    }
```

(d)

```
    int ival = 512, jval = 1024, kval = 4096;
    int chunksize;
    // ...
    switch (swt) {
```

```
case ival:
    chunksize = ival * sizeof(int);
    break;
case jval:
    chunksize = jval * sizeof(int);
    break;
case kval:
    chunksize = kval * sizeof(int);
    break;
}
```

A case label must be a constant expression.

```
const int ival = 512, jval = 1024, kval = 4096;
int chunksize;
// ...
switch (swt) {
case ival:
    chunksize = ival * sizeof(int);
    break;
case jval:
    chunksize = jval * sizeof(int);
    break;
case kval:
    chunksize = kval * sizeof(int);
    break;
}
```

(Note that chunksize = swt * sizeof(int); yields the same results if swt has one of the three values listed.)

(e)

```
enum { illustrator = 1, photoshop, photostyler = 2 };

switch (ival) {
case illustrator:
    --illus_license;
    break;
case photoshop:
    --pshop_license;
    break;
case photostyler:
    --pstyler_license;
    break;
}
```

No two case labels can have the same value.

```
enum { illustrator = 1, photoshop, photostyler };

switch (ival) {
case illustrator:
    --illus_license;
    break;
case photoshop:
    --pshop_license;
    break;
case photostyler:
    --pstyler_license;
    break;
}
```

Exercise 5.8

Which of the following `for` **loop declarations, if any, are in error?**

```
(a) for (int *ptr = &ia, ix = 0;
         ix < size && ptr != ia+size;
         ++ix, ++ptr)
         // ...

(b) for ( ; ; ) {
         if (some_condition)
             break;
         // ...
    }

(c) for (int ix = 0; ix < sz; ++ix)
         // ...
    if (ix != sz)
         // ...

(d) int ix;
    for (ix < sz; ++ix)
         // ...

(e) for (int ix = 0; ix < sz; ++ix, ++sz)
         // ...
```

(a) and (b) are correct. Corrections for (c), (d), and (e) are as follows.

```
(c) for (int ix = 0; ix < sz; ++ix)
        // ...
    if (ix != sz)
        // ...
```

Incorrect. ix is local to the for loop. To correct this, declare ix outside the loop:

```
    int ix;

    for (ix = 0; ix < sz; ++ix)
        // ...
    if (ix != sz)
        // ...
```

```
(d) int ix;
    for (ix < sz; ++ix)
        // ...
```

Incorrect. ix is not initialized, and a null statement is required for the init statement portion of the for loop.

```
    int ix = 0;
    for (; ix < sz; ++ix)
        // ...
```

```
(e) for (int ix = 0; ix < sz; ++ix, ++sz)
        // ...
```

Incorrect. Unless ix or sz (or both) is modified within the body of the for loop, the condition ix < sz will always be true.

```
    for (int ix = 0; ix < sz; ++ix)
        // ...
```

Exercise 5.9

You have been asked to devise a style guide for the projectwide use of the for loop. Explain and illustrate usage rules, if any, for each of the three parts. If you believe strongly against usage rules — or at least with regard to the for loop — explain and illustrate why.

Programming style is largely a matter of opinion, although some style guidelines have been shown to reduce certain kinds of errors. Here are some possible usage rules.

- Initialize the iteration variable(s) as close to the for loop as possible, preferably in the init statement.

- Avoid modification of the iteration variable(s) in the loop body.

- Avoid infinite loops that use break to terminate.

Exercise 5.10

Given the function declaration

```
bool is_equal(const vector<int> &v1,
              const vector<int> &v2);
```

write the body of the function to determine whether the two vectors are equal. For vectors of unequal length, compare the number of elements of the smaller vector. For example, given the vectors (0,1,1,2) and (0,1,1,2,3,5,8), is_equal() returns true. v1.size() and v2.size() return the size of the vectors.

Here is our function.

```
bool is_equal(const vector<int> &v1, const vector<int> &v2)
{
    int i = 0;

    for (vector<int>::const_iterator it1 = v1.begin(), it2 = v2.begin();
            it1 != v1.end() && it2 != v2.end();
            ++it1, ++it2) {

        // if we find an inequality return immediately
        if (*it1 != *it2)
            return false;
    }
    return true;
}
```

We chose not to use size() and instead use iterators to traverse the two vectors. If either iterator reaches the end of its vector before the other, the loop ends. Because an inequality causes an immediate return, any time the loop terminates we have equal vectors.

Here is a small test program.

```
int main()
{
    int ia6ne[6] = { 0, 1, 1, 3, 3, 5 };
    int ia[7] = { 0, 1, 1, 2, 3, 5, 8 };
    int iane[7] = { 1, 1, 1, 2, 3, 5, 8 };
    int ia8eq[8] = { 0, 1, 1, 2, 3, 5, 8, 13 };
    int ia8ne[8] = { 0, 1, 1, 2, 3, 5, 9, 13 };
```

```
vector<int> v1(ia, ia+7);
vector<int> vs6(ia, ia+6);
vector<int> vs6ne(ia6ne, ia6ne+6);
vector<int> vs7(ia, ia+7);
vector<int> vs8(ia8eq, ia8eq+8);
vector<int> vs8ne(ia8ne, ia8ne+8);

cout << "is_equal(v1, vs7): ";
if (is_equal(v1, vs7))
    cout << "equal\n";
else
    cout << "not equal\n";

cout << "is_equal(v1, vs6): ";
if (is_equal(v1, vs6))
    cout << "equal\n";
else
    cout << "not equal\n";

cout << "is_equal(v1, vs6ne): ";
if (is_equal(v1, vs6ne))
    cout << "equal\n";
else
    cout << "not equal\n";

cout << "is_equal(v1, vs8): ";
if (is_equal(v1, vs8))
    cout << "equal\n";
else
    cout << "not equal\n";

cout << "is_equal(v1, vs8ne): ";
if (is_equal(v1, vs8ne))
    cout << "equal\n";
else
    cout << "not equal\n";

return 0;
}
```

Exercise 5.11

Which of the following `while` loop declarations, if any, are incorrect or in error?

```
(a) string bufString, word;
    while (cin >> bufString >> word)
        // ...

(b) while (vector<int>::iterator iter != ivec.end())
        // ...

(c) while (ptr = 0)
        ptr = find_a_value();

(d) while (bool status = find(word)) {
        word = get_next_word();
        if (word.empty())
            break;
        // ...
    }

    if (!status)
        cout << "Did not find any words\n";
```

(a) is correct. The corrections for (b), (c), and (d) are as follows.

```
(b) while (vector<int>::iterator iter != ivec.end())
        // ...
```

This is incorrect because we cannot have a declaration in the expression part of a `while` loop, and `iter` has not been initialized. A correct way is

```
    vector<int>::iterator iter = ivec.begin();
    while (iter != ivec.end()) {
        // ...
        ++iter;
    }
```

```
(c) while (ptr = 0)
        ptr = find_a_value();
```

This is incorrect because = assigns the value 0 to ptr, and the expression evaluates to false, terminating the loop. We use == to test whether ptr is equal to zero:

```
    while (ptr == 0)
        ptr = find_a_value();
```

```
(d) while (bool status = find(word)) {
        word = get_next_word();
        if (word.empty())
            break;
        // ...
    }

    if (!status)
        cout << "Did not find any words\n";
```

This is incorrect because status is not visible outside the while loop. A correct way is

```
bool status;
while (status = find(word)) {
    word = get_next_word();
    if (word.empty())
        break;
    // ...
}

if (!status)
    cout << "Did not find any words\n";
```

Exercise 5.12

The while **loop is particularly good at executing while some condition holds; for**
example, while the end of file is not reached, read a next value. The for **loop is gen-**
erally thought of as a step loop: an index steps through a range of values in a collection.
Write an idiomatic use of each loop and then rewrite each using the other loop construct.
If you were able to program with only one loop, which construct would you choose?
Why?

Here is a typical for loop:

```
for (int i = 0; i < SIZE; ++i) {
    // ...
}
```

An equivalent while loop would be

```
int i = 0;
while (i < SIZE) {
    // ...
    ++i;
}
```

Here is a typical `while` loop:
```
bool found = false;
while (!found) {
    // ...
    found = search();
    // ...
}
```
An equivalent `for` loop would be
```
for (bool found = false; !found; ) {
    // ...
    found = search();
    // ...
}
```

Using only `while` loops is preferable. In general, it is easier to simulate a `for` loop with a `while` loop than vice versa.

Exercise 5.13

Write a small function to read a sequence of strings from standard input until either the same word occurs in succession or all the words have been read. Use a `while` loop to read the text one word at a time. Use the break statement to terminate the loop if a word occurs in succession. Print the word if it occurs in succession, or else print a message saying that no word was repeated.

Here is our solution.
```
#include <iostream>
#include <string>
using namespace std;

int main()
{
    string word, lastword;

    while (cin >> word) {
        if (word == lastword)
            // word word occurred
            break;

        // remember the word we just read
        lastword = word;
    }
```

```
        if (word != "" && word == lastword)
            cout << word << " occurred in succession.\n";
        else
            cout << "No word was repeated.\n";

        return 0;
    }
```

Exercise 5.14

Which of the following do-while **loops, if any, are in error?**

```
(a) do
            string rsp;
            int val1, val2;
            cout << "please enter two values: ";
            cin >> val1 >> val2;
            cout << "The sum of " << val1
                << " and " << val2
                << " = " << val1 + val2 << "\n\n"
                << "More? [yes][no] ";
            cin >> rsp;
        while (rsp[0] != 'n');

(b) do {
            // ...
        } while (int ival = get_response());

(c) do {
            int ival = get_response();
            if (ival == some_value())
                break;
        } while (ival);

        if (!ival)
            // ...
```

The corrections are as follows.

```
(a) do
            string rsp;
            int val1, val2;
            cout << "please enter two values: ";
```

```
            cin >> val1 >> val2;
            cout << "The sum of " << val1
                    << " and " << val2
                    << " = " << val1 + val2 << "\n\n"
                    << "More? [yes][no] ";
            cin >> rsp;
        while (rsp[0] != 'n');
```

Incorrect. A statement block is required:

```
        do {
            string rsp;
            int val1, val2;
            cout << "please enter two values: ";
            cin >> val1 >> val2;
            cout << "The sum of " << val1
                    << " and " << val2
                    << " = " << val1 + val2 << "\n\n"
                    << "More? [yes][no] ";
            cin >> rsp;
        } while (rsp[0] != 'n');
```

(b)
```
    do {
        // ...
    } while (int ival = get_response());
```

Incorrect. Object definitions are not allowed in the condition.

```
    int ival;
    do {
        // ...
    } while (ival = get_response());
```

(c)
```
    do {
        int ival = get_response();
        if (ival == some_value())
            break;
    } while (ival);

    if (!ival)
        // ...
```

Incorrect. ival is not visible outside the do-while loop.

```
    int ival;
    do {
        ival = get_response();
```

```
    if (ival == some_value())
         break;
} while (ival);

if (!ival)
    // ...
```

Exercise 5.15

Write a small program that requests two strings from the user and reports which string is lexicographically less than the other (that is, comes before the other alphabetically). Continue to solicit the user until the user requests to quit. Use the string type, the string less-than operator, and the `do-while` loop.

We need a way for the user to request program termination. If the user enters quit as the first string we will use that as an indication to end the program.

Here is our solution.

```cpp
#include <iostream>
#include <string>
using namespace std;

int main()
{
    string word1, word2;

    cout << "This program requests two strings at a time and\n"
         << "reports which is lexicographically less than the\n"
         << "other.  Entering \"quit\" for the first string will\n"
         << "end the program.\n\n";

    do {
        cout << "Enter the first string: ";
        cin >> word1;
        if (word1 != "quit") {
            cout << "Enter the second string: ";
            cin >> word2;
            if (word1 < word2)
                cout << word1 << " < " << word2 << endl;
            else
                cout << word2 << " <= " << word1 << endl;
        }
    } while (word1 != "quit");
```

```
    return 0;
}
```

Inside the `do-while` loop the user is asked for the first string. If this string is not `quit`, the user is asked for the second string. The two strings are compared and the result printed. The loop condition checks whether the first string is `quit` and, if it is not, continues to loop.

Exercise 5.16

We do not define an `ilist_item` destructor, although the class contains a pointer member. The reason is that the `ilist_item` class does not allocate the object addressed by `_next`, so it is not responsible for its deallocation. A common beginner error is to provide an `ilist` destructor defined as follows:

```
// a bad design choice
ilist_item::~ilist_item()
{
    delete _next;
}
```

Looking at `remove_all()` or `remove_front()`, explain why the presence of this destructor is a bad design choice.

The two statements

```
ilist_item *ptr = _at_front;
_at_front = _at_front->next();
```

from `remove_front()` set ptr to point to the element being removed and set the new front element to be `_at_front->next()`, which is the same as `ptr->next()`.

When `delete ptr;` invokes the destructor, it would also deallocate the `ilist_item` that `_at_front` is now pointing to. This is obviously an error.

Exercise 5.17

Our `ilist` class does not support either of these statements:

```
void ilist::remove_end();
void ilist::remove(ilist_item*);
```

Why do you think we excluded them? Sketch out an algorithm to support these two operations.

Because `ilist` does not keep track of pointers to previous items in the list, removing the last item or a specific item would require traversing the entire list up to the item being removed.

Here are the two new operations.

```
void
ilist::remove_end()
{
    remove(_at_end);
}

void
ilist::remove(ilist_item* item)
{
    ilist_item *plist = _at_front;
    ilist_item *prev = 0;

    while (plist && plist != item) {
        prev = plist;
        plist = plist->next();
    }

    if (plist) {
        if (_current == plist)
            _current = plist->next();

        if (!plist->next()) // item is at the end of the list
            _at_end = prev;

        if (!prev)          // item is at the front of the list
            _at_front = plist->next();
        else
            prev->next(plist->next());

        bump_down_size();

        delete plist;
    }
}
```

Exercise 5.18

Modify find() to take a second argument, an ilist_item*, which, if set, indicates where
to begin searching for the item. If it is not set, the search should begin as before at the
front of the list. (By providing this new parameter as the second argument and specifying
a zero default argument, we preserve the original public interface. Code that uses the
previous definition of find() does not need to be modified.)

```
class ilist {
public:
    // ...
    ilist_item* find(int value, ilist_item *start_at = 0);
    // ...
};
```

We need only change the initialization of ptr to use a non-null start_at.

```
ilist_item*
ilist::find(int value, ilist_item *start_at)
{
    ilist_item *ptr = start_at ? start_at : _at_front;
    while (ptr) {
        if (ptr->value() == value)
            break;
        ptr = ptr->next();
    }
    return ptr;
}
```

Exercise 5.19

Using this new version of find(), implement count(), which returns a count of the occurrences of a value in an ilist. Write a small program to test your implementation.

count() calls find() in a while loop until find() returns null. The body of the loop keeps track of the number of times value is found and increments the value of i, which keeps track of where we are in the list.

```
inline int
ilist::count(int value)
{
    int cnt = 0;
    ilist_item *i = 0;

    while (i = find(value, i)) {
        i = i->next();
        cnt++;
    }

    return cnt;
}
```

Exercise 5.20

Revise `insert(ilist_item *ptr, int value)` **to return the** `ilist_item` **pointer it has just inserted.**

Our new function is as follows:

```
inline ilist_item *
ilist::insert(ilist_item *ptr, int value)
{
    if (!ptr)
        return insert_front(value);
    else {
        bump_up_size();
        ilist_item *p = new ilist_item(value, ptr);
        if (ptr == _at_end)
            _at_end = p;
        return p;
    }
}
```

Because `insert_front()` is called, we also need to modify it by adding `return ptr;` at the end of the function.

```
inline ilist_item *
ilist::insert_front(int value)
{
    ilist_item *ptr = new ilist_item(value);

    if (!_at_front)
        _at_front = _at_end = ptr;
    else {
        ptr->next(_at_front);
        _at_front = ptr;
    }
    bump_up_size();
    return ptr;
}
```

Exercise 5.21

Using the revised `insert()` **function, implement**

```
void ilist::
insert(ilist_item *begin, int *array_of_value, int elem_cnt);
```

in which `array_of_value` addresses an array of values to be inserted in the ilist, `elem_cnt` is the number of elements in the array, and `begin` indicates where to begin inserting the elements. For example, given an ilist of the values

    (3)(0 1 21)

and an array such as the following

    int ia[] = { 1, 2, 3, 5, 8, 13 };

the new insert operation might be called as follows:

    ilist_item *it = mylist.find(1);
    mylist.insert(it, ia, 6);

It would modify `mylist` as follows:

    (9)(0 1 1 2 3 5 8 13 21)

Here is our new function.

```
inline void
ilist::insert(ilist_item *begin, int *array_of_value, int elem_cnt)
{
    while (elem_cnt > 0) {
        begin = insert(begin, *array_of_value);
        array_of_value++;
        elem_cnt--;
    }
}
```

`insert()` is called repeatedly for each of the `elem_cnt` elements we are inserting. Because `insert()` returns a pointer to the item we just inserted, we can use that in each subsequent call to `insert()` as the new insertion point.

Here is our test program.

```
#include <iostream>
using namespace std;

#include "ilist.h"

int main()
{
    ilist mylist;
    int ia[] = { 1, 2, 3, 5, 8, 13 };

    ilist_item *p;

    p = mylist.insert_front(21);
    mylist.insert_front(1);
    mylist.insert_front(0);
    cout << "mylist: ";
    mylist.display();
```

```
    mylist.insert(0, -3);
    cout << "mylist: ";
    mylist.display();

    mylist.insert(p, -33);
    cout << "mylist: ";
    mylist.display();

    mylist.insert_end(-55);
    cout << "mylist: ";
    mylist.display();

    ilist_item *it = mylist.find(1);
    mylist.insert(it, ia, 6);

    cout << "mylist: ";
    mylist.display();

    return 0;
}
```

Exercise 5.22

One problem with concat() and reverse() is that both of them modify the original list. This is not always desirable. Provide an alternative pair of operations that returns a new ilist object:

```
    ilist ilist::reverse_copy();
    ilist ilist::concat_copy(const ilist &rhs);
```

For reverse_copy() we traverse the list and insert each value at the front of a new list.

```
    ilist
    ilist::reverse_copy()
    {
        ilist newilist;

        ilist_item *ptr = _at_front;

        while (ptr) {
            newilist.insert_front(ptr->value());
            ptr = ptr->next();
        }
```

chapter six

Abstract Container Types

Exercise 6.1

Which is the most appropriate — a vector, deque, or a list — for the following program tasks, or is neither preferred?

   a.   Read an unknown number of words from a file for the purpose of generating random English language sentences.

   b.   Read a fixed number of words, inserting them in the container alphabetically as they are entered.

   c.   Read an unknown number of words. Always insert new words at the back. Remove the next value from the front.

   d.   Read an unknown number of integers from a file. Sort the numbers and then print them to standard output.

   a.   Read an unknown number of words from a file for the purpose of generating random English language sentences.

Because the number of words is unknown and the words will be accessed in any order to generate random English language sentences, a vector, which supports random access, is more appropriate.

   b.   Read a fixed number of words, inserting them in the container alphabetically as they are entered.

A list is more appropriate when we have a fixed number of words (the length is fixed) and the insertion of the words occurs anywhere in the list.

c.   Read an unknown number of words. Always insert new words at the back. Remove the next value from the front.

   The most appropriate choice is a deque because we remove elements from the front and insert elements in the back of the list.

d.   Read an unknown number of integers from a file. Sort the numbers and then print them to standard output.

   Here we choose a vector because of the random access required for sorting.

Exercise 6.2

Explain the difference between a vector's capacity and its size. Why is it necessary to support the notion of capacity in a container that stores elements contiguously but not, for example, in a list?

   "A vector represents a contiguous area of memory in which each element is stored in turn" (L&L, page 255).

   Capacity is the number of elements that a vector can contain without allocating more memory, whereas size is the current number of elements that a vector contains.

   Vector implementations store elements in contiguous memory. STL lists are implemented as doubly linked lists in which every node has a pointer to the next node and a pointer to the previous node. Unlike the elements of a vector, the elements of a list are not stored contiguously. Every time we exceed the capacity of a vector, the system must reallocate space for the contiguous elements. Vectors involve reallocation, copying, and deallocation of the old container, so it is necessary to have the capacity of the vector available.

Exercise 6.3

Why is it more efficient to store a collection of a large, complex class object by pointer but less efficient to store a collection of integer objects by pointer?

   For a large, complex class object, a pointer is a small number of bytes when compared with the size of the object, and it is more efficient when you are copying objects. For a collection of integer objects, we double the amount of space required: space for the pointer and space for the integer object that the pointer points to. The heap overhead may be substantial.

Exercise 6.4

In the following situations, which is the more appropriate container type, a list or a vector? In each case, an unknown number of elements are inserted. Explain your answer.

(a) Integer values
(b) Pointers to a large, complex class object
(c) Large, complex class objects

(a) Integer values

A vector is preferred because it does not use extra pointers as a list does. The amount of information stored is small when compared with the pointers required by a list. Caveat: A large number of random insert operations can be expensive for vectors.

(b) Pointers to a large, complex class object

A vector is a better choice for the same reasons as in (a).

(c) Large, complex class objects

List. Using a vector could involve reallocation, copying, and deallocation of the container. If we use a list, we pay for the pointers but we avoid the extra work at run-time.

Exercise 6.5

Explain what the following program does:

```
#include <string>
#include <vector>
#include <iostream>

int main()
{
    vector< string > svec;
    svec.reserve( 1024 );

    string text_word;
    while ( cin >> text_word )
        svec.push_back( text_word );

    svec.resize( svec.size() + svec.size() / 2 );
    // ...
}
```

Let's look at the program starting with the definition of svec:

```
vector< string > svec;
svec.reserve( 1024 );
```

svec is a vector of strings. The default constructor creates an empty vector with no associated memory storage.

svec.reserve(1024) preallocates space for 1,024 strings. This is the current capacity of the vector.

```
while ( cin >> text_word )
    svec.push_back( text_word );
```

The while loop reads a string into text_word. As long as cin succeeds — that is, it does not encounter EOF — the statement in the body of the loop is executed: it adds the string at the end of the vector.

```
svec.resize( svec.size() + svec.size() / 2 );
```

Upon EOF, the while loop terminates. The program then uses resize() to make the capacity of the vector 1.5 times the current size of the vector.

Exercise 6.6

Can a container have a capacity less than its size? Is a capacity equal to its size desirable? Initially? After an element is inserted? Why or why not?

A container cannot have a capacity less than its size because a capacity is the number of elements that a vector can contain without allocating more memory, whereas size is the current number of elements that a vector contains. A container causes reallocation, copy, and deallocation every time the size exceeds the original capacity. Usually, the capacity exceeds the vector size and thereby avoids the extra reallocation, copy, and deallocation.

Exercise 6.7

In Exercise 6.5, if the program reads 256 words, what is its likely capacity after it is resized? If it reads in 512? 1,000? 1,048?

This is a trick question. Because the program specifies a reserve of 1,024, reading 256, 512, or 1,000 all result in a 1.5 × 1,024 size. The 1,048 causes an internal reallocation, so that is likely 1.5 × 1,048.

Exercise 6.8

Given the following class definitions, which cannot be used for defining a vector?

```
(a) class cl1 {                    (b) class cl2 {
        public:                            public:
            cl1(int = 0);                      cl2(int = 0);
            bool operator==();                 bool operator!=();
            bool operator!=();                 bool operator<=();
```

```
        bool operator<=();              // ...
        bool operator<();             };
        // ...
    };
```

```
(c) class cl3 {                  (d) class cl4 {
        public:                          public:
            int ival;                        cl4(int, int = 0);
            bool operator==();               bool operator==();
            // ...                           // ...
    };                               };
```

For a container to be used for defining a vector, it must meet three criteria (L&L, page 263):

- The element type must support the equality operator.
  cl2 does not support the equality operator.

- The element type must support the less-than operator.
  cl1 is the only container that supports the less-than operator (operator<()).

- The element type must support a default constructor or have no constructor at all.
  cl4 does not support a default constructor; cl3 does not have any constructor.

cl2, cl3, and cl4 cannot be used for defining a vector. Only cl1 in (a) can be used for defining a vector.

Exercise 6.9

Which, if any, of the following iterator uses are in error?

```
    const vector< int > ivec;
    vector< string >    svec;
    list< int >         ilist;
```

```
(a) vector<int>::iterator it = ivec.begin();
(b) list<int>::iterator it = ilist.begin() + 2;
(c) vector<string>::iterator it = &svec[0];
(d) for ( vector<string>::iterator it = svec.begin();
            it != 0; ++it )
                // ...
```

(a) vector<int>::iterator it = ivec.begin();

Error. it is an iterator for ivec, which is a const vector. It should read

```
    vector<int>::const_iterator it = ivec.begin();
```

(b) `list<int>::iterator it = ilist.begin() + 2;`

   Error. A list iterator cannot do pointer addition to offset into another element because the elements are not guaranteed to be contiguous (as in vectors).

(c) `vector<string>::iterator it = &svec[0];`

   Error. Iterators must be initialized with `begin()` instead of the address of a vector. It should read

```
vector<string>::iterator it = svec.begin();
```

(d) `for ( vector<string>::iterator it = svec.begin();`
           `it != 0; ++it )`

   Error. Iterators should be compared with `end()` instead of 0. It should read

```
for ( vector<string>::iterator it = svec.begin();
        it != svec.end(); ++it )
```

Exercise 6.10

Which, if any, of the following iterator uses are in error?
```
int ia[7] = { 0, 1, 1, 2, 3, 5, 8 };
string sa[6] = {
    "Fort Sumter", "Manassas", "Perryville", "Vicksburg",
    "Meridian", "Chancellorsville" };
```

(a) `vector<string> svec( sa, &sa[6] );`
(b) `list<int> ilist( ia+4, ia+6 );`
(c) `list<int> ilist2( ilist.begin(), ilist.begin()+2 );`
(d) `vector<int> ivec( &ia[0], ia+8 );`
(e) `list<string> slist( sa+6, sa );`
(f) `vector<string> svec2( sa, sa+6 );`

(a), (b), and (f) are correct.
(c), (d), and (e) are incorrect.

(c) `list<int> ilist2( ilist.begin(), ilist.begin()+2 );`

   Error. The iterator for a list cannot use a scalar (+2) because the elements of a list are not guaranteed to be adjacent (as in vectors).

(d) `vector<int> ivec( &ia[0], ia+8 );`

Error. The array ia is not long enough to support ia+8. It should read

```
vector<int> ivec( &ia[0], ia+7 );
```

(e) `list<string> slist( sa+6, sa );`

Error. The arguments for the constructor for a list should go from "first" to "last." It should read

```
list<string> slist( sa, sa+6 );
```

Exercise 6.11

Write a program that accepts the following definitions:

```
int ia[] = { 1, 5, 34 };
int ia2[] = { 1, 2, 3 };
int ia3[] = { 6, 13, 21, 29, 38, 55, 67, 89 };
```

Using the various insertion operations and the appropriate values of ia2 **and** ia3, **modify** ivec **to hold the sequence**

```
{ 0, 1, 1, 2, 3, 5, 8, 13, 21, 55, 89 }
```

Here's one solution:

```
#include    <iostream>
#include    <vector>
using namespace std;

int main()
{
    int ia[] = { 1, 5, 34 };
    int ia2[] = { 1, 2, 3 };
    int ia3[] = { 6, 13, 21, 29, 38, 55, 67, 89 };
    vector<int> ivec;

    // 0
    ivec.push_back(0);
    // 0, 1
    ivec.insert(ivec.end(), ia, ia+1);
    // 0, 1, 1, 2, 3
    ivec.insert(ivec.end(), ia2, ia2+3);
    // 0, 1, 1, 2, 3, 5
    ivec.insert(ivec.end(), ia+1, ia+2);
    // 0, 1, 1, 2, 3, 5, 8
```

```
    ivec.push_back(8);
    // 0, 1, 1, 2, 3, 5, 8, 13, 21
    ivec.insert(ivec.end(), ia3+1, ia3+3);
    // 0, 1, 1, 2, 3, 5, 8, 13, 21, 55
    ivec.insert(ivec.end(), ia3+5, ia3+6);
    // 0, 1, 1, 2, 3, 5, 8, 13, 21, 55, 89
    ivec.insert(ivec.end(), ia3+7, ia3+8);

    int size = ivec.size();

    cout << "{ ";
    for (int i = 0; i < size; ++i) {
        cout << ivec[i];
        if (i < size - 1)
            cout << ", ";
    }
    cout << " }\n";
    return 0;
}
```

Exercise 6.12

Write a program that accepts the following definitions:

```
    int ia[] = { 0, 1, 1, 2, 3, 5, 8, 13, 21, 55, 89 };
    list<int> ilist( ia, ia+11 );
```

Using the single iterator form of erase(), **remove all the odd-numbered elements in**
ilist.

Here's one solution:

```
    #include    <iostream>
    #include    <list>
    using namespace std;

    int main()
    {
        int ia[] = { 0, 1, 1, 2, 3, 5, 8, 13, 21, 55, 89 };

        // our compiler does not provide a constructor that
        // works with the better initialization below; so
        // we used the for loop that follows...

        // list<int> ilist(ia, ia+11);
```

```
        list<int> ilist;

        for (int i = 0; i < 11; ++i)
            ilist.push_back(ia[i]);

        list<int>::iterator iter;

        for (iter = ilist.begin(); iter != ilist.end(); ++iter)
            if (*iter % 2 != 0)
                ilist.erase(iter);

        cout << "{ ";
        for (iter = ilist.begin(); iter != ilist.end(); ++iter)
            cout << *iter << ", ";
        cout << "}\n";

        return 0;
    }
```

Exercise 6.13

Write a program that, given the string

    `"ab2c3d7R4E6"`

finds each numeric character and then each alphabet character first using `find_first_of()` **and then** `find_first_not_of()`.

Here's one possible solution:

```
    #include    <iostream>
    #include    <string>
    using namespace std;

    int main()
    {
        string s("ab2c3d7R4E6");
        string numerics("0123456789");
        string alphabetic("abcdefghijklmnopqrstuvwxyz"
                          "ABCDEFGHIJKLMNOPQRSTUVWXYZ");
        string::size_type pos = 0;

        // (a) find each numeric character using find_first_of()
        while ((pos = s.find_first_of(numerics, pos)) != string::npos)
            cout << "s[ " << pos << " ] = " << s[pos++] << "\n";
```

```
    // (a) find each numeric character using find_first_not_of()
    pos = 0;
    while ((pos = s.find_first_not_of(alphabetic, pos)) != string::npos)
        cout << "s[ " << pos << " ] = " << s[pos++] << "\n";

    // (b) find each alphabet character using find_first_of()
    pos = 0;
    while ((pos = s.find_first_of(alphabetic, pos)) != string::npos)
        cout << "s[ " << pos << " ] = " << s[pos++] << "\n";

    // (b) find each alphabet character using find_first_not_of()
    pos = 0;
    while ((pos = s.find_first_not_of(numerics, pos)) != string::npos)
        cout << "s[ " << pos << " ] = " << s[pos++] << "\n";

    return 0;
}
```

Exercise 6.14

Write a program that, given the string

```
    string line1 = "We are her pride of 10 she named us --";
    string line2 = " Benjamin, Phoenix, the Prodigal ";
    string line3 = "and perspicacious pacific Suzanne";

    string sentence = line1 + line2 + line3;
```

counts the number of words in the sentence and identifies the largest and smallest words. If more than one word is either the largest or smallest, keep track of all of them.

This version is similar to the code that appears in L&L, Section 6.8.

```
    #include    <iostream>
    #include    <string>
    #include    <vector>
    #include    <map>
    using namespace std;

    int main()
    {
        string line1 = "We were her pride of 10 she named us --";
        string line2 = " Benjamin, Phoenix, the Prodigal ";
        string line3 = "and perspicacious pacific Suzanne";
        string sentence = line1 + line2 + line3;
```

```cpp
cout << '"' << sentence << '"' << endl;

string::size_type pos = 0, prev_pos = 0;
typedef pair<short,string> track;
vector<track>              words;
string                     word;
short                      len;

// collect the words in sentence
while ((pos = sentence.find_first_of(' ', pos)) != string::npos) {
    len = pos - prev_pos;
    word = sentence.substr(prev_pos, len);
    cout << word << endl;
    words.push_back(make_pair(len, word));
    prev_pos = ++pos;
}
// collect the last word
len = sentence.size() - prev_pos;
word = sentence.substr(prev_pos, len);
cout << word << endl;
words.push_back(make_pair(len, word));

int min = words[0].first;
int max = words[0].first;
int i;

// determine min and max count
for (i = 0; i < words.size(); ++i) {
    if (min > words[i].first)
        min = words[i].first;
    if (max < words[i].first)
        max = words[i].first;
}
cout << "MIN\n";
for (i = 0; i < words.size(); ++i) {
    if (min == words[i].first)
        cout << words[i].first << " " << words[i].second << endl;
}
cout << "MAX\n";
for (i = 0; i < words.size(); ++i) {
    if (max == words[i].first)
        cout << words[i].first << " " << words[i].second << endl;
}
```

```
        return 0;
    }
```

The next version is simpler because we added an extra character (\n) at the end of the string and modified the arguments passed to find_first_not_of() to include a blank and a newline character. We also determine min and max in the same loop that acquires the words.

```
#include     <iostream>
#include     <string>
#include     <vector>
#include     <map>
using namespace std;

int main()
{
    string line1 = "We were her pride of 10 she named us --";
    string line2 = " Benjamin, Phoenix, the Prodigal ";
    string line3 = "and perspicacious pacific Suzanne\n";
    string sentence = line1 + line2 + line3;

    cout << '"' << sentence << '"' << endl;

    string::size_type pos = 0, prev_pos = 0;
    typedef pair<short,string> track;
    vector<track>              words;
    string                     word;
    short                      len;
    int min = sentence.length();
    int max = 0;

    // collect the words in sentence
    while ((pos = sentence.find_first_of(" \n", pos)) != string::npos) {
        len = pos - prev_pos;
        word = sentence.substr(prev_pos, len);
        cout << word << endl;
        words.push_back(make_pair(len, word));

        // determine min and max count
        if (min > len)
            min = len;
        if (max < len)
            max = len;
```

```
            prev_pos = ++pos;
        }

        int i;
        cout << "MIN\n";
        for (i = 0; i < words.size(); ++i) {
            if (min == words[i].first)
                cout << words[i].first << " " << words[i].second << endl;
        }
        cout << "MAX\n";
        for (i = 0; i < words.size(); ++i) {
            if (max == words[i].first)
                cout << words[i].first << " " << words[i].second << endl;
        }

        return 0;
    }
```

Exercise 6.15

Write a program that, given the string

```
"/.+(STL).*$1/"
```

erases all the characters except STL first using erase(pos, count) **and then using** erase(iter,iter).

This is a Perl regular expression in which the $1 refers to the field in parentheses.
The original exercise statement uses

```
"/.+(STL).*$1/"
```

We use

```
"/.+(STL).*$1STL/"
```

to make sure we catch STL in more than one place in the string.

```
#include      <iostream>
#include      <string>
using namespace std;

int main()
{
    string s = "/.+(STL).*$1STL/";
    string filter = "STL";
    string t = s;
```

```
cout << t << endl;
string::size_type pos  = 0;
string::size_type last = 0;

while ((pos = t.find(filter, pos)) != string::npos) {
    t.erase(last, pos - last);
    pos = last = last + filter.size();
    cout << '\t' << t << "pos: " << pos << endl;
}
// erase the remaining non-STL characters
t.erase(last, t.size() - last);
cout << t << endl;

t = s;
string::iterator here = t.begin();
string::iterator there;
string::size_type cur = 0;  // current position remaining string
pos = 0;

while ((pos = t.find(filter, pos)) != string::npos) {
    there = here + pos - cur;
    t.erase(here, there);
    cur += filter.size();
    pos = cur;
    here = t.begin() + cur;
}
// erase the remaining non-STL characters
t.erase(here, t.end());
cout << t << endl;

return 0;
}
```

The find() method works properly in this solution. Stan Lippman pointed out that the find_first_not_of() method would not work as part of the solution for this exercise. Why not? It is because the latter method returns the index of the first character that does not occur in filter. So any permutation of STL succeeds, and that is not what we want. We wish to erase all the characters except STL but not its permutations.

Exercise 6.16

Write a program that accepts these definitions:

```
string sentence( "kind of" );
string s1( "whistle" );
string s2( "pixie" );
```

Using the various insert string functions, provide sentence **with the value**

```
"A whistling-dixie kind of walk."
```

One solution uses straightforward calls:

```
string sentence("kind of");
string s1("whistle");
string s2("pixie");

sentence.insert(0, "A ");
cout << sentence << endl;
sentence.insert(2, s1);
cout << sentence << endl;
sentence.erase(8, 1);
cout << sentence << endl;
sentence.insert(8, "ing-d");
cout << sentence << endl;
sentence.insert(13, s2, 1, s2.size()-1);
cout << sentence << endl;
sentence.insert(17, " ");
cout << sentence << endl;
sentence.insert(sentence.size(), " walk.");
cout << sentence << endl;
```

Another solution combines a number of calls:

```
string sentence("kind of");
string s1("whistle");
string s2("pixie");

sentence.insert(0, "A ").insert(2, s1).erase(8, 1).
    insert(8, "ing-d").insert(13, s2, 1, s2.size()-1).
    insert(17, " ");
sentence.insert(sentence.size(), " walk.");
cout << sentence << endl;
```

Exercise 6.17

Our program does not handle suffixes ending in ed, **as in** surprised; ly, **as in** surprisingly; **and** ing, **as in** surprising. **Add one of the following suffix handlers to the program: (a)** suffix_ed(), **(b)** suffix_ly(), **or (c)** suffix_ing().

We added `suffix_ed()`:

```
void suffix_ed(vector<string> *words)
{
    vector<string>::iterator iter = words->begin();
    vector<string>::iterator iter_end = words->end();

    while (iter != iter_end)
    {
        // if 3 or less characters, let it be
        if (iter->size() <= 3) {
            ++iter;
            continue;
        }
        // does the word end with ed? drop 'ed'
        if (iter->compare(iter->size()-2, 2, "ed") == 0)
            *iter = iter->substr(0, iter->size()-2);
        ++iter;
    }
}
```

This solution does not address all situations. For example, "tried -> try" is not covered here.

Exercise 6.18

Write a program that accepts the following two strings:

```
string quote1( "When lilacs last in the dooryard bloom'd" );
string quote2( "The child is father of the man" );
```

Using the `assign()` **and** `append()` **operations, create the string**

```
string sentence( "The child is in the dooryard" );
```

```
#include    <iostream>
#include    <string>
using namespace std;

int main()
{
    string quote1("When lilacs last in the dooryard bloom'd");
    string quote2("The child is father of the man");
    string sentence;

    // our compiler does not allow assign() with a string argument
    //sentence.assign(quote2, 13);
```

```
// use c_str() to obtain char *
sentence.assign(quote2.c_str(), 13);
cout << "sentence is '" << sentence << "'\n";
sentence.append(quote1.c_str()+17, 15);
cout << "sentence is '" << sentence << "'\n";

return 0;
}
```

Exercise 6.19

Write a program that, given the strings

```
string generic1( "Dear Ms Daisy:" );
string generic2( "MrsMsMissPeople" );
```

implements the function

```
string generate_salutation( string generic1,
                            string lastName,
                            string generic2,
                            string::size_type pos,
                            int length );
```

using the `replace()` **operations, where** `lastname` **replaces** Daisy **and** pos **indexes into** generic2 **of** length **characters replacing** Ms. **For example, the following**

```
string lastName( "AnnaP" );
string greetings =
        generate_salutation( generic1, lastName, generic2,
                5, 4 );
```

returns the string

```
Dear Miss AnnaP:
```

Here's the function:

```
string generate_salutation(string generic1,
                           string lastName,
                           string generic2,
                           string::size_type pos,
                           int length)
{
    // replace the last name first
    generic1.replace(8, 5, lastName);
    // replace the title
    generic1.replace(5, 2, generic2, pos, length);
    return generic1;
}
```

Exercise 6.20

Define a map for which the index is the family surname and the key is a vector of the children's names. Populate the map with at least six entries. Test it by supporting user queries based on a surname, adding a child to one family and triplets to another, and printing out all the map entries.

```
int main()
{
    typedef vector<string> children;
    typedef string surname;
    map<surname, children> family;

    // populate the map
    family["a"].push_back("a1");
    family["b"].push_back("b1");
    family["b"].push_back("b2");
    family["c"].push_back("c1");
    family["c"].push_back("c2");
    family["c"].push_back("c3");
    family["d"].push_back("d1");
    family["d"].push_back("d2");
    family["d"].push_back("d3");
    family["d"].push_back("d4");
    family["e"].push_back("e1");
    family["e"].push_back("e2");
    family["e"].push_back("e3");
    family["f"].push_back("f1");
    family["f"].push_back("f2");
    family["g"].push_back("g1");

    map<surname, children>::iterator mi;
    children::iterator vi;
    string s;

    // print out all the map entries
    for (mi = family.begin(); mi != family.end(); ++mi) {
        s = mi->first;
        cout << s << endl;
        for (vi = mi->second.begin(); vi != mi->second.end(); ++vi)
            cout << s << "\t" << *vi << endl;
    }
```

```
            // allow for queries based on family surnames
            cout << "Please enter family name: ";
            string name;
            cin >> name;
            while (! name.empty()) {
                cout << name << endl;
                for (vi = family[name].begin();
                        vi != family[name].end(); ++vi)
                    cout << name << "\t" << *vi << endl;
                cout << "Please enter family name: ";
                cin >> name;
            }

            return 0;
    }
```

Exercise 6.21

Extend the map of Exercise 6.20 by having the vector store a pair of strings: the child's name and birthday. Revise the Exercise 6.20 implementation to support the new pair vector. Test your modified test program to verify its correctness.

The vector children now contains a pair: an object that contains two other objects. The two objects are of type string: the child's name and birthday.

```
    typedef pair<string, string> child;
    typedef vector<child> children;
```

To populate the map we use make_pair() to create an object that will be pushed back into the vector of pairs.

```
    family["a"].push_back(make_pair(string("a1"), string("01/01")));
    family["b"].push_back(make_pair(string("b1"), string("02/02")));
    family["b"].push_back(make_pair(string("b2"), string("02/03")));
    family["c"].push_back(make_pair(string("c1"), string("03/04")));
    family["c"].push_back(make_pair(string("c2"), string("03/05")));
    family["c"].push_back(make_pair(string("c3"), string("03/06")));
```

When displaying the map entries we traverse the vector of pairs and display each pair:

```
    map<surname, children>::iterator mi;
    children::iterator vi;
    string s;

    // print all the map entries
    for (mi = family.begin(); mi != family.end(); ++mi) {
```

```
        s = mi->first;
        cout << s << endl;
        for (vi = mi->second.begin(); vi != mi->second.end(); ++vi)
            cout << s << "\t" << vi->first << "\t" << vi->second << endl;
}
```

Exercise 6.22

List at least three possible applications in which the map type might be of use. Write
the definition of each map and indicate how the elements are likely to be inserted and
retrieved.

1.   Create a map from employee name to wages:

```
        map< string, double > employee;
        employee["name"] = wage;
```

2.   Create a map from wages to a vector of employee names, representing all employees
      that receive the same wages:

```
        map< float, vector<string> > employee;
        employee[wage].push_back(name);
```

3.   Create a map from strings to ints, representing phone book entries:

```
        map< string, int > phone_book;
        phone_book["your name"] = 5551212;
```

For more information on this example, see *The C++ Programming Language*, third
edition, Bjarne Stroustrup, Addison-Wesley, 1997, pages 55 and 487.

Exercise 6.23

Add an exclusion set of handling words in which the trailing 's' should not be removed
but for which there exists no general rule. For example, three words to place in this set are
the proper names Pythagoras, Brahms, and Burne_Jones. Fold the use of this exclusion
set into the suffix_s() function of Section 6.10.

Here's the exclusion set:
```
    set<string> exclusion_set;
    exclusion_set.insert("Pythagoras");
    exclusion_set.insert("Brahms");
    exclusion_set.insert("Burne_Jones");
```

We modified `suffix_s()` to take one more argument containing the exclusion set. While iterating through the words in the vector that `words` points to, we invoke `count()` to check whether the word is part of the exclusion set.

```
void suffix_s(vector<string> *words,
              const set<string> &exclusion_set)
{
    vector<string>::iterator iter = words->begin();
    vector<string>::iterator iter_end = words->end();

    while (iter != iter_end)
    {
        // word part of exclusion set?
        if (exclusion_set.count(*iter))
            cout << "\texclude\t" << *iter << endl;

        // ...
        ++iter;
    }
}
```

Exercise 6.24

Define a vector of books you'd like to read within the next virtual six months, and a set of titles that you've read. Write a program that chooses a next book for you to read from the vector provided you have not yet read it. When it returns the selected title to you, it should enter the title in the set of books read. If in fact you end up putting the book aside, provide support for removing the title from the set of books read. At the end of our virtual six months, print the set of books read and those books that were not read.

We create a small vector of books to read and then randomly pick six books. We remove from the vector each book selected, but we choose to put back every fourth book, to indicate that we picked it but did not read it.

Finally, we list the books read and the books that were not read.

Here's the program:

```
#include    <iostream>
#include    <string>
#include    <vector>
#include    <set>
using namespace std;

int main()
{
    set<string> books_read;
    vector<string> books_to_read;
```

```
books_to_read.push_back("AAA");
books_to_read.push_back("BBBB");
books_to_read.push_back("CCCCC");
books_to_read.push_back("DDDDDD");
books_to_read.push_back("EEEEEEE");
books_to_read.push_back("FFFFFFFF");

// initialize random number generator
srand(33);

int i;
// try to pick 6 books
for (i = 0; i < 6; ++i) {
    // generate a pseudo-random number
    int j = rand() % books_to_read.size();

    string book = books_to_read[j];
    cout << "\t" << book << endl;
    books_to_read.erase(books_to_read.begin() + j);

    if (books_read.count(book))
        cout << "\talready read\t" << book << endl;
    else {
        if (i % 4 != 0)      // not a fourth book: read it
            books_read.insert(book);
        else {                 // put back every fourth book
            cout << "putting back book " << book << endl;
            books_to_read.push_back(book);
        }
    }
}
cout << "Books read:\n";

set<string>::iterator iter;
for (iter = books_read.begin(); iter != books_read.end(); ++iter)
    cout << "\t" << *iter << endl;

cout << "Books not read:\n";

for (i = 0; i < books_to_read.size(); ++i)
    cout << "\t" << books_to_read[i] << endl;

return 0;
}
```

Exercise 6.25

Explain why we need to use the special inserter iterator to populate the exclusion word set. (It is briefly explained in Section 6.13.1, and discussed in detail in Section 12.4.1.)

```
set<string> exclusion_set;
ifstream    infile( "exclusion_set" );
// ...
copy( default_excluded_words, default_excluded_words+25,
      inserter( exclusion_set, exclusion_set.begin() ));
```

The `inserter()` iterator is necessary because we wish to insert data into the set exclusion_set, but the set does not yet have any space allocated. The iterator causes the container's `insert()` operation to be invoked in place of the assignment operator. This means that the iterator indirectly causes the necessary space to be allocated as needed.

Exercise 6.26

Our original implementation reflects a procedural solution — that is, a collection of global functions operating on an independent set of unencapsulated data structures. Our final program reflects an alternative solution in which we wrap the functions and data structures within a TextQuery class. Compare the two approaches. What are the drawbacks and strengths of each?

An alternative solution using a class would improve the program. Some of the reasons are as follows.

- The data could be private, and only the methods in the class would have access to it.

- Some of the methods will not be invoked by the user but only by other public methods; consequently, some of the methods could be private.

- We could reimplement the class while maintaining the same interface. The user would not have access to the data or access to the implementation details of the methods.

Exercise 6.27

In this version of the program, the user is prompted for the text file to be handled. A more convenient implementation would allow the user to specify the file on the program

command line — we'll see how to support command line arguments to a program in Chapter 7. What other command line options should our program support?

The program could support a few options, each followed by a file name, to inform the program about

- Exclusion words
- Words terminated with 's'
- Words terminated with 'ed'

Exercise 6.28

Reimplement the text query program of Section 6.14 to use a multimap in which each location is entered separately. What are the performance and design characteristics of the two solutions? Which do you feel is the preferred design solution? Why?

We make a few changes to go from a `map` to a `multimap`. The advantage is that by using `multimap` we simplify the data structure that remembers each word and the line/location pairs indicating where the word appears.

The original class `TextQuery` defined

```
map<string,loc*,less<string> >  *word_map;
```

Each map entry would contain a string and a pointer to `loc`, where `loc` was a typedef:

```
typedef pair<short,short>  location;
typedef vector<location>   loc;
```

That is, `loc` is a synonym for a vector that contains pairs of `shorts` (each pair indicates the line number and location of the word within the line). So for each word, there is an associated vector of pairs of line numbers and locations.

The modified class `TextQuery` uses `multimap`:

```
multimap<string,location,less<string> >  *word_map;
```

Each multimap entry contains a string and a `location` that is a pair consisting of a line number and a location. The multimap allows us to store multiple occurrences of the same word in the text as separate entries in the multimap.

The declarations in `build_word_map()` were modified to use `multimap`:

```
word_map = new multimap< string, location, less<string> >;
typedef multimap<string,location,less<string> >::value_type value_type;
```

The original code checked whether a word was not in the map yet; that is, it checked whether `count()` returned the value zero. If it did, the code added the word to the map and created the vector that would contain the line numbers and locations. If the word already appeared in the map, the code added only the line number and location to the vector.

```
    if (! word_map->count((*text_words)[ix]))
    { // not present, add it:
        loc *ploc = new vector<location>;
        ploc->push_back((*text_locs)[ix]);
        word_map->insert(value_type((*text_words)[ix], ploc));
    }
    else (*word_map)[(*text_words)[ix]]->push_back((*text_locs)[ix]);
```

Using multimap, the preceding code is replaced with

```
    word_map->insert(value_type((*text_words)[ix], (*text_locs)[ix]));
```

The second half of query_code() must be modified to reflect our new way of storing the information in a multimap.

```
    set<short,less<short> >  occurrence_lines;
    int size = word_map->count(query_text);
    multimap<string,location,less<string> >::iterator iter;

    iter = word_map->find(query_text);


    while (size--) {
        occurrence_lines.insert(occurrence_lines.end(),
                                (*iter).second.first);
        ++iter;
    }


    size = occurrence_lines.size();
    cout << "\n" << query_text
         << " occurs " << size
         << (size == 1 ? " time:" : " times:")
         << "\n\n";

    set<short,less<short> >::iterator  it = occurrence_lines.begin();
    for (; it != occurrence_lines.end(); ++it) {
        int line = *it;

        cout << "\t( line "
             // don't confound user with text lines starting at 0 ...
             << line + 1 << " ) "
             << (*lines_of_text)[line] << endl;
    }
```

The `display_map_text()` becomes simpler with `multimap`:

```
void
TextQuery::
display_map_text()
{
    typedef multimap<string,location,less<string> >  map_text;
    map_text::iterator iter = word_map->begin(),
                       iter_end = word_map->end();
    for ( ; iter != iter_end; iter++) {
        cerr << "word: " << (*iter).first << " (";
        cerr << (*iter).second.first << ",";
        cerr << (*iter).second.second << ")\n";
    }

    cerr << endl;
}
```

The rest of the code remains the same.

The design of the program became simpler with `multimap`. We prefer this solution over the original one.

Exercise 6.29

Reimplement the `peek()` function (Exercise 4.23 of Section 4.15) for our dynamic Stack class template.

Here's the new `peek()` function:

```
bool iStack::peek(int &top_value)
{
    if (empty())
        return false;

    top_value = _stack[ size()-1 ];    // only modification
    cout << "iStack::peek(): " << top_value << endl;
    return true;
}
```

Exercise 6.30

Provide the revised member operations for our Stack class template. Run the test program of Section 4.15 against the new implementation.

We modified `stack.h` and reimplemented the member operations for the template.

```cpp
#include    <vector>
using namespace std;

template <class elemType>
class Stack {
  public:
    Stack(int capacity = 0) : _stack(capacity) { }
    bool pop(elemType &value);
    bool push(elemType value);
    bool peek(elemType &value);

    bool full();
    bool empty();
    void display();

    int size();
  private:
    vector< elemType > _stack;
};

template <class elemType>
inline bool Stack<elemType>::empty() { return _stack.empty(); }

template <class elemType>
inline int Stack<elemType>::size() { return _stack.size(); }

template <class elemType>
inline bool Stack<elemType>::full()
{
    return _stack.max_size() == _stack.size();
}

template <class elemType>
bool Stack<elemType>::pop(elemType &top_value)
{
    if (empty())
        return false;

    top_value = _stack[ size()-1 ];
    _stack.pop_back();
    cout << "Stack::pop(): " << top_value << endl;
    return true;
}
```

```
template <class elemType>
bool Stack<elemType>::push(elemType value)
{

    if (full())
        return false;

    cout << "Stack::push( " << value << " )\n";
    _stack.push_back(value);
    return true;
}


template <class elemType>
void Stack<elemType>::display()
{
    cout << "( " << size() << " )(bot: ";

    for (int ix = 0; ix < size(); ++ix)
        cout << _stack[ix] << " ";

    cout << ":top )\n";
}


template <class elemType>
bool Stack<elemType>::peek(elemType &top_value)
{
    if (empty())
        return false;

    top_value = _stack[ size()-1 ];
    cout << "Stack::peek(): " << top_value << endl;
    return true;
}
```

Exercise 6.31

Using the model of the List class in Section 5.11.1, encapsulate our Stack class template in the Primer_Third_Edition namespace.

We created the namespace encapsulating the template `Stack`:

```
namespace Primer_Third_Edition
{
    template <class elemType>
    class Stack {
        // ...
    }
}
```

We could use

```
template <typename elemType>
```

instead of

```
template <class elemType>
```

with the same results.

chapter seven

Functions

Exercise 7.1

Which, if any, of the following function prototypes are invalid? Why?

```
(a) set(int *, int);
(b) void func();
(c) string error(int);
(d) arr[10] sum(int *, int);
```

(b) and (c) are correct.

```
(a) set(int *, int);
```

   Invalid. Functions must specify a return type.

```
(d) arr[10] sum(int *, int);
```

   Invalid. Functions cannot return arrays.

Exercise 7.2

Write the prototypes for each of the following functions:

  (a) A function named `compare` with two parameters that are references to a class named `matrix` and with a return value of type `bool`

  (b) A function named `extract` with no parameters and returning a set of integers (where `set` is the container type defined in Section 6.13)

We build each prototype step-by-step.

(a)   A function named `compare` with two parameters that are references to a class named
       `matrix` and with a return value of type `bool`

First, we write a function named `compare`.

```
compare()
```

We add two parameters that are `const` references to a class named `matrix` (the parameters
are declared `const` because the function will not change the values of the matrices).

```
compare(const matrix &, const matrix &)
```

Then we add a return value of type `bool`.

```
bool compare(const matrix &, const matrix &);
```

(b)   A function named `extract` with no parameters and returning a set of integers (where
       set is the container type defined in Section 6.13)

We write a function named `extract`.

```
extract()
```

It has no parameters.

```
extract(void)
```

Note that the `void` is optional when we're declaring a function with no parameters. We will
omit the `void` in our declarations.

The function returns a set of integers.

```
set<int> extract();
```

Exercise 7.3

Given the following declarations, which function calls, if any, are in error? Why?

```
double calc(double);
int count(const string &, char);
void sum(vector<int> &, int);
vector<int> vec(10);
```

(a) `calc(23.4, 55.1);`
(b) `count("abcda", 'a');`
(c) `sum(vec, 43.8);`
(d) `calc(66);`

(b), (c), and (d) are correct.

(a) `calc(23.4, 55.1);`

Error. `calc()` takes only one argument.

(b) `count("abcda", 'a');`

OK. The string literal "abcda" is converted from type `const char *` to the type `string` using an implicit conversion.

(c) `sum(vec, 43.8);`

OK. The value `43.8` is converted from type `double` to type `int`. As a result of this conversion, the value is truncated to 43.

(d) `calc(66);`

OK. The value 66 is promoted to type `double`.

Exercise 7.4

Which, if any, of the following declarations are errors? Why?
```
(a) void print(int arr[][], int size);
(b) int ff(int a, int b = 0, int c = 0);
(c) void operate(int *matrix[]);
(d) char *screenInit(int height = 24, int width,
                     char background);
(e) void putValues(int (&ia)[]);
```

(b) and (c) are correct.

(a) `void print(int arr[][], int size);`

Error. The size of the second dimension of `arr` must be specified. The general rule is this: If a parameter is of array type, only the first dimension can be omitted.

(d) `char *screenInit(int height = 24, int width,`
                     `char background);`

Error. `height` cannot be given a default argument unless all arguments that follow it (`width` and `background`) also have default arguments.

(e) `void putValues(int (&ia)[]);`

Error. Because `ia` is a reference to an array parameter, its size must be specified.

Exercise 7.5

The redeclaration of each of these functions is an error. Why?

```
(a) char *screenInit(int height, int width,
                     char background = ' ');
    char *screenInit(int height = 24, int width,
                     char background);

(b) void print(int (*arr)[6], int size);
    void print(int (*arr)[5], int size);

(c) void manip(int *pi, int first, int end = 0);
    void manip(int *pi, int first = 0, int end = 0);
```

Here are the answers.

```
(a) char *screenInit(int height, int width,
                     char background = ' ');
    char *screenInit(int height = 24, int width,
                     char background);
```

For `height` to have a default parameter, all the parameters that follow it must also have default values. The default value for `background` is set in the first declaration, but none is given for `width` in either declaration.

```
(b) void print(int (*arr)[6], int size);
    void print(int (*arr)[5], int size);
```

The size of an array is not part of its parameter type. Only for parameters of array type is there a conversion from array to pointer (and hence the value of the first dimension is lost). In this case, because the parameter is already a pointer, there is no conversion and all other dimensions must be specified. (Note: Our compiler accepted the redeclaration in (b).)

```
(c) void manip(int *pi, int first, int end = 0);
    void manip(int *pi, int first = 0, int end = 0);
```

The default argument for `end` should not be respecified. The correct redeclaration is

```
    void manip(int *pi, int first = 0, int end);
```

Exercise 7.6

Given the following function declarations, which ones, if any, of the following function calls are errors? Why?

```
// declarations
void print(int arr[][5], int size);
void operate(int *matrix[7]);
char *screenInit(int height = 24, int width = 80,
                 char background = ' ');
```

(a) `screenInit();`

(b) `int *matrix[5];`
    `operate(matrix);`

(c) `int arr[5][5];`
    `print(arr, 5);`

All three function calls are syntactically correct. (b) could have potential run-time problems because the function is expecting an array of size 7.

Exercise 7.7

Rewrite the `putValues()` function provided for `vector<int>` and presented in Subsection 7.3.4 to handle `list<string>` instead. Print one string per line so that a list of two strings would print as follows:

```
( 2 )
<
"first string"
"second string"
>
```

Write a function `main()` that invokes this new `putValues()` function for a list of strings containing the following values:

```
"put function declarations in header files"
"use abstract container types instead of built-in arrays"
"declare class parameters as references"
"use reference to const types for invariant parameters"
"use less than eight parameters"
```

The changes are straightforward. We use an iterator instead of an index variable to traverse the list. `main()` initializes the list and calls `putValues()`.

Here is the complete program.

```
#include <iostream>
#include <list>
#include <string>
using namespace std;
```

```
    void putValues(const list<string> &strlist)
    {
        cout << "( " << strlist.size() << " )\n<\n";

        for (list<string>::const_iterator i = strlist.begin();
             i != strlist.end(); ++i)
            cout << '"' << *i << '"' << endl;

        cout << ">\n";
    }

    int main()
    {
        list<string> strlist;

        strlist.push_back("put function declarations in header files");
        strlist.push_back("use abstract container types "
                          "instead of built-in arrays");
        strlist.push_back("declare class parameters as references");
        strlist.push_back("use reference to const types for invariant "
                          "parameters");
        strlist.push_back("use less than eight parameters");

        putValues(strlist);

        return 0;
    }
```

Exercise 7.8

When would you use a parameter that is a pointer? When would you use a parameter that is a reference? Explain the advantages and disadvantages of each.

Both pointer and reference parameters are used when the function must modify the argument or when the argument is large and passing it by value would be inefficient. If the argument is being passed by reference for reasons of efficiency alone, it is best to declare the parameter as const.

A pointer is better suited for a parameter that may not point to an object or may be used to point to more than one object at different times.

A reference parameter has the advantage of not requiring the caller to explicitly pass the address of an argument, and the function does not have to use the dereference operator to access the value of the argument.

Exercise 7.9

What are the two forms of the `return` statement? Explain when you would use each form.

The two forms of `return` are `return;` and `return` *expression*`;`.

The first form is used to return from a function with a `void` return type. The second form is used when a function returns a value. The *expression* must be the same type as the function return type, or there must be a conversion available to convert *expression* to the return type.

Exercise 7.10

What potential run-time problem do you see with the following function definition?

```
vector<string> &readText()
{
    vector<string> text;

    string word;
    while (cin >> word) {
        text.push_back(word);
        // ...
    }

    // ...
    return text;
}
```

`text` is an automatic `vector` of `strings` that will go out of scope and have its destructor called when `readText()` returns. Because `readText()` returns a reference to `text`, any attempt by the caller to use the return value is likely to lead to a run-time error.

Exercise 7.11

How would you return more than one value from a function? Describe the advantages and disadvantages of your approach.

One method to return more than one value from a function is to use a reference parameter for each of the return values. This technique has the advantage of freeing the caller from having to explicitly pass an address and also allows the caller to control the storage allocation of the objects. Conversely, this may be a disadvantage if the function needs the freedom to dynamically allocate the returned objects; in this case, a reference to a pointer parameter should be used. Another possible way to return more than one value is to return a `pair` object or some other composite structure.

Exercise 7.12

Rewrite `factorial()` **as an iterative function.**

Here is the iterative version. It holds the partial result in a local variable `product`. `val` is decremented in the loop until it reaches the same stopping condition as the recursive version.

```
unsigned long
iter_factorial(int val)
{
    int product;

    for (product = 1; val > 1; --val)
        product *= val;
    return product;
}
```

Exercise 7.13

What would happen if the stopping condition of `factorial()` **were as follows?**

```
if (val != 0)
```

On the recursive call, `val` is equal to 1 at the call site. This results in the inbound expression, `val-1`, being equal to zero, and `factorial()` will return zero. This result is propagated back through the recursive calls, and thus `factorial()` will always return zero.

Here is a look at part of the call and return sequence.

```
...
return 3 * factorial(2)
            return 2 * factorial(1)
                        return 1 * factorial(0)
                                    return 0
                        return 1 * 0
            return 2 * 0
return 3 * 0
...
```

Although `factorial` is not defined for negative numbers, this change would cause an infinite loop to occur if `factorial()` were called with a negative value.

Exercise 7.14

exit(), printf(), malloc(), strcpy(), and strlen() are C language library routines.
Modify the following C program so that it compiles and links under C++.

```
const char *str = "hello";

void *malloc(int);
char *strcpy(char *, const char *);
int printf(const char *, ...);
int exit(int);
int strlen(const char *);

int main()
{   /* C language program */

    char *s = malloc(strlen(str)+1);
    strcpy(s, str);
    printf("%s, world\n", s);

    exit(0);
}
```

We need only wrap the function prototypes in an extern "C" linkage directive.
Here is the modified program.

```
const char *str = "hello";

extern "C" {
    void *malloc(int);
    char *strcpy(char *, const char *);
    int printf(const char *, ...);
    int exit(int);
    int strlen(const char *);
}

int main()
{   /* C language program */

    char *s = (char *)malloc(strlen(str)+1);
    strcpy(s, str);
    printf("%s, world\n", s);

    return 0;
}
```

Exercise 7.15

Add handling for a -t option (which turns on a timer), and a -b option (which takes a bufsize **argument). Be sure to update** usage() **as well. For example:**

```
prog -t -b 512 data0
```

We model the handling of -t after that of -d and the handling of -b after that of -1. Three new variables are introduced:

```
bool timer_on = false;
bool bufsize_on = false;
int bufsize = -1;
```

Here is the new version:

```cpp
#include <iostream>
#include <string>
#include <vector>
#include <ctype.h>
using namespace std;

const char *const program_name = "comline";
const char *const program_version = "version 7.15";

inline void usage(int exit_value = 0)
{
    // prints a formatted usage message
    // and exits using the exit_value ...

    cerr << "usage:\n"
         << program_name << " "
         << "[-d] [-h] [-v] [-t]\n\t"
            // change begins
         << "[-b bufsize] [-o output_file] [-l limit] \n\t"
            // change ends
         << "file_name\n\t[file_name [file_name [...]]]\n\n"
         << "where [] indicates optional option:\n\n\t"
         << "-h: help.\n\t\t"
         << "generates this message and exits\n\n\t"
         << "-v: version.\n\t\t"
         << "prints version information and exits\n\n\t"
         << "-d: debug.\n\t\tturns debugging on\n\n\t"
         << "-t: timer.\n\t\tturns timer on\n\n\t"
            // change begins
         << "-b bufsize\n\t\t"
```

```
            << "bufsize must be a non-negative integer\n\n\t"
               // change ends
            << "-l limit\n\t\t"
            << "limit must be a non-negative integer\n\n\t"
            << "-o ofile\n\t\t"
            << "file within which to write out results\n\t\t\t"
            << "by default, results written to standard output\n\n"
            << "file_name\n\t\t"
            << "the name of the actual file to process\n\t\t"
            << "at least one file_name is required --\n\t\t"
            << "any number may be specified\n\n"
            << "examples:\n\t\t"
            << "$command chapter7.doc\n\t\t"
            << "$command -d -l 1024 -o test_7_8 "
            << "chapter7.doc chapter8.doc\n\n";

    exit(exit_value);
}

int main(int argc, char *argv[])
{
    bool debug_on = false;
    bool ofile_on = false;
    bool limit_on = false;
    int limit = -1;
    // change begins
    bool timer_on = false;
    bool bufsize_on = false;
    int bufsize = -1;
    // change ends

    string ofile;
    vector<string> file_names;

    cout << "illustration of handling command line arguments:\n"
         << "argc: " << argc << endl;

    for (int ix = 1; ix < argc; ++ix) {
        cout << "argv[" << ix << "]: "
             << argv[ix] << endl;

        char *pchar = argv[ix];
        switch (pchar[0]) {
```

```
case '-':
{
    cout << "case \'-\' found\n";
    switch (pchar[1]) {
    case 'd':
        cout << "-d found: "
             << "debugging turned on\n";
        debug_on = true;
        break;

    // change begins
    case 't':
        cout << "-t found: "
             << "timer turned on\n";
        timer_on = true;
        break;
    // change ends

    case 'v':
        cout << "-v found: "
             << "version info displayed\n";
        cout << program_name
             << "::"
             << program_version
             << endl;
        return 0;

    case 'h':
        cout << "-h found: "
             << "help information\n";
        // no break necessary: usage() exits
        usage();

    case 'o':
        cout << "-o found: output file\n";

        ofile_on = true;
        break;

    case 'l':
        cout << "-l found: "
             << "resource limit\n";
        limit_on = true;
        break;
```

```
    // change begins
    case 'b':
        cout << "-b found: "
            << "bufsize\n";
        bufsize_on = true;
        break;
    // change ends

    default:
        cerr << program_name
            << " : error : "
            << "unrecognized option: - "
            << pchar << "\n\n";

        // no break necessary: usage() exits
        usage(-1);
    }
    break;
}
default:
    cout << "default non-hyphen argument: "
        << pchar << endl;

    if (ofile_on) {
        ofile_on = false;
        ofile = pchar;
    } else if (limit_on) {
        limit_on = false;
        limit = atoi(pchar);
        if (limit < 0) {
            cerr << program_name
                << " : error : "
                << "negative value for limit.\n\n";

            usage(-2);
        }
    // change begins
    } else if (bufsize_on) {
        bufsize_on = false;
        bufsize = atoi(pchar);
        if (bufsize < 0) {
            cerr << program_name
                << " : error : "
                << "negative value for bufsize.\n\n";
```

```
                    usage(-4);
                }
          // change ends
          } else
                file_names.push_back(string(pchar));
          break;
       }
}


if (file_names.empty()) {
    cerr << program_name
         << " : error : "
         << "no file specified for processing.\n\n";


    usage(-3);
}


if (limit != -1)
    cout << "User-specified limit: "
         << limit << endl;


// change begins
if (bufsize != -1)
    cout << "User-specified bufsize: "
         << bufsize << endl;
// change ends


if (!ofile.empty())
    cout << "User-specified output file: "
         << ofile << endl;


cout << (file_names.size() == 1 ? "File " : "Files ")
     << "to be processed are the following:\n";


for (int inx = 0; inx < file_names.size(); ++inx)
    cout << "\t" << file_names[inx] << endl;


return 0;
}
```

Exercise 7.16

Our implementation currently fails to handle the case of there being no space between the option and its associated value. Ideally, we would accept the option with or without the space. Modify our implementation to do this.

We need to make modifications for the three options that accept a value: o, l, and b. We discuss o here, but l and b are similar and are shown in the complete listing.

```
case 'o':
    cout << "-o found: output file\n";

    if (pchar[2] == '\0')
        ofile_on = true;
```

We check whether o is the last character in the string. If it is, we continue as before. Otherwise, we process the remainder of the argument.

```
    else {
        cout << "argument immediately following: "
             << &pchar[2] << endl;
        ofile = &pchar[2];
    }
    break;
```

If the associated value is present, we assign the value to ofile but do *not* set ofile_on to true.

Here is the complete version:

```
#include <iostream>
#include <string>
#include <vector>
#include <ctype.h>
using namespace std;

const char *const program_name = "comline";
const char *const program_version = "version 7.16";

inline void usage(int exit_value = 0)
{
    // prints a formatted usage message
    // and exits using the exit_value ...

    cerr << "usage:\n"
         << program_name << " "
         << "[-d] [-h] [-v] [-t]\n\t"
         << "[-b bufsize] [-o output_file] [-l limit] \n\t"
```

```
            << "file_name\n\t[file_name [file_name [...]]]\n\n"
            << "where [] indicates optional option:\n\n\t"
            << "-h: help.\n\t\t"
            << "generates this message and exits\n\n\t"
            << "-v: version.\n\t\t"
            << "prints version information and exits\n\n\t"
            << "-d: debug.\n\t\tturns debugging on\n\n\t"
            << "-t: timer.\n\t\tturns timer on\n\n\t"
            << "-b bufsize\n\t\t"
            << "bufsize must be a non-negative integer\n\n\t"
            << "-l limit\n\t\t"
            << "limit must be a non-negative integer\n\n\t"
            << "-o ofile\n\t\t"
            << "file within which to write out results\n\t\t"
            << "by default, results written to standard output\n\n"
            << "file_name\n\t\t"
            << "the name of the actual file to process\n\t\t"
            << "at least one file_name is required --\n\t\t"
            << "any number may be specified\n\n"
            << "examples:\n\t\t"
            << "$command chapter7.doc\n\t\t"
            << "$command -d -l 1024 -o test_7_8 "
            << "chapter7.doc chapter8.doc\n\n";

    exit(exit_value);
}

int main(int argc, char *argv[])
{
    bool debug_on = false;
    bool ofile_on = false;
    bool limit_on = false;
    int limit = -1;
    bool timer_on = false;
    bool bufsize_on = false;
    int bufsize = -1;

    string ofile;
    vector<string> file_names;

    cout << "illustration of handling command line arguments:\n"
         << "argc: " << argc << endl;
```

```
for (int ix = 1; ix < argc; ++ix) {
    cout << "argv[" << ix << "]: "
         << argv[ix] << endl;

    char *pchar = argv[ix];
    switch (pchar[0]) {
    case '-':
    {
        cout << "case \'-\' found\n";
        switch (pchar[1]) {
        case 'd':
            cout << "-d found: "
                 << "debugging turned on\n";
            debug_on = true;
            break;

        case 't':
            cout << "-t found: "
                 << "timer turned on\n";
            timer_on = true;
            break;

        case 'v':
            cout << "-v found: "
                 << "version info displayed\n";
            cout << program_name
                 << "::"
                 << program_version
                 << endl;
            return 0;

        case 'h':
            cout << "-h found: "
                 << "help information\n";
            // no break necessary: usage() exits
            usage();

        // change begins
        case 'o':
            cout << "-o found: output file\n";

            if (pchar[2] == '\0')
                ofile_on = true;
            else {
```

```
            cout << "argument immediately following: "
                    << &pchar[2] << endl;
            ofile = &pchar[2];
        }
        break;

    case 'l':
        cout << "-l found: "
                << "resource limit\n";
        if (pchar[2] == '\0')
            limit_on = true;
        else {
            cout << "argument immediately following: "
                    << &pchar[2] << endl;
            limit = atoi(&pchar[2]);
            if (limit < 0) {
                cerr << program_name
                        << " : error : "
                        << "negative value for limit.\n\n";

                usage(-2);
            }
        }
        break;

    case 'b':
        cout << "-b found: "
                << "bufsize\n";
        if (pchar[2] == '\0')
            bufsize_on = true;
        else {
            cout << "argument immediately following: "
                    << &pchar[2] << endl;
            bufsize = atoi(&pchar[2]);
            if (bufsize < 0) {
                cerr << program_name
                        << " : error : "
                        << "negative value for bufsize.\n\n";

                usage(-4);
            }
        }
        break;
// change ends
```

```
                default:
                    cerr << program_name
                            << " : error : "
                            << "unrecognized option: - "
                            << pchar << "\n\n";

                    // no break necessary: usage() exits
                    usage(-1);
                }

                break;
            }
            default:
                cout << "default non-hyphen argument: "
                        << pchar << endl;

                if (ofile_on) {
                    ofile_on = false;
                    ofile = pchar;
                } else if (limit_on) {
                    limit_on = false;
                    limit = atoi(pchar);
                    if (limit < 0) {
                        cerr << program_name
                                << " : error : "
                                << "negative value for limit.\n\n";

                        usage(-2);
                    }
                } else if (bufsize_on) {
                    bufsize_on = false;
                    bufsize = atoi(pchar);
                    if (bufsize < 0) {
                        cerr << program_name
                                << " : error : "
                                << "negative value for bufsize.\n\n";

                        usage(-4);
                    }
                } else
                    file_names.push_back(string(pchar));
                break;
        }
    }
```

```
            if (file_names.empty()) {
                cerr << program_name
                    << " : error : "
                    << "no file specified for processing.\n\n";

                usage(-3);
            }

            if (limit != -1)
                cout << "User-specified limit: "
                    << limit << endl;

            if (bufsize != -1)
                cout << "User-specified bufsize: "
                    << bufsize << endl;

            if (!ofile.empty())
                cout << "User-specified output file: "
                    << ofile << endl;

            cout << (file_names.size() == 1 ? "File " : "Files ")
                << "to be processed are the following:\n";

            for (int inx = 0; inx < file_names.size(); ++inx)
                cout << "\t" << file_names[inx] << endl;

            return 0;
        }
```

Exercise 7.17

Our implementation currently fails to handle the user error of adding a space between the hyphen and the option, as in

```
    prog - d data0
```

Modify our implementation to recognize and explicitly flag this error.

If the option letter does not immediately follow the hyphen, pchar[1] is the null character '\0'. We need only add a case for this that prints an error message and exits.

Here is the new version:

```
    #include <iostream>
    #include <string>
    #include <vector>
    #include <ctype.h>
    using namespace std;
```

```cpp
const char *const program_name = "comline";
const char *const program_version = "version 7.17";

inline void usage(int exit_value = 0)
{
    // prints a formatted usage message
    // and exits using the exit_value ...

    cerr << "usage:\n"
        << program_name << " "
        << "[-d] [-h] [-v] [-t]\n\t"
        << "[-b bufsize] [-o output_file] [-l limit] \n\t"
        << "file_name\n\t[file_name [file_name [...]]]\n\n"
        << "where [] indicates optional option:\n\n\t"
        << "-h: help.\n\t\t"
        << "generates this message and exits\n\n\t"
        << "-v: version.\n\t\t"
        << "prints version information and exits\n\n\t"
        << "-d: debug.\n\t\tturns debugging on\n\n\t"
        << "-t: timer.\n\t\tturns timer on\n\n\t"
        << "-b bufsize\n\t\t"
        << "bufsize must be a non-negative integer\n\n\t"
        << "-l limit\n\t\t"
        << "limit must be a non-negative integer\n\n\t"
        << "-o ofile\n\t\t"
        << "file within which to write out results\n\t\t"
        << "by default, results written to standard output\n\n"
        << "file_name\n\t\t"
        << "the name of the actual file to process\n\t\t"
        << "at least one file_name is required --\n\t\t"
        << "any number may be specified\n\n"
        << "examples:\n\t\t"
        << "$command chapter7.doc\n\t\t"
        << "$command -d -l 1024 -o test_7_8 "
        << "chapter7.doc chapter8.doc\n\n";

    exit(exit_value);
}

int main(int argc, char *argv[])
{
    bool debug_on = false;
    bool timer_on = false;
```

```cpp
bool ofile_on = false;
bool limit_on = false;
int limit = -1;
bool bufsize_on = false;
int bufsize = -1;

string ofile;
vector<string> file_names;

cout << "illustration of handling command line arguments:\n"
     << "argc: " << argc << endl;

for (int ix = 1; ix < argc; ++ix) {
    cout << "argv[" << ix << "]: "
         << argv[ix] << endl;

    char *pchar = argv[ix];
    switch (pchar[0]) {
    case '-':
    {
        cout << "case \'-\' found\n";
        switch (pchar[1]) {
        case 'd':
            cout << "-d found: "
                 << "debugging turned on\n";
            debug_on = true;
            break;

        case 't':
            cout << "-t found: "
                 << "timer turned on\n";
            timer_on = true;
            break;

        case 'v':
            cout << "-v found: "
                 << "version info displayed\n";
            cout << program_name
                 << "::"
                 << program_version
                 << endl;
            return 0;
```

```
        case 'h':
            cout << "-h found: "
                 << "help information\n";
            // no break necessary: usage() exits
            usage();

        case 'o':
            cout << "-o found: output file\n";

            if (pchar[2] == '\0')
                ofile_on = true;
            else {
                cout << "argument immediately following: "
                     << &pchar[2] << endl;
                ofile = &pchar[2];
            }
            break;

        case 'l':
            cout << "-l found: "
                 << "resource limit\n";
            if (pchar[2] == '\0')
                limit_on = true;
            else {
                cout << "argument immediately following: "
                     << &pchar[2] << endl;
                limit = atoi(&pchar[2]);
                if (limit < 0) {
                    cerr << program_name
                         << " : error : "
                         << "negative value for limit.\n\n";

                    usage(-2);
                }
            }
            break;

        case 'b':
            cout << "-b found: "
                 << "bufsize\n";
            if (pchar[2] == '\0')
                bufsize_on = true;
            else {
                cout << "argument immediately following: "
```

```
                << &pchar[2] << endl;
            bufsize = atoi(&pchar[2]);
            if (bufsize < 0) {
                cerr << program_name
                    << " : error : "
                    << "negative value for bufsize.\n\n";

                usage(-4);
            }
        }
        break;

    // change begins
    case '\0':
        cerr << program_name
            << " : error : "
            << "space following hyphen not allowed\n\n";

        usage(-5);
    // change ends

    default:
        cerr << program_name
            << " : error : "
            << "unrecognized option: - "
            << pchar << "\n\n";

        // no break necessary: usage() exits
        usage(-1);
    }

    break;
}
default:
    cout << "default non-hyphen argument: "
        << pchar << endl;

    if (ofile_on) {
        ofile_on = false;
        ofile = pchar;
    } else if (limit_on) {
        limit_on = false;
        limit = atoi(pchar);
        if (limit < 0) {
            cerr << program_name
                << " : error : "
                << "negative value for limit.\n\n";
```

```
                                usage(-2);
                    }
            } else if (bufsize_on) {
                bufsize_on = false;
                bufsize = atoi(pchar);
                if (bufsize < 0) {
                    cerr << program_name
                            << " : error : "
                            << "negative value for bufsize.\n\n";

                    usage(-4);
                }
            } else
                file_names.push_back(string(pchar));
            break;
        }
    }

    if (file_names.empty()) {
        cerr << program_name
                << " : error : "
                << "no file specified for processing.\n\n";

        usage(-3);
    }

    if (limit != -1)
        cout << "User-specified limit: "
                << limit << endl;

    if (bufsize != -1)
        cout << "User-specified bufsize: "
                << bufsize << endl;

    if (!ofile.empty())
        cout << "User-specified output file: "
                << ofile << endl;

    cout << (file_names.size() == 1 ? "File " : "Files ")
            << "to be processed are the following:\n";

    for (int inx = 0; inx < file_names.size(); ++inx)
        cout << "\t" << file_names[inx] << endl;

    return 0;
}
```

Exercise 7.18

Our implementation currently fails to recognize multiple instances of the −l or −o option. Modify our implementation to do this. What should the policy be?

Although our implementation does not "recognize" multiple instances of −l, −o, or −b, it accepts them and sets the appropriate object to the latest value. We will adopt this as our policy and simply add warnings to alert the user to the multiple instances.

Here is the new version:

```
#include <iostream>
#include <string>
#include <vector>
#include <ctype.h>
using namespace std;

const char *const program_name = "comline";
const char *const program_version = "version 7.18";

inline void usage(int exit_value = 0)
{
    // prints a formatted usage message
    // and exits using the exit_value ...

    cerr << "usage:\n"
        << program_name << " "
        << "[-d] [-h] [-v] [-t]\n\t"
        << "[-b bufsize] [-o output_file] [-l limit] \n\t"
        << "file_name\n\t[file_name [file_name [...]]]\n\n"
        << "where [] indicates optional option:\n\n\t"
        << "-h: help.\n\t\t"
        << "generates this message and exits\n\n\t"
        << "-v: version.\n\t\t"
        << "prints version information and exits\n\n\t"
        << "-d: debug.\n\t\tturns debugging on\n\n\t"
        << "-t: timer.\n\t\tturns timer on\n\n\t"
        << "-b bufsize\n\t\t"
        << "bufsize must be a non-negative integer\n\n\t"
        << "-l limit\n\t\t"
        << "limit must be a non-negative integer\n\n\t"
        << "-o ofile\n\t\t"
        << "file within which to write out results\n\t\t"
        << "by default, results written to standard output\n\n"
        << "file_name\n\t\t"
```

```
                     << "the name of the actual file to process\n\t\t"
                     << "at least one file_name is required --\n\t\t"
                     << "any number may be specified\n\n"
                     << "examples:\n\t\t"
                     << "$command chapter7.doc\n\t\t"
                     << "$command -d -l 1024 -o test_7_8 "
                     << "chapter7.doc chapter8.doc\n\n";

        exit(exit_value);
    }

int main(int argc, char *argv[])
{
    bool debug_on = false;
    bool timer_on = false;
    bool ofile_on = false;
    bool limit_on = false;
    int limit = -1;
    bool bufsize_on = false;
    int bufsize = -1;

    string ofile;
    vector<string> file_names;

    cout << "illustration of handling command line arguments:\n"
         << "argc: " << argc << endl;

    for (int ix = 1; ix < argc; ++ix) {
        cout << "argv[" << ix << "]: "
             << argv[ix] << endl;

        char *pchar = argv[ix];
        switch (pchar[0]) {
        case '-':
        {
            cout << "case \'-\' found\n";
            switch (pchar[1]) {
            case 'd':
                cout << "-d found: "
                     << "debugging turned on\n";
                debug_on = true;
                break;
```

```
case 't':
    cout << "-t found: "
        << "timer turned on\n";
    timer_on = true;
    break;

case 'v':
    cout << "-v found: "
        << "version info displayed\n";
    cout << program_name
        << "::"
        << program_version
        << endl;
    return 0;

case 'h':
    cout << "-h found: "
        << "help information\n";
    // no break necessary: usage() exits
    usage();

case 'o':
    cout << "-o found: output file\n";

    if (!ofile.empty()) {
        cerr << "Warning: multiple -o options specified. "
            << "Using latest value.\n";
    }

    if (pchar[2] == '\0')
        ofile_on = true;
    else {
        cout << "argument immediately following: "
            << &pchar[2] << endl;
        ofile = &pchar[2];
    }
    break;

case 'l':
    cout << "-l found: "
        << "resource limit\n";
```

```
        // change begins
        if (limit != -1) {
            cerr << "Warning: multiple -l options specified. "
                << "Using latest value.\n";
        }
        // change ends

        if (pchar[2] == '\0')
            limit_on = true;
        else {
            cout << "argument immediately following: "
                << &pchar[2] << endl;
            limit = atoi(&pchar[2]);
            if (limit < 0) {
                cerr << program_name
                        << " : error : "
                        << "negative value for limit.\n\n";

                usage(-2);
            }
        }
        break;

    case 'b':
        cout << "-b found: "
            << "bufsize\n";

        // change begins
        if (bufsize != -1) {
            cerr << "Warning: multiple -b options specified. "
                << "Using latest value.\n";
        }
        // change ends

        if (pchar[2] == '\0')
            bufsize_on = true;
        else {
            cout << "argument immediately following: "
                << &pchar[2] << endl;
            bufsize = atoi(&pchar[2]);
            if (bufsize < 0) {
                cerr << program_name
                        << " : error : "
                        << "negative value for bufsize.\n\n";
```

```
                    usage(-4);
                }
            }
            break;
        case '\0':
            cerr << program_name
                << " : error : "
                << "space following hyphen not allowed\n\n";
            usage(-5);
        default:
            cerr << program_name
                << " : error : "
                << "unrecognized option: - "
                << pchar << "\n\n";

            // no break necessary: usage() exits
            usage(-1);
        }

        break;
    }
default:
    cout << "default non-hyphen argument: "
         << pchar << endl;
    if (ofile_on) {
        ofile_on = false;
        ofile = pchar;
    } else if (limit_on) {
        limit_on = false;
        limit = atoi(pchar);
        if (limit < 0) {
            cerr << program_name
                << " : error : "
                << "negative value for limit.\n\n";
            usage(-2);
        }
    } else if (bufsize_on) {
        bufsize_on = false;
        bufsize = atoi(pchar);
        if (bufsize < 0) {
            cerr << program_name
                << " : error : "
                << "negative value for bufsize.\n\n";
```

```
                    usage(-4);
                }
            } else
                file_names.push_back(string(pchar));
            break;
        }
    }


    if (file_names.empty()) {
        cerr << program_name
            << " : error : "
            << "no file specified for processing.\n\n";


        usage(-3);
    }


    if (limit != -1)
        cout << "User-specified limit: "
            << limit << endl;


    if (bufsize != -1)
        cout << "User-specified bufsize: "
            << bufsize << endl;


    if (!ofile.empty())
        cout << "User-specified output file: "
            << ofile << endl;


    cout << (file_names.size() == 1 ? "File " : "Files ")
        << "to be processed are the following:\n";


    for (int inx = 0; inx < file_names.size(); ++inx)
        cout << "\t" << file_names[inx] << endl;


    return 0;
}
```

Exercise 7.19

Our implementation generates a fatal error if the user specifies an unknown option. Do you think this is reasonable? What else might we do?

Generating a fatal error may be reasonable because an appropriate error message plus the usage message are displayed. Another way to handle an unknown option is to issue a warning and ignore the option. One problem with this approach is that we don't know whether the user specified a value for the unknown option. If the user specified a value without an intervening space, it, too, will be ignored. If the user specified a value with an intervening space, it will be interpreted as a file name.

Here is the new version:

```
#include <iostream>
#include <string>
#include <vector>
#include <ctype.h>
using namespace std;

const char *const program_name = "comline";
const char *const program_version = "version 7.19";

inline void usage(int exit_value = 0)
{
    // prints a formatted usage message
    // and exits using the exit_value ...

    cerr << "usage:\n"
        << program_name << " "
        << "[-d] [-h] [-v] [-t]\n\t"
        << "[-b bufsize] [-o output_file] [-l limit] \n\t"
        << "file_name\n\t[file_name [file_name [...]]]\n\n"
        << "where [] indicates optional option:\n\n\t"
        << "-h: help.\n\t\t"
        << "generates this message and exits\n\n\t"
        << "-v: version.\n\t\t"
        << "prints version information and exits\n\n\t"
        << "-d: debug.\n\t\tturns debugging on\n\n\t"
        << "-t: timer.\n\t\tturns timer on\n\n\t"
        << "-b bufsize\n\t\t"
        << "bufsize must be a non-negative integer\n\n\t"
        << "-l limit\n\t\t"
        << "limit must be a non-negative integer\n\n\t"
        << "-o ofile\n\t\t"
```

```
                << "file within which to write out results\n\t\t"
                << "by default, results written to standard output\n\n"
                << "file_name\n\t\t"
                << "the name of the actual file to process\n\t\t"
                << "at least one file_name is required --\n\t\t"
                << "any number may be specified\n\n"
                << "examples:\n\t\t"
                << "$command chapter7.doc\n\t\t"
                << "$command -d -l 1024 -o test_7_8 "
                << "chapter7.doc chapter8.doc\n\n";

        exit(exit_value);
}

int main(int argc, char *argv[])
{
        bool debug_on = false;
        bool timer_on = false;
        bool ofile_on = false;
        bool limit_on = false;
        int limit = -1;
        bool bufsize_on = false;
        int bufsize = -1;

        string ofile;
        vector<string> file_names;

        cout << "illustration of handling command line arguments:\n"
                << "argc: " << argc << endl;

        for (int ix = 1; ix < argc; ++ix) {
                cout << "argv[" << ix << "]: "
                        << argv[ix] << endl;

                char *pchar = argv[ix];
                switch (pchar[0]) {
                case '-':
                {
                        cout << "case \'-\' found\n";
                        switch (pchar[1]) {
                        case 'd':
                                cout << "-d found: "
                                        << "debugging turned on\n";
                                debug_on = true;
                                break;
```

```
    case 't':
        cout << "-t found: "
             << "timer turned on\n";
        timer_on = true;
        break;

    case 'v':
        cout << "-v found: "
             << "version info displayed\n";
        cout << program_name
             << "::"
             << program_version
             << endl;
        return 0;

    case 'h':
        cout << "-h found: "
             << "help information\n";
        // no break necessary: usage() exits
        usage();

    case 'o':
        cout << "-o found: output file\n";

        if (!ofile.empty()) {
            cerr << "Warning: multiple -o options specified. "
                 << "Using latest value.\n";
        }

        if (pchar[2] == '\0')
            ofile_on = true;
        else {
            cout << "argument immediately following: "
                 << &pchar[2] << endl;
            ofile = &pchar[2];
        }
        break;

    case 'l':
        cout << "-l found: "
             << "resource limit\n";

        if (limit != -1) {
            cerr << "Warning: multiple -l options specified. "
                 << "Using latest value.\n";
        }
```

```
        if (pchar[2] == '\0')
            limit_on = true;
        else {
            cout << "argument immediately following: "
                 << &pchar[2] << endl;
            limit = atoi(&pchar[2]);
            if (limit < 0) {
                cerr << program_name
                     << " : error : "
                     << "negative value for limit.\n\n";

                usage(-2);
            }
        }
        break;

    case 'b':
        cout << "-b found: "
             << "bufsize\n";

        if (bufsize != -1) {
            cerr << "Warning: multiple -b options specified. "
                 << "Using latest value.\n";
        }

        if (pchar[2] == '\0')
            bufsize_on = true;
        else {
            cout << "argument immediately following: "
                 << &pchar[2] << endl;
            bufsize = atoi(&pchar[2]);
            if (bufsize < 0) {
                cerr << program_name
                     << " : error : "
                     << "negative value for bufsize.\n\n";

                usage(-4);
            }
        }
        break;

    case '\0':
        cerr << program_name
             << " : error : "
             << "space following hyphen not allowed\n\n";
```

```
                usage(-5);

            // change begins
            default:
                cerr << "Warning: ignoring unrecognized option: - "
                    << pchar << "\n";

                break;
            }
            // change ends

            break;
        }
    default:
        cout << "default non-hyphen argument: "
            << pchar << endl;

        if (ofile_on) {
            ofile_on = false;
            ofile = pchar;
        } else if (limit_on) {
            limit_on = false;
            limit = atoi(pchar);
            if (limit < 0) {
                cerr << program_name
                    << " : error : "
                    << "negative value for limit.\n\n";

                usage(-2);
            }
        } else if (bufsize_on) {
            bufsize_on = false;
            bufsize = atoi(pchar);
            if (bufsize < 0) {
                cerr << program_name
                    << " : error : "
                    << "negative value for bufsize.\n\n";

                usage(-4);
            }
        } else
            file_names.push_back(string(pchar));
        break;
    }
}
```

```
        if (file_names.empty()) {
            cerr << program_name
                << " : error : "
                << "no file specified for processing.\n\n";

            usage(-3);
        }

        if (limit != -1)
            cout << "User-specified limit: "
                << limit << endl;

        if (bufsize != -1)
            cout << "User-specified bufsize: "
                << bufsize << endl;

        if (!ofile.empty())
            cout << "User-specified output file: "
                << ofile << endl;

        cout << (file_names.size() == 1 ? "File " : "Files ")
            << "to be processed are the following:\n";

        for (int inx = 0; inx < file_names.size(); ++inx)
            cout << "\t" << file_names[inx] << endl;

        return 0;
    }
```

Exercise 7.20

Add support for options beginning with a plus (+), providing handling for the options +s and +p as well as +sp and +ps. Let's presume that +s turns strict handling on and that +p supports previous constructs that are now obsolete. For example:

```
    prog +s +p -d -b 1024 data0
```

First, we update usage() (see complete listing) and add two new variables.

```
    bool strict_on = false;
    bool previous_on = false;
```

Next, we add a new label, case '+':, to the outer switch. Because we want to be able to recognize options in the form +ps, we use a loop to process all the option letters following the +.

```
int pix = 1;

while (pchar[pix] != '\0')
    switch (pchar[pix++]) {
    case 's':
        // ...
        break;
    case 'p':
        // ...
        break;
    // ...
    }
```

This code has the effect of allowing options such as +spss. Although this may cause some unnecessary processing, it will also report any unrecognized options in the entire argument.

Here is the complete program:

```
#include <iostream>
#include <string>
#include <vector>
#include <ctype.h>
using namespace std;

const char *const program_name = "comline";
const char *const program_version = "version 7.20";

inline void usage(int exit_value = 0)
{
    // prints a formatted usage message
    // and exits using the exit_value ...

    cerr << "usage:\n"
         << program_name << " "
         << "[-d] [-h] [-v] [-t]\n\t"
         << "[+p] [+s]\n\t"
         << "[-b bufsize] [-o output_file] [-l limit] \n\t"
         << "file_name\n\t[file_name [file_name [...]]]\n\n"
         << "where [] indicates optional option:\n\n\t"
         << "-h: help.\n\t\t"
         << "generates this message and exits\n\n\t"
         << "-v: version.\n\t\t"
         << "prints version information and exits\n\n\t"
         << "-d: debug.\n\t\tturns debugging on\n\n\t"
         << "-t: timer.\n\t\tturns timer on\n\n\t"
         << "+p: previous constructs.\n\t\t"
```

```
                    << "turns on support for obsolete constructs\n\n\t"
                    << "+s: strict.\n\t\tturns strict handling on\n\n\t"
                    << "-b bufsize\n\t\t"
                    << "bufsize must be a non-negative integer\n\n\t"
                    << "-l limit\n\t\t"
                    << "limit must be a non-negative integer\n\n\t"
                    << "-o ofile\n\t\t"
                    << "file within which to write out results\n\t\t"
                    << "by default, results written to standard output\n\n"
                    << "file_name\n\t\t"
                    << "the name of the actual file to process\n\t\t"
                    << "at least one file_name is required --\n\t\t"
                    << "any number may be specified\n\n"
                    << "examples:\n\t\t"
                    << "$command chapter7.doc\n\t\t"
                    << "$command -d -l 1024 -o test_7_8 "
                    << "chapter7.doc chapter8.doc\n\n";

        exit(exit_value);
    }


    int main(int argc, char *argv[])
    {
        bool debug_on = false;
        bool timer_on = false;
        bool ofile_on = false;
        bool limit_on = false;
        int limit = -1;
        bool bufsize_on = false;
        int bufsize = -1;
        bool strict_on = false;
        bool previous_on = false;

        string ofile;
        vector<string> file_names;

        cout << "illustration of handling command line arguments:\n"
             << "argc: " << argc << endl;

        for (int ix = 1; ix < argc; ++ix) {
            cout << "argv[" << ix << "]: "
                 << argv[ix] << endl;
```

```
char *pchar = argv[ix];
switch (pchar[0]) {
case '-':
{
    cout << "case \'-\' found\n";
    switch (pchar[1]) {
    case 'd':
        cout << "-d found: "
            << "debugging turned on\n";
        debug_on = true;
        break;

    case 't':
        cout << "-t found: "
            << "timer turned on\n";
        timer_on = true;
        break;

    case 'v':
        cout << "-v found: "
            << "version info displayed\n";
        cout << program_name
            << "::"
            << program_version
            << endl;
        return 0;

    case 'h':
        cout << "-h found: "
            << "help information\n";
        // no break necessary: usage() exits
        usage();

    case 'o':
        cout << "-o found: output file\n";

        if (!ofile.empty()) {
            cerr << "Warning: multiple -o options specified. "
                << "Using latest value.\n";
        }

        if (pchar[2] == '\0')
            ofile_on = true;
        else {
```

```
            cout << "argument immediately following: "
                << &pchar[2] << endl;
            ofile = &pchar[2];
        }
        break;

    case 'l':
        cout << "-l found: "
            << "resource limit\n";

        if (limit != -1) {
            cerr << "Warning: multiple -l options specified. "
                << "Using latest value.\n";
        }

        if (pchar[2] == '\0')
            limit_on = true;
        else {
            cout << "argument immediately following: "
                << &pchar[2] << endl;
            limit = atoi(&pchar[2]);
            if (limit < 0) {
                cerr << program_name
                    << " : error : "
                    << "negative value for limit.\n\n";

                usage(-2);
            }
        }
        break;

    case 'b':
        cout << "-b found: "
            << "bufsize\n";

        if (bufsize != -1) {
            cerr << "Warning: multiple -b options specified. "
                << "Using latest value.\n";
        }

        if (pchar[2] == '\0')
            bufsize_on = true;
        else {
            cout << "argument immediately following: "
```

```
                                << &pchar[2] << endl;
                    bufsize = atoi(&pchar[2]);
                    if (bufsize < 0) {
                        cerr << program_name
                                << " : error : "
                                << "negative value for bufsize.\n\n";

                        usage(-4);
                    }
                }
                break;

        case '\0':
            cerr << program_name
                    << " : error : "
                    << "space following hyphen not allowed\n\n";

            usage(-5);

        default:
            cerr << program_name
                    << " : error : "
                    << "unrecognized option: - "
                    << pchar << "\n\n";

            // no break necessary: usage() exits
            usage(-1);
        }

        break;
    }
    // change begins
    case '+':
    {
        cout << "case \'+\' found\n";

        int pix = 1;

        while (pchar[pix] != '\0')
            switch (pchar[pix++]) {
            case 's':
                cout << "+s found: "
                        << "strict handling turned on\n";
                strict_on = true;
```

```
                    break;
             case 'p':
                 cout << "+p found: "
                        << "support for obsolete constructs turned on\n";
                 previous_on = true;
                 break;
             default:
                 cerr << program_name
                        << " : error : "
                        << "unrecognized option: +"
                        << pchar[pix] << "\n\n";

                 // no break necessary: usage() exits
                 usage(-6);
             }
        break;
    }
    // change ends
    default:
        cout << "default non-hyphen argument: "
               << pchar << endl;

        if (ofile_on) {
            ofile_on = false;
            ofile = pchar;
        } else if (limit_on) {
            limit_on = false;
            limit = atoi(pchar);
            if (limit < 0) {
                cerr << program_name
                        << " : error : "
                        << "negative value for limit.\n\n";

                usage(-2);
            }
        } else if (bufsize_on) {
            bufsize_on = false;
            bufsize = atoi(pchar);
            if (bufsize < 0) {
                cerr << program_name
                        << " : error : "
                        << "negative value for bufsize.\n\n";
```

```
                        usage(-4);
                }
            } else
                file_names.push_back(string(pchar));
            break;
        }
    }

    if (file_names.empty()) {
        cerr << program_name
            << " : error : "
            << "no file specified for processing.\n\n";

        usage(-3);
    }

    if (limit != -1)
        cout << "User-specified limit: "
            << limit << endl;

    if (bufsize != -1)
        cout << "User-specified bufsize: "
            << bufsize << endl;

    if (!ofile.empty())
        cout << "User-specified output file: "
            << ofile << endl;

    cout << (file_names.size() == 1 ? "File " : "Files ")
        << "to be processed are the following:\n";

    for (int inx = 0; inx < file_names.size(); ++inx)
        cout << "\t" << file_names[inx] << endl;

    return 0;
}
```

Exercise 7.21

Section 7.5 defines the function `factorial()`. **Define a pointer to a function that can point to `factorial()`. Invoke the function through this pointer to generate the factorial of number 11.**

The pointer definition is

```
unsigned long (*pfac)(int);
```

We build the definition as follows: `pfac` is a pointer

```
*pfac
```

...to a function

```
(*pfac)()
```

...taking an `int` parameter

```
(*pfac)(int);
```

...and returning an `unsigned long`.

```
unsigned long (*pfac)(int);
```

The invocation is

```
(*pfac)(11);
```

or

```
pfac(11);
```

Exercise 7.22

What are the types of the following declarations?

```
(a) int  (*mpf)(vector<int>&);
(b) void (*apf[20])(double);
(c) void (*(*papf)[2])(int);
```

How would you use typedef names to make the declarations easier to read?

(a) `int  (*mpf)(vector<int>&);`

Let's look at it step-by-step.
`mpf` is a pointer

```
*mpf
```

...to a function

```
(*mpf)()
```

...taking a reference parameter of type `vector<int>`

```
(*mpf)(vector<int>&)
```

...taking a reference parameter of type `vector<int>` and returning an `int`.

```
int (*mpf)(vector<int>&);
```

(b) `void (*apf[20])(double);`

Let's look at it step-by-step.

```
apf[20]
```

apf is an array with 20 elements.

```
*apf[20]
```

apf is an array with 20 elements that are pointers.

```
(*apf[20])()
```

apf is an array with 20 elements that are pointers to functions.

```
(*apf[20])(double)
```

apf is an array with 20 elements that are pointers to functions taking a parameter of type double.

```
void (*apf[20])(double);
```

apf is an array with 20 elements that are pointers to functions taking a parameter of type double and returning no value.

```
(c) void (*(*papf)[2])(int);
```

Let's look at it step-by-step.

```
*papf
```

papf is a pointer.

```
(*papf)[2]
```

papf is a pointer to an array with two elements.

```
*(*papf)[2]
```

papf is a pointer to an array with two elements that are pointers.

```
(*(*papf)[2])()
```

papf is a pointer to an array with two elements that are pointers to functions.

```
(*(*papf)[2])(int)
```

papf is a pointer to an array with two elements that are pointers to functions taking one parameter of type int.

```
void (*(*papf)[2])(int);
```

papf is a pointer to an array with two elements that are pointers to functions taking one parameter of type int and returning no value.

Defining a typedef name for each of the function pointer types in (b) and (c) would make them easier to read.

```
(b) void (*apf[20])(double);
    typedef void (*PF1)(double);
    PF1 apf[20];

(c) void (*(*papf)[2])(int);
    typedef void (*PF2)(int);
    PF2 (*papf)[2];
```

Exercise 7.23

The following functions are C library functions defined in the header <cmath>.

```
double abs(double);
double sin(double);
double cos(double);
double sqrt(double);
```

How would you declare an array of pointer to C functions and initialize this array to contain the four functions? Write a main() **function that will call** sqrt() **through the array element with the argument** 97.9.

We declare our array and initialize it as follows:

```
double (*mfunc[4])(double) = { abs, sin, cos, sqrt };
```

Here is the complete program.

```
#include <iostream>
#include <cmath>
using namespace std;

int main()
{
    double (*mfunc[4])(double) = { abs, sin, cos, sqrt };

    cout << (*mfunc[3])(97.9) << endl;

    // alternate method of invocation

    cout << mfunc[3](97.9) << endl;

    return 0;
}
```

Exercise 7.24

Let's go back to the sort() **example. Provide the definition for the function**

```
    int sizeCompare(const string &, const string &);
```

so that if the two parameters refer to strings of the same size, then sizeCompare() **returns 0; otherwise, if the string represented by the first parameter is shorter than the string represented by the second parameter, a negative number is returned; if it is greater, a positive number is returned. Remember that the string operation** size() **yields the size of a string. Change** main() **to call** sort() **with a third argument that is a pointer to** sizeCompare().

The definition of sizeCompare() is straightforward.

```
int sizeCompare(const string &s1, const string &s2)
{
    if (s1.size() == s2.size())
        return 0;
    else if (s1.size() < s2.size())
        return -1;
    else
        return 1;
}
```

The modified call to sort() is

```
sort(as, as + sizeof(as)/sizeof(as[0]) - 1, sizeCompare);
```

Here is sort() and a test program.

```
void sort(string *s1, string *s2, PFI compare)
{
    if (s1 < s2) {
        string elem = *s1;
        string *low = s1;
        string *high = s2 + 1;

        for (;;) {
            while (compare(*++low, elem) < 0 && low < s2);
            while (compare(elem, *--high) < 0);

            if (low < high)
                low->swap(*high);
            else
                break;
        }

        s1->swap(*high);
        sort(s1, high-1, compare);
        sort(high+1, s2, compare);
    }
}

int main()
{
    string as[10] = { "a", "light", "drizzle", "was", "falling",
                      "when", "they", "left", "the", "museum" };

    sort(as, as + sizeof(as)/sizeof(as[0]) - 1);
```

```
        cout << "Sort with default lexicoCompare\n";
        for (int i = 0; i < sizeof(as)/sizeof(as[0]); ++i)
            cout << "\t\"" << as[i].c_str() << "\"\n";

        cout << "\n";
        sort(as, as + sizeof(as)/sizeof(as[0]) - 1, sizeCompare);

        cout << "Sort with sizeCompare\n";
        for (int j = 0; j < sizeof(as)/sizeof(as[0]); ++j)
            cout << "\t\"" << as[j].c_str() << "\"\n";

        return 0;
    }
```

chapter eight

Scope and Lifetime

Exercise 8.1

In the following code sample, identify the different scopes. Which of the following declarations of ix, if any, are errors? Explain why.

```
int ix = 1024;
int ix();

void func( int ix, int iy ) {
    int ix = 255;

    if (int ix = 0 ) {
        int ix = 79;
        {
            int ix = 89;
        }
    }
    else {
        int ix = 99;
    }
}
```

We first look at the different scopes in the program, and then we discuss them.

```
int ix = 1024;                  // global scope
int ix();

void func( int ix, int iy ) {   // local scope 1
    int ix = 255;
```

```
    if (int ix = 0 ) {              // local scope 2
        int ix = 79;                // local scope 3
        {
            int ix = 89;            // local scope 4
        }
    }
    else {
        int ix = 99;                // local scope 5
    }
}
```

Now let's look at the individual instances of ix in the different scopes. The expression

```
    int ix = 1024;
```

declares ix to be an int, with initial value 1,024, that has global scope. It is a valid declaration.

The expression

```
    int ix();
```

is a function prototype that redeclares ix in the global scope. It is an error because a name must be declared to refer to single entity within a given scope (L&L, page 389). An exception to that rule is overloaded functions that have the same name and exist in the same scope; the compiler can distinguish the functions because of their parameter lists.

The expression

```
    void func( int ix, int iy ) {
```

is a valid declaration of parameters to func(): ix and iy.

```
    int ix = 255;
```

The function parameters are local variables that belong to the outermost local scope of the function. The parameter ix and the local variable ix are declared in the same scope, and this is an error.

The ix that appears in

```
    if (int ix = 0 ) {
```

is in the outermost scope of the statements associated with the if statement. So ix cannot be defined in the local scopes 3 and 5 but can be redefined in scopes nested within the local scopes 3 and 5. (Note: our compiler flagged this error.)

The redeclaration of ix in local scope 3,

```
    int ix = 79;
```

is an error for the reasons already mentioned. (Note: our compiler flagged this error.)

The redeclaration of ix in local scope 4,

```
    int ix = 89;
```

hides the earlier redeclaration of ix in local scope 3.

Exercise 8.2

In the following code sample, to which declarations do the uses of ix and iy refer?

```
int ix = 1024;

void func( int ix, int iy ) {
    ix = 100;

    for ( int iy = 0; iy < 400; iy += 100 ) {
        iy += 100;
        ix = 300;
    }
    iy = 400;
}
```

We refer to the uses of ix and iy in terms of scopes:

```
int ix = 1024;                    // global scope

void func( int ix, int iy ) {     // first local scope
    ix = 100;                     // first local scope

                                  // redeclares iy
    for ( int iy = 0; iy < 400; iy += 100 ) {
        iy += 100;                // second local scope
        ix = 300;                 // first local scope
    }
    iy = 400;                     // first local scope
}
```

Exercise 8.3

Identify which ones of the following are declarations and which ones are definitions. Explain why they are declarations or definitions.

```
(a) extern int ix = 1024;
(b) int iy;
(c) extern void reset( void *p ) { /* ... */ }
(d) extern const int *pi;
(e) void print( const matrix & );
```

(a) `extern int ix = 1024;`

It is a definition because `ix` has an initial value.

(b) `int iy;`

It is a definition because `iy` is not preceded by the keyword `extern`.

(c) `extern void reset( void *p ) { /* ... */ }`

It is a definition because the function `reset()` has a body.

(d) `extern const int *pi;`

It is a declaration because `pi` is an `extern` pointer to a `const int`, and it is not initialized.

(e) `void print( const matrix & );`

It is a declaration of a function because, unlike (c), the body of the function is not present.

Exercise 8.4

Which one of the following declarations and definitions would you put in a header file? In a program text file? Explain why.

```
(a) int var;
(b) inline bool is_equal(const SmallInt &, const SmallInt &) { }
(c) void putValues( int *arr, int size );
(d) const double pi = 3.1416;
(e) extern int total = 255;
```

(a) `int var;`

It is a definition because it is not preceded by `extern`. It should appear in a text file because definitions should appear only once in a program.

(b) `inline bool is_equal(const SmallInt &, const SmallInt &) { }`

It is a definition of an `inline` function. It should appear in a header file because the compiler must have the actual definition of an `inline` function to do the inlining when it encounters the calls to the function in the text files.

(c) `void putValues( int *arr, int size );`

It is a function prototype and should appear in a header file so that it can be used by different text files.

(d) `const double pi = 3.1416;`

It is a symbolic constant. The definitions of symbolic constants should be placed in header files to guarantee that the same value is given to a symbolic constant in different text files.

(e) `extern int total = 255;`

It is a definition for `total` because of the initial value and because it is not `const`; it should appear in a text file. A definition for an ordinary object must appear only once in a program and therefore should be placed in a text file.

Exercise 8.5

Explain why the following new expressions are errors.
    (a) `const float *pf = new const float[100];`
    (b) `double *pd = new double[10][getDim()];`
    (c) `int (*pia2)[ 1024 ] = new int[ ][ 1024 ];`
    (d) `const int *pci = new const int;`

(a) `const float *pf = new const float[100];`

A `const` object created on the free store must be initialized. Because we cannot initialize arrays of built-in types created with a new expression, `new const float[100]` is an error.

(b) `double *pd = new double[10][getDim()];`

The second and higher dimensions for an array allocation must be constants. The second dimension in this example is a nonconstant expression: `getDim()`.

The other error is that pd is a pointer to `double`, whereas new, if correct, would return a pointer to an array of `doubles`. The pointer would have to look something like pia2 in (c).

(c) `int (*pia2)[ 1024 ] = new int[ ][ 1024 ];`

The first dimension for the array allocation is missing. The first dimension for an array can be either a constant value or a value evaluated at run-time, but the value of the first dimension cannot be omitted; otherwise, the compiler would not know how large a memory area it should allocate. For example, if we wish to create a matrix 10×1024, we would write

    `int (*pia2)[ 1024 ] = new int[ 10 ][ 1024 ];`

(d) `const int *pci = new const int;`

A `const` object created on the free store must be initialized. For example, if we wanted the const int object to have the value 1,234, we could use

    `const int *pci = new const int(1234);`

Exercise 8.6

Given the following new expression, how would you delete pa?

```
typedef int arr[10];
int *pa = new arr;
```

We must use

```
delete [] pa;
```

because pa is a pointer to an array of ints.

Exercise 8.7

Which ones of the following delete expressions, if any, are potential run-time errors? Why?

```
int globalObj;
char buf[1000];

void f() {
    int *pi = &globalObj;
    double *pd = 0;
    float *pf = new float(0);
    int *pa = new(buf) int[20];

    delete pi;          // (a)
    delete pd;          // (b)
    delete pf;          // (c)
    delete [] pa;       // (d)
}
```

```
delete pi;        // (a)
```

It is a potential run-time error because pi points to an int in the global space; that is, the int was not allocated using new.

```
delete pd;        // (b)
```

OK. pd is set to 0, but the language guarantees that operator delete is not called by a delete expression if the pointer operand is set to 0.

```
delete pf;        // (c)
```

OK. pf points to one object of type float that was allocated with new.

```
delete [] pa;     // (d)
```

It is a potential run-time error because pa points to an object created in the storage location of buf, which is a global array. Deleting pa means deleting the memory for buf, which was not allocated using new.

Exercise 8.8

Which of the following `auto_ptr` **declarations are illegal or likely to result in subsequent program error? Explain what the problem is with each one.**

```
int ix = 1024;
int *pi = &ix;
int *pi2 = new int( 2048 );
```

```
(a) auto_ptr<int> p0(ix);
(b) auto_ptr<int> p1(pi);
(c) auto_ptr<int> p2(pi2);
(d) auto_ptr<int> p3(&ix);
(e) auto_ptr<int> p4(new int( 2048 ) );
(f) auto_ptr<int> p5(p2.get());
(g) auto_ptr<int> p6(p2.release());
(h) auto_ptr<int> p7(p2);
```

```
(a) auto_ptr<int> p0(ix);
```

This is illegal because p0 can be initialized only with the address of an object created with a new expression or with another `auto_ptr`.

```
(b) auto_ptr<int> p1(pi);
```

This is illegal for the same reasons as in (a).

```
(c) auto_ptr<int> p2(pi2);
```

Valid.

```
(d) auto_ptr<int> p3(&ix);
```

This is illegal because the initial value for p3 was not obtained through new.

```
(e) auto_ptr<int> p4(new int( 2048 ) );
```

Valid.

(f) `auto_ptr<int> p5(p2.get());`

This is valid, but it is likely to result in a subsequent program error because both p5 and p2 will have ownership of the same object. The reason is that `get()` returns a pointer to an object without relinquishing ownership of the object.

This answer assumes that p2 is a valid `auto_ptr`.

(g) `auto_ptr<int> p6(p2.release());`

This is valid because `release()` returns a valid pointer to an object and then relinquishes ownership of the object. Notice that this is different from `get()` in (f).

This answer assumes that p2 is a valid `auto_ptr`.

(h) `auto_ptr<int> p7(p2);`

This is valid because when we initialize an `auto_ptr` with another valid `auto_ptr`, both pointers refer to the same object, but only the second pointer (p7) has ownership of the object.

This answer assumes that p2 is a valid `auto_ptr`.

Exercise 8.9

Explain the difference between these two statements:

```
int *pi0 = p2.get();
int *pi1 = p2.release();
```

Under what conditions would each respective invocation be more appropriate?

The assumption here is that p2 is a valid `auto_ptr`.

The method `get()` returns a pointer to an object without relinquishing ownership of the object. So both pi0 and p2 point to the same object. Whenever p2 goes out of scope, it will deallocate the space for the object. If we invoke the `delete()` operator on pi0, the object will be deleted twice. We use `get()` when we want to have two pointers referring to the same object but we want the first `auto_ptr` object to retain the ownership of the object and to handle the deallocation of the object automatically.

The method `release()` returns a pointer to an object and relinquishes ownership of the object. So we must make sure that we explicitly invoke the operator `delete()` on pi1 to deallocate the space for the object. We use `release()` when we transfer ownership of an object.

Exercise 8.10

Suppose we have the following:

```
auto_ptr<string> ps( new string( "Daniel" ) );
```

What is the difference, if any, between the following two invocations of assign()**? Which do you think is preferable? Why?**

```
ps->get()->assign( "Danny" );
ps->assign( "Danny" );
```

get() returns a pointer to an object. assign() changes the value in the object that the pointer points to. So

```
ps->get()->assign( "Danny" );
```

takes two explicit steps to change the value of the object that ps points to. In the second invocation,

```
ps->assign( "Danny" );
```

all the work happens underneath the covers; the auto_ptr<string>::assign() calls the string::assign() to modify the string. That is, the two steps are implicit.

The second method is preferable. The point of the auto_ptr is to transparently wrap the otherwise vulnerable heap pointer.

Exercise 8.11

Why would you define your own namespace in your programs?

If we were library vendors we might want to provide a library to be used by many customers. To avoid polluting the global namespace in these customers' programs, they could use namespaces to hide the library's global names.

Users may also use namespaces, but they will mainly use using directives and using declarations to access the names within the libraries they use.

Exercise 8.12

Suppose we have the following declaration of the operator*() **that is a member of the nested namespace** cplusplus_primer::MatrixLib**:**

```
namespace cplusplus_primer {
    namespace MatrixLib {
        class matrix { /* ... */ };
        matrix operator* (const matrix &, const matrix &);
        // ...
    }
}
```

How would you define this operator in global scope? Provide only the prototype for the operator's definition.

```
using cplusplus_primer::MatrixLib::matrix;
matrix cplusplus_primer::MatrixLib::operator* (
                const matrix &, const matrix &);
```

Exercise 8.13

Explain why you would use an unnamed namespace in your programs.

One reason is to localize a name to a specific text file and not to make it visible (for linking purposes) to other text files. Another reason is that we would derive the benefits of namespaces without creating yet another namespace.

Exercise 8.14

Explain the differences between using declarations and using directives.

A using declaration introduces a name in the scope in which the using declaration appears. So we can refer to a name of a namespace member using its unqualified form. In L&L, Section 8.6, the example

```
namespace cplusplus_primer {
    namespace MatrixLib {
        class matrix { /* ... */ };
        matrix operator* (const matrix &, const matrix &);
        // ...
    }
}
using cplusplus_primer::MatrixLib::matrix;
using cplusplus_primer::MatrixLib::operator* (
                const matrix &, const matrix &);
```

makes the two members `matrix` and `operator*()` visible using the unqualified form.

A using directive allows us to make all the names from a specific namespace visible in their short form. For the same example in L&L, we could use

```
using namespace cplusplus_primer::MatrixLib;
```

to make all the members visible in the current scope using the unqualified form.

Exercise 8.15

Given the full example in Section 6.14, write the using declarations necessary to make the member of namespace `std` visible in this example.

We must come up with all the using declarations like

```
using std::string;
using std::cin;
// ...
```

The simplest solution is to add a using directive following the #include directives (L&L, page 441):

```
using namespace std;
```

This solution is dangerous. See L&L, page 439. The safe solution is to come up with all the using declarations.

Exercise 8.16

Consider the following code sample:

```
namespace Exercise {
    int ivar = 0;
    double dvar = 0;
    const int limit = 1000;
}
int ivar = 0;

// 1
void manip() {
    // 2
    double dvar = 3.1416;
    int    iobj = limit + 1;

    ++ivar;
    ++::ivar;
}
```

What are the effects of the declarations and expressions in this code sample if using declarations for all the members of namespace Exercise are located at //1? At //2 instead? Now answer the same question but replace the using declarations with a using directive for name space Exercise.

Using declarations

- At //1 causes the redefinition of ivar

- At //2 causes the redefinition of dvar

Using directives

- At //1 causes ivar to become an ambiguous symbol, but ++::ivar increments ivar declared in the global namespace.

- At //2

  – dvar is not used in manip(), and ambiguities caused by using directives are detected only at the point of use; there is no ambiguity for dvar.

  – If dvar was used in manip() it would still be fine; the using directive in manip() makes Exercise::dvar appear as if it were declared in global scope. The declaration of dvar in manip() hides this declaration.

chapter nine

Overloaded Functions

Exercise 9.1

Why would you declare overloaded functions?

We declare overloaded functions when we want to "define a set of functions that perform the same general action but that apply to different parameter types" (L&L, page 444).

Exercise 9.2

How should a set of overloaded functions for the following error() **function be declared to handle the following calls?**

```
int index;
int upperBound;
char selectVal;
// ...

error("Array out of bounds: ", index, upperBound);
error("Division by zero");
error("Invalid selection", selectVal);
```

There are three different calls we need to consider. All three take a string as their first parameter and differ in the remaining parameters. A string literal in C++ is actually const char *, so the first parameter could instead be of that type. We take advantage of the implicit conversion from const char * to string.

```
void error(const string &, int, int);
void error(const string &);
void error(const string &, char);
```

Exercise 9.3

Explain the effect of the second declaration in each one of the following sets of declarations.

```
(a) int calc(int, int);
    int calc(const int, const int);

(b) int get();
    double get();

(c) int *reset(int *);
    double *reset(double *);

(d) extern "C" int compute(int *, int);
    extern "C" double compute(double *, double);
```

We need to consider the parameter and return types.

```
(a) int calc(int, int);
    int calc(const int, const int);
```

The second declaration is considered a redeclaration. It is not an error. The `const` qualifiers in the second declaration are ignored because the parameters are neither pointers nor references. It is as if we had written

```
    int calc(int, int);
    int calc(int, int);
```

Because two declarations of the same function are allowed in any given text file, the second declaration is valid.

```
(b) int get();
    double get();
```

The second declaration is an error because the "return type is not enough to distinguish between two overloaded functions" (L&L, page 445).

```
(c) int *reset(int *);
    double *reset(double *);
```

These are valid declarations for the overloaded function `reset()`.

```
(d) extern "C" int compute(int *, int);
    extern "C" double compute(double *, double);
```

The second declaration is an error because "a linkage directive may be specified only for one function in a set of overloaded functions" (L&L, page 452).

Exercise 9.4

Which ones of the following initializations, if any, are errors? Why?

```
(a) void reset(int *);
    void (*pf)(void *) = reset;

(b) int calc(int, int);
    int (*pf1)(int, int) = calc;

(c) extern "C" int compute(int *, int);
    int (*pf3)(int *, int) = compute;

(d) void (*pf4)(const matrix &) = 0;
```

The initializations (a) and (c) are incorrect.

```
(a) void reset(int *);
    void (*pf)(void *) = reset;
```

reset() is a function with a single parameter of type int *, whereas pf is a pointer to a function with a single parameter of type void *. The pointer type and the function type must be exactly the same. Even if there exists a conversion between the type of the function parameter and the type of the parameter of the function pointer (as is the case here, where a conversion exists between int * and void *), the assignment is in error.

```
(c) extern "C" int compute(int *, int);
    int (*pf3)(int *, int) = compute;
```

extern "C" is part of the function type, and the pointer must also be declared with extern "C" for the initialization to be valid. It should read

```
    extern "C" int (*pf3)(int *, int) = compute;
```

Many compilers do not require this. They allow the extern "C" part to be omitted as an extension.

Exercise 9.5

What happens during the last (third) step of the function overload resolution process?

During the last step of the function overload resolution process, the function that best matches the call is selected from the set of viable functions. The conversions used to convert the arguments are ranked to determine the best viable function.

Exercise 9.6

Name two of the minor conversions allowed in an exact match.

The four minor conversions allowed in an exact match are

- Lvalue-to-rvalue conversion
- Array-to-pointer conversion
- Function-to-pointer conversion
- Qualification conversions

Exercise 9.7

What is the rank of each conversion on the arguments in the following function calls?

```
(a) void print(int *, int);
    int arr[6];
    print(arr, 6);              // function call

(b) void manip(int, int);
    manip('a', 'z');            // function call

(c) int calc(int, int);
    double dobj;
    double = calc(55.4, dobj);  // function call

(d) void set(const int *);
    int *pi;
    set(pi);                    // function call
```

The possible ranks for each conversion are an exact match, a promotion, and a standard conversion. (User-defined conversions are described in Chapter 15.)

```
(a) void print(int *, int);
    int arr[6];
    print(arr, 6);              // function call
```

Both arguments are an exact match. arr requires an array-to-pointer conversion.

(b) `void manip(int, int);`
    `manip('a', 'z');`   `// function call`

Both arguments require a promotion from `char` to `int`.

(c) `int calc(int, int);`
    `double dobj;`
    `dobj = calc(55.4, dobj);` `// function call`

Both arguments require a standard conversion from `double` to `int`.

(d) `void set(const int *);`
    `int *pi;`
    `set(pi);`   `// function call`

The argument `pi` is an exact match and requires a qualification conversion from `int * to const int *`.

Exercise 9.8

Which ones of the following function calls, if any, are errors because no conversion exists between the type of the argument and the function parameter?

(a) `enum Stat(Fail, Pass);`
    `void test(Stat);`
    `test(0);`   `// function call`

(b) `void reset(void *);`
    `reset(0);`   `// function call`

(c) `void set(void *);`
    `int *pi;`
    `set(pi);`   `// function call`

(d) `#include <list>`
    `list<int> oper();`
    `void print(list<int> &);`
    `print(oper());`   `// function call`

(e) `void print(const int);`
    `int iobj;`
    `print(iobj);`   `// function call`

Only (a) and (d) are errors.

```
(a) enum Stat(Fail, Pass);
    void test(Stat);
    test(0);                    // function call
```

Error. The literal constant 0 is of type int, but there is no conversion from int to an enumeration type.

```
(d) #include <list>
    list<int> oper();
    void print(list<int> &);
    print(oper());             // function call
```

Error. A function return value is not a valid initializer for a non-const reference parameter.

Exercise 9.9

Explain what happens during function overload resolution for the call to compute() **in** main(). **Which functions are candidate functions? Which functions are viable functions? What is the type conversion sequence applied to the argument to match the parameter in each viable function? Which function (if any) is the best viable function?**

```
namespace primerLib {
    void compute();
    void compute(const void *);
}

using primerLib::compute;
void compute(int);
void compute(double, double = 3.4);
void compute(char*, char* = 0;

int main() {
    compute(0);
    return 0;
}
```

What would happen if the using **declaration were located in** main(), **before the call to** compute()? **Answer the same questions as before.**

Because the using declaration is in the global scope, all function declarations are visible within main().

1.   Candidate functions:

   •   void compute();

   •   void compute(const void *);

- void compute(int);
- void compute(double, double = 3.4);
- void compute(char*, char* = 0);

2. Viable functions:

- void compute(const void *);
   - Conversion sequence: pointer standard conversion -> qualification conversion from void * to const void *
- void compute(int);
   - Conversion sequence: exact match
- void compute(double, double = 3.4);
   - Conversion sequence: floating-to-integral standard conversion
- void compute(char*, char* = 0);
   - Conversion sequence: pointer standard conversion

3. Best viable function:

- void compute(int);

By placing the using declaration in main(), the global function declarations are hidden.

1. Candidate functions:

- void compute();
- void compute(const void *);

2. Viable functions:

- void compute(const void *);
   - Conversion sequence: pointer standard conversion -> qualification conversion from void * to const void *

3. Best viable function:

- void compute(const void *);

chapter ten

Function Templates

Exercise 10.1

Identify which, if any, of the following function template definitions are illegal. Correct each one that you identify.

```
(a) template <class T, U, class V>
        void foo( T, U, V );

(b) template <class T>
        T foo( int *T );

(c) template <class T1, typename T2, class T3>
        T1 foo( T2, T3 );

(d) inline template <typename T>
        T foo( T, unsigned int * );

(e) template <class myT, class myT>
        void foo( myT, myT );

(f) template <class T>
        foo( T, T );

(g) typedef char Ctype;
        template <class Ctype>
          Ctype foo( Ctype a, Ctype b);
```

The illegal template definitions are (a), (d), and (e).

```
(a) template <class T, U, class V>
        void foo( T, U, V );
```

Each type listed in a template must be preceded by either `class` or `typename` or must be a built-in type. One possible way to correct the template declaration is

```
template <class T, class U, class V>
        void foo( T, U, V );
```

```
(d) inline template <typename T>
            T foo( T, unsigned int * );
```

"A function template can be declared `inline` or `extern` in the same way as a nontemplate function. The specifier is placed following the template parameter list and not in front of the `template` keyword" (L&L, page 496). The correct declaration is

```
template <typename T> inline
        T foo( T, unsigned int * );
```

```
(e) template <class myT, class myT>
        void foo( myT, myT );
```

"The name of a template parameter can be used only once within the same template parameter list" (L&L, page 494). The correct declaration is

```
template <class myT>
        void foo( myT, myT );
```

Exercise 10.2

Which ones, if any, of the following template redeclarations are errors? Why?

```
(a) template <class Type>
            Type bar(Type, Type);

    template <class Type>
            Type bar(Type, Type);
```

```
(b) template <class T1, class T2>
            void bar(T1, T2);

    template <typename C1, typename C2>
            void bar(C1, C2);
```

Both redeclarations are correct.

(a) is correct because the declarations are identical. (b) is correct because "the names of the template parameters do not need to be the same across declarations and the definition of the template" (L&L, page 494). The keywords `class` and `typename` have the same meaning and can be used interchangeably (L&L, page 495).

Exercise 10.3

Rewrite the function `putValues()`, introduced in Section 7.3.3, as a function template. Parameterize the function template so that it has two template parameters (one for the type of the array element and one for the size of the array) and one function parameter that is a reference to an array. Provide the function template definition as well.

```
template <class Type>
void putValues(Type *ia, int sz)
{
    cout << "( " << sz << " )<";
    for (int i = 0; i < sz; ++i)
    {
        if (i % lineLength == 0 && i)
            cout << "\n\t";       // line filled
        cout << ia[i];


        // separate all but last element
        if (i % lineLength != lineLength-1 && i != sz-1)
            cout << ", ";
    }
    cout << " >\n";
}
```

The changes are straightforward.

- We add the line
  ```
  template <class Type>
  ```
  before the function.

- The first argument changes from `int *` to `Type *`.

- Pointer types, such as `Type *`, also support `operator[]`; the only assumption left is that `Type` also supports `operator<<` because of the line
  ```
  cout << ia[i];
  ```

To meet the requirements specified in the question, the answer should be

```
template <class Type, int sz>
void putValues(Type (&ia)[sz])
    . . .
```

but our compiler does not yet support this construct.

Exercise 10.4

Name two type conversions allowed on function arguments involved in template argument deduction.

1. Lvalue transformation; "an lvalue transformation is either an lvalue-to-rvalue conversion, an array-to-pointer conversion, or a function-to-pointer conversion" (L&L, page 501).

2. Qualification conversion; "a qualification conversion adds `const` or `volatile` qualifiers to pointers" (L&L, page 502).

Exercise 10.5

Given the following template definitions

```
template <class Type>
    Type min3(const Type* array, int size) { /* ... */ }
template <class Type>
    Type min5(Type p1, Type p2) { /* ... */ }
```

which one of the following calls, if any, are errors? Why?

```
double dobj1, dobj2;
float  fobj1, fobj2;
char   cobj1, cobj2;
int ai[5] = { 511, 16, 8, 63, 34 };

(a) min5( cobj2, 'c' );
(b) min5( dobj1, fobj1 );
(c) min3( ai, cobj1 );
```

We get a syntax error in (b) and a possible run-time error in (c).

```
(b) min5( dobj1, fobj1 );
```

This call is an error. The call is ambiguous because using the first function argument, the type deduced for the template parameter `Type` is `double`, whereas the type deduced for the second function argument is `float`. Two different types are deduced for `Type`, and the call is ambiguous. See L&L, page 504.

```
(c) min3( ai, cobj1 );
```

This call is syntactically correct because all type conversions are allowed for function arguments in a call to a function template when the argument does not participate in template argument deduction. The conversion for the second argument is a promotion from char to `int`. Because the type of the second function parameter is fixed to `int` and does not depend on a template parameter `Type`, all conversions are considered for this function argument. Another point to consider: using an uninitialized variable for the "size" of `ai` is likely to give unexpected results or a run-time error.

Exercise 10.6

Name two situations in which the use of explicit template arguments is necessary.

In template functions, explicit template arguments are necessary in the following situations.

1. When the argument deduction would fail; for example, in Exercise 10.5, the code

    ```
    min5( dobj1, fobj1 );
    ```

    produced an error message indicating that this is an ambiguous call. We could explicitly specify the arguments:

    ```
    min5< double >( dobj1, fobj1 );
    ```

2. When the return type cannot be deduced from the argument list; for example, from L&L, page 507,

    ```
    template <class T1, class T2, class T3>
    T1 sum( T2, T3 );
    ```

Exercise 10.7

Given the following template definition for `sum()`

```
template <class T1, class T2, class T3>
    T1 sum( T2, T3 );
```

which ones of the following calls, if any, are errors? Why?

```
    double dobj1, dobj2;
    float  fobj1, fobj2;
    char   cobj1, cobj2;

(a) sum ( dobj1, dobj2 );
(b) sum< double, double, double >( fobj1, fobj2 );
(c) sum< int >( cobj1, cobj2 );
(d) sum< double, , double >( fobj2, dobj2 );
```

The calls (a) and (d) are errors.

```
(a) sum ( dobj1, dobj2 );
```

This call is invalid because the compiler cannot deduce the return type for sum(). We could explicitly specify the first template argument:

```
    sum< double >( dobj1, dobj2 );
```

Or we could specify all the template arguments:

```
    sum< double, double, double >( dobj1, dobj2 );
```

```
(d) sum< double, , double >( fobj2, dobj2 );
```

This call is invalid because we are allowed to omit only trailing arguments. Examples of valid calls are

```
    sum< double >( fobj2, dobj2 );
    sum< double, double >( fobj2, dobj2 );
    sum< double, double, double >( fobj2, dobj2 );
```

Exercise 10.8

Name the two template compilation models supported in C++. Explain how programs with function template definitions are organized under each template compilation model.

1. Inclusion compilation model: "the definition of the function template [is included] in every file in which a template is instantiated" (L&L, page 509). The *definition* of the function template appears within a header file.

2. Separation compilation model: "the declarations of the function templates are placed in a header file and their definitions in a program text file" (L&L, page 510). Only the function template *declaration* appears within a header file.

Exercise 10.9

Given the following template definition for sum()

```
    template <typename Type>
        Type sum( Type op1, char op2 );
```

how would you declare an explicit instantiation declaration for a template argument of type string?

We declare an explicit instantiation declaration as

```
    template string sum< string >( string, char );
```

Exercise 10.10

Define a function template count() **to count the number of occurrences of some value in an array. Write a program to call it. Pass it in turn an array of** doubles, ints, **and** chars.

Introduce a specialized template instance of the count() **function to handle strings. Rerun the program you wrote to call the function template instantiations.**

The function template count takes three arguments: a pointer to an array, the array size, and a const reference to the element to count:

```
template <class Type>
int count(Type *a, int sz, const Type &which)
{
    int n = 0;
    for (int i = 0; i < sz; ++i)
        if (a[i] == which)
            n++;
    return n;
}
```

The main program tests the function template with doubles, ints, and chars. Finally, we test the function template with strings. The specialized template instance of count() to handle strings is not required (count() will handle arrays of strings automatically, and there is nothing in the generic template definition that requires a specialization for arrays of strings), but we include it because that is a requirement in the exercise. This means that not all declarations of a function template specialization must be definitions. See L&L, page 515.

```
// we should have written an explicit specialization
// template <> int count< string >(string *, int, string);

// our compiler supports only explicit instantiations
template int count< string >(string *, int, string);

int main()
{
    double a[] = { 10., 20., 30., 40., 50., 30., 70., 80., 30. };
    cout << "count(a, 9, 30.) should return 3: "
        << count(a, 9, 30.) << endl;

    int b[] = { 10, 20, 30, 40, 50, 30, 70, 80, 30 };
    cout << "count(b, 9, 30) should return 3: "
        << count(b, 9, 30) << endl;

    char c[] = { 'a', 'a', 'c', 'a' };
    cout << "count(c, 4, 'a') should return 3: "
        << count(c, 4, 'a') << endl;
```

```
    string d[] = { "aa", "aa", "aa" };
    cout << "count(d, 3, \"aa\") should return 3: "
         << count(d, 3, string("aa")) << endl;

    string e[] = { "bb", "aa", "aa" };
    cout << "count(e, 3, \"aa\") should return 2: "
         << count(e, 3, string("aa")) << endl;

    return 0;
}
```

Another alternative is to have an explicit specialization definition for count() (see L&L, page 514):

```
template <class Type>
int count(Type *a, int sz, const char *which)
{
    int n = 0;
    for (int i = 0; i < sz; ++i)
        if (strcmp(a[i], which) == 0)
            n++;
    return n;
}
```

Exercise 10.11

Let's return to the example presented earlier:

```
template <class Type>
    Type max( Type, Type ) { ... }

double max( double, double );

int main()
{
    int ival;
    double dval;
    float fd;

    max(0, ival);
    max(0.25, dval);
    max(0, fd);
}
```

The following function template specialization is added to the set of declarations in global scope:

```
template <> char max< char >( char, char ) { ... }
```

Revisit the function calls in `main()` **and list the candidate functions and list the viable functions for each call.**

Suppose that the following function call is added within `main()`**. To which function does the call resolve? Why?**

```
int main() {
    // ...
    max(0, 'J');
}
```

We address the calls to `max()` in the order they appear in `main()`.

`max(0, ival);`

1. Candidate functions:

    • `int max( int, int );`   // external function

    • `int max <int>( int, int );` // template instantiation

    • `double max( double, double );`

2. Viable functions:

    • `int max( int, int );`

    The call would be ambiguous because the external function and template instantiation are equally good. However, the template instantiation is ignored and the external function becomes the best viable function. See L&L, page 526.

`max(0.25, dval);`

1. Candidate functions:

    • `double max( double, double );`

    • `double max <double>( double, double );`

    • `int max( int, int );`

2. Viable functions:

    • `double max( double, double);`

    It is viable for the reasons we discussed previously.

`max(0, fd);`

1. Candidate functions:

- `int max( int, int );`
- `double max( double, double );`

2. Viable functions: the call is ambiguous because the best function for the first argument is as follows.

    ```
    int max( int, int );
    ```

    That is because the argument is an exact match. The best function for the second argument is as follows.

    ```
    double max( double, double );
    ```

    That is because the argument is promoted from `float` to `double`. Because no function is better for all arguments, the call is ambiguous.

`max(0, 'J');`

1. Candidate functions:

    - `int max( int, int );`
    - `double max( double, double );`

2. Viable functions:

    - `int max( int, int );`

    This is an exact match for the first argument and an integral promotion for the second argument.

Exercise 10.12

Suppose we have the following set of template definitions and specializations and variable and function declarations:

```
int i;
unsigned int ui;
char str[24];
int ia[24];

template <class T> T calc( T*, int );
template <class T> T calc( T, T );
template <> char calc( char*, int );
double calc( double, double );
```

Identify which, if any, template instantiation or function is invoked for each of the following calls. For each call, list the candidate functions, list the viable functions, explain why the best viable function is selected.

```
(a) calc( str, 24 );      (d) calc( i, ui );
(b) calc( ia, 24 );      (e) calc( ia, ui );
(c) calc( ia[0], i );    (f) calc( &i, i);
```

(a) calc(str, 24);

1. Candidate functions:

    •   `template <> char calc( char *, int );`

    •   `double calc( double, double );`

    Using

    ```
    template <class T> T calc( T*, int );
    ```

    the instantiation

    ```
    char <char>( char *, int );
    ```

    becomes a candidate function. However, because an explicit specialization is provided for this instantiation, it is the explicit specialization that is entered instead in the set of candidate functions.

2. Viable functions:

    •   `template <> char calc( char*, int );`

3. Best viable function:

    •   `template <> char calc( char*, int );`

    It is the only exact match.

(b) calc(ia, 24);

1. Candidate functions:

    •   `int calc( int *, int );`
        `// from template <class T> T calc( T*, int );`

    •   `double calc( double, double );`

2. Viable functions:

    •   `int calc( int *, int );`

3. Best viable function:

    •   `int calc( int *, int );`

    It is the only exact match.

(c) `calc( ia[0], i );`

1.   Candidate functions:
     - `int calc( int, int );`
       `// from template <class T> T calc( T, T );`
     - `double calc( double, double );`

2.   Viable functions:
     - `int calc( int, int );`
     - `double calc( double, double );`

3.   Best viable function:
     - `int calc( int, int );`

     It is an exact match.

(d) `calc( i, ui );`

1.   Candidate functions:
     - `double calc( double, double );`

2.   Viable functions:
     - `double calc( double, double );`

3.   Best viable function:
     - `double calc( double, double );`

(e) `calc( ia, ui );`

1.   Candidate functions:
     - `int calc( int *, int );`
       `// from template <class T> T calc( T*, int );`
     - `double calc( double, double );`

2.   Viable functions:
     - `int calc( int *, int );`

3.   Best viable function:
     - `int calc( int *, int );`

It is a match because there exists a type conversion from unsigned int to int for parameter ui.

(f) calc(&i, i);

1. Candidate functions:

    •   int calc(int *, int);
         // from template <class T> T calc(T*, int);

    •   double calc(double, double);

2. Viable functions:

    •   int calc(int *, int);

3. Best viable function:

    •   int calc(int *, int);

    It is an exact match.

Exercise 10.13

List the two steps of name resolution in template definitions. Explain how the first step addresses the concerns of library designers and how the second step provides the flexibility needed for template users.

1. "The names that do not depend on a template parameter are resolved when the template is defined" (L&L, page 533).
    A library designer wants a function print() that does not depend on a template parameter and that appears in a template definition to be retrieved from the library. In this way, the template definition will not use some other print() function that the user may have created later.

2. "The names that depend on a template parameter are resolved when the template is instantiated" (L&L, page 533).
    When a function print(T) depends on a template parameter T, the function will be resolved when the template is instantiated and the type T is known. If the type T for which the template is intantiated is a type defined by the user (and not a type defined in the library), the template instantiation must take into account the operations defined for T in the user code.

Exercise 10.14

To which declarations do the names display **and** SIZE **refer to in the instantiation of**
max(LongDouble*, SIZE)?

```
// ---- exercise.h ----
void display(const void *);
typedef unsigned int SIZE;

template <typename Type>
    Type max(Type * array, SIZE size)
{
    Type max_val = array[0];
    for (SIZE i = 1; i < size; ++i)
        if (array[i] > max_val)
            max_val = array[i];
    display("Maximum value found: ");
    display(max_val);

    return max_val;
}
// ---- user.h ----
class LongDouble { /* ... */ };
void display(const LongDouble &);
void display(const char *);
typedef int SIZE;

// ---- user.C ----
#include  <exercise.h>
#include  "user.h"

LongDouble ad[7];

int main() {
    // set the elements of ad

    // instantiation of max(LongDouble *, SIZE)
    SIZE size = sizeof(ad) / sizeof(LongDouble);
    max(&ad[0], size);
}
```

In the first place, the compiler will produce an error message when it detects the redefinition of the SIZE. The typedef for SIZE is unsigned int in exercise.h. There is an attempt in user.h to change it to int. That's a syntax error.

If we comment out SIZE in user.h, then

- SIZE in max() is the one in exercise.h.

- In exercise.h,
  display("Maximum value found: ");
  refers to
  void display(const void *);

- In exercise.h,
  display(max_val);
  refers to
  void display(const LongDouble &);

Exercise 10.15

We now place the content of the header file `<exercise.h>` provided in Exercise 10.14 in namespace `cplusplus_primer`. How would you change the function `main()` so that it can instantiate the function template `max()` located in namespace `cplusplus_primer`?

We add a using declaration:

```
using cplusplus_primer::max;
```

Exercise 10.16

Again referring to Exercise 10.14, given that the content of the header file `exercise.h` is placed in namespace `cplusplus_primer`, we want to specialize the function template `max()` for arrays of objects of class `LongDouble`. We want the template specialization to use the function `compareGreater()` defined to compare two objects class type `LongDouble` like this:

```
// comparison function for LongDouble objects
// returns true if parm1 is greater than parm2
bool compareGreater(const LongDouble &parm1,
                    const LongDouble &parm2);
```

The definition of our class `LongDouble` looks as follows:

```
class LongDouble {
  public:
    LongDouble(double dval) : value(dval) { }
    void set(double dval) { value = dval; }
    friend bool compareGreater(const LongDouble &,
                               const LongDouble &);
```

```
    private:
      double value;
  };
```

Provide the definition for the function `compareGreater()` **and the definition for the specialization of** `max()` **that uses this function. Write a function** `main()` **that sets the elements
of the array** `ad` **and then calls the specialization of** `max()` **to obtain the maximum value
in** `ad`**; the values to initialize the elements of the array** `ad` **should be obtained by reading
the values from the standard input** `cin`**.**

We enhance the class `LongDouble` a bit.

-   We add a default constructor that initializes `value` and allows us to create an array
    of elements of type `LongDouble`; whenever we create an array of objects of some
    class type, the class is expected to provide a default constructor to initialize each
    element of the array (unless we use an initialization list to initialize the array — see
    L&L, page 709).

-   We add a `get()` function that returns a copy of `value` and add the prototypes for
    the two `display()` functions that are used in `max()`.

```
    class LongDouble {
      public:
        LongDouble() { value = 0.; }
        LongDouble(double dval) : value(dval) { }
        void set(double dval) { value = dval; }
        double get() const { return value; }
        friend bool compareGreater(const LongDouble &,
                                   const LongDouble &);
      private:
        double value;
    };
    void display(const LongDouble &);
    void display(const char *);
```

The function `compareGreater()` compares two `LongDouble` objects and returns true if
the first object is greater than the second:

```
    inline bool compareGreater(const LongDouble &a,
                               const LongDouble &b)
    {
        return a.value > b.value;
    }
```

We place `max()` in the namespace `cplusplus_primer` and create a specialized version of
the function that uses `compareGreater()`:

```
namespace cplusplus_primer {
    template <typename Type>
        Type max(Type *array, SIZE size)
    {
        Type max_val = array[0];
        for (SIZE i = 1; i < size; ++i)
            if (array[i] > max_val)
                max_val = array[i];

        display("Maximum value found: ");
        display(max_val);

        return max_val;
    }

    template<>
        LongDouble max<LongDouble>(LongDouble *array, SIZE size)
    {
        LongDouble max_val = array[0];
        for (SIZE i = 1; i < size; ++i)
            if (compareGreater(array[i], max_val))
                max_val = array[i];

        display("Maximum value found: ");
        display(max_val);

        return max_val;
    }
}
```

We write the two display() functions that we declared earlier:

```
void display(const char *s)
{
    cout << s << "\n";
}

void display(const LongDouble &ld)
{
    cout << ld.get() << "\n";
}
```

Finally, here's the function main():

```
using namespace cplusplus_primer;

LongDouble ad[7];
```

```
int main() {
    int i;
    double d;

    // set the elements of ad
    for (i = 0; i < 7; ++i) {
        cout << "value for ad[" << i << "] ? ";
        cin >> d;
        ad[i].set(d);
    }
    for (i = 0; i < 7; ++i)
        cout << "\tad[" << i << "] = " << ad[i].get() << "\n";

    // instantiation of max(LongDouble *, SIZE)
    SIZE size = sizeof(ad) / sizeof(LongDouble);
    max(&ad[0], size);

    return 0;
}
```

chapter eleven

Exception Handling

Exercise 11.1

Which, if any, of the following throw expressions are errors? Why? For the valid throw expressions, indicate the type of the exception thrown.

```
(a) class exceptionType {};
    throw exceptionType();

(b) int excpObj;
    throw excpObj;

(c) enum mathErr { overflow, underflow, zeroDivide };
    throw zeroDivide();

(d) int* pi = excpObj;
    throw pi;
```

Parts (c) and (d) contain errors.

```
(a) class exceptionType {};
    throw exceptionType();
```

This expression throws an exception of type class exceptionType. The parentheses in exceptionType() are required because an exception is an object, and to create an object of type exceptionType we must call the class constructor. See L&L, page 549.

```
(b) int excpObj;
    throw excpObj;
```

This expression throws an exception of type int.

(c) `enum mathErr { overflow, underflow, zeroDivide };`
    `throw zeroDivide();`

The correct expression is

   `throw zeroDivide;`

`zeroDivide` is an `enum` constant and not a class or a function.
   This statement throws an exception of type `enum mathErr`.

(d) `int* pi = &excpObj;`
    `throw pi;`

The `throw` expression throws an exception of type `int *` (pointer to `int`).

Exercise 11.2

The `IntArray` class defined in Section 2.3 has a member operator function `operator[]()` that uses `assert()` to indicate that the index is outside the bounds of the array. Change the definition of `operator[]()` to instead throw an exception in this situation. Define an exception class to be used as the type of the exception thrown.

The `assert()` expression ensures that `index` is in bounds before continuing. We change the sense of the expression to check whether `index` is out of bounds and, if it is, throw the exception.
   Here is the exception class and the modified `operator[]()`:

```
class outOfBounds { };

int& IntArray::
operator[](int index)
{
    if (index < 0 || index >= size())
        throw outOfBounds();

    return ia[index];
}
```

Exercise 11.3

Write a program that defines an `IntArray` object (where `IntArray` is the class type defined in Section 2.3) and performs the following actions. We have three files containing integer values.

1. Read the first file and assign the first, third, fifth, . . . , nth value read (where n is an odd number) to the `IntArray` object; then display the content of the `IntArray` object.

2. Read the second file and assign the fifth, tenth, . . . , nth value read (where n is a multiple of 5) to the `IntArray` object; then display the content of the `IntArray` object.

3. Read the third file and assign the second, fourth, sixth, ..., nth value read (where n is an even number) to the `IntArray` object; then display the content of the `IntArray` object.

Use the `IntArray operator[]()` defined in Exercise 11.2 to store values into and read values from the `IntArray` object. Because `operator[]()` may throw an exception, use one or more try blocks and catch clauses in your program to handle the possible exceptions thrown by `operator[]()`. Explain the reasoning behind where you located the try block(s) in your program.

We have one exception to consider — `outOfBounds` — in two possible instances. In the first instance, we are reading values and assigning them to the `IntArray` object. In the second, we are displaying the contents of the array and reading the values from the `IntArray` object.

We use two try blocks: one around the code assigning the array values and a second one around the display code. Each try block has a single catch clause associated with it. By using two try blocks we can do a small amount of error recovery for each case.

If an exception is thrown while assigning values, we display an error message and adjust the number of elements assigned, `ix`. Because program execution resumes following the catch clause, the remainder of the file being read is ignored.

If an exception is thrown while displaying the contents of the array, we print an error message and continue to the next file or, if there are no more files to process, exit the program.

Note that this program uses the exception from `IntArray::operator[]` to find out when the array is full. This is usually viewed as bad style because exception handling is expensive (see L&L, Section 11.1).

Here is the program:

```
#include <iostream>
#include <fstream>
#include <cstdlib>
#include "IntArray.h"
using namespace std;

int main(int argc, char *argv[])
{
    if (argc != 4) {
        cerr << "usage: " << argv[0] << " <file1> <file2> <file3>\n";
        exit(-1);
    }
```

```
IntArray ia(10);
int ix;          // index for ia
int cnt;         // count values read from file
int val;         // value read from file
ifstream infile;

for (int i = 1; i <= 3; ++i) {
    infile.open(argv[i], ios::in);
    if (!infile) {
        cerr << "Error: unable to open " << argv[i] << " for input\n";
        exit(-2);
    }
    cout << "Reading values from " << argv[i] << endl;

    try {
        ix = cnt = 0;
        while (infile >> val) {
            switch (i) {
            case 1:
                // assign odd elements
                if (++cnt % 2)
                    ia[ix] = val;
                break;
            case 2:
                // assign every fifth element
                if (++cnt % 5 == 0)
                    ia[ix] = val;
                break;
            case 3:
                // assign even elements
                if (++cnt % 2 == 0)
                    ia[ix] = val;
                break;
            }
            ix++;
        }
    }
    catch (outOfBounds) {
        cerr << "Attempted to assign value outside of array bounds.  "
             << "Skipping remainder of file.\n";
    }

    infile.close();
```

```
            cout << ix << " values assigned.\n";
            for (int j = 0; j < ix; ++j)
                cout << ia[j] << endl;
            cout << endl;
        }

        return 0;
    }
```

`IntArray.h` remains unchanged.

Exercise 11.4

Explain why we say that the C++ exception handling model is nonresumptive.

An exception handling model is nonresumptive if, after the exception has been handled, the program continues execution at the point where the exception is handled and not at the point in the program where the exception was thrown. In C++, the program execution resumes following the last `catch` clause in the list.

Exercise 11.5

Given the following exception declarations, provide a throw expression that creates an exception object that can be caught by the following catch clauses.

```
(a) class exceptionType {};
    catch(exceptionType *pet) {}

(b) catch(...) {}

(c) enum mathErr { overflow, underflow, zeroDivide };
    catch(mathErr &ref) {}

(d) typedef int EXCPTYPE;
    catch(EXCPTYPE) {}
```

Here are the appropriate throw expressions.

```
(a) class exceptionType {};
    catch(exceptionType *pet) {}

    exceptionType *eT = new exceptionType;
    throw eT;
```

(b) `catch(...) {}`

   This `catch` clause catches any exception that is thrown. For example:
   ```
   throw 3;
   ```

(c) ```
    enum mathErr { overflow, underflow, zeroDivide };
    catch(mathErr &ref) {}
    ```

   ```
   throw zeroDivide;
   ```

   Remember that an exception is an object, so we cannot use `throw mathErr;`.

(d) ```
    typedef int EXCPTYPE;
    catch(EXCPTYPE) {}
    ```

   ```
   throw 13;
   ```

   Again, we cannot use only the type `EXCPTYPE`.

Exercise 11.6

Explain what happens during stack unwinding.

Stack unwinding is "the process by which compound statements and function definitions exit because of a thrown exception in the search for a catch clause to handle the exception" (L&L, page 559). Destructors for local class objects are called, and the lifetime of local objects ends as compound statements, in which the variables are declared, are exited because of an unhandled exception. In other words, there is a synchronization aspect between the exit of a compound statement and the destruction of its local variables.

Exercise 11.7

Give three reasons that the exception declaration of a catch clause should declare a reference.

The three reasons that the exception declaration of a catch clause should declare a reference are as follows:

1.   "To prevent unnecessary copying of large class objects" (L&L, page 558)

2.   "To ensure that modifications applied to the exception object within the catch clause are reflected in the exception object that is rethrown" (L&L, page 561)

3.   To avoid slicing of derived class objects (L&L, page 1040)

Exercise 11.8

Using the code you developed for Exercise 11.3, modify the exception class you created so that the invalid index used with operator [] () is stored in the exception object when the exception is thrown and later displayed by the catch clause. Modify your program so that operator [] () throws an exception during the execution of the program.

Here is our new exception class and modified operator [] ().

```
class outOfBounds {
public:
    outOfBounds(int ix) : _index(ix) {};
    int index() { return _index; }

private:
    int _index;
};

int& IntArray::
operator[](int index)
{
    if (index < 0 || index >= _size)
        throw outOfBounds(index);

    return ia[index];
}
```

Exercise 11.9

Using the code you developed for Exercise 11.8, change the declaration of class IntArray operator [] () to add an appropriate exception specification to describe the exception this operator can throw. Modify your program so that operator [] () throws an exception not listed in its exception specification. What happens then?

Here is our new declaration of operator [] ().

```
int& IntArray::
operator[](int index) throw(outOfBounds)
{
    if (index < 0 || index >= _size)
        throw outOfBounds(index);

    return ia[index];
}
```

The exception specification must also appear in the member function declaration located in the class definition. If it is not also included there, the program is in error. Also, note that the definition of the class outOfBounds is needed before its name can be used in an exception specification.

```
class IntArray {
  public:
    // ...
    int &operator[](int) throw(outOfBounds);
    // ...
};
```

Here we modify our program to throw an unlisted exception:

```
class badIndex {};

int& IntArray::
operator[](int index) throw(outOfBounds)
{
    if (index < 0 || index >= _size)
        throw badIndex();

    return ia[index];
}
```

When the program executes and throws the exception, the run-time library function unexpected() is called and the program terminates.

Exercise 11.10

What exceptions may a function throw if it has an exception specification of the form throw()? If it has no exception specification?

A function with an exception specification of the form throw() is not allowed to throw any exception. Doing so results in the library function unexpected() to be called and the program terminates.

A function with no exception specification has no restrictions on the exceptions it may throw.

Exercise 11.11

Which one, if any, of the following pointer assignments is in error? Why?

```
    void example() throw(string);
(a) void (*pf1)() = example;

(b) void (*pf2)() throw() = example;
```

(b) is in error because pf2's exception specification is more restrictive than example's.

chapter twelve

The Generic Algorithms

Exercise 12.1

One criticism of the generic algorithms is that their design, although elegant, places the burden of correctness on the programmer. For example, an invalid iterator or iterator pair marking an invalid range results in undefined run-time behavior. How valid is this criticism? Should use of the algorithms be limited to only the more-experienced programmers? In general, should programmers be protected against potentially error-prone constructs, such as the generic algorithms, pointers, and explicit casts?

The burden of correctness is always on programmers no matter which construct we choose to use. Some languages do extra work at run-time to make sure that the programmer does not, for example, access an element past the boundaries of an array. That is useful and may help the programmer, but it comes at a price: it may take a bit longer to run the program because of the extra checking.

Programmers can always add their own checks on top of the generic algorithms. If the checks were part of a function in a library, the programmer would not be able to remove them without rewriting the function.

The designers of the C and C++ languages emphasized efficiency and relied on programmers to ensure program correctness.

Exercise 12.2

Word length is not the only nor possibly the best complexity measure of a piece of text. Another possible test is the length of a sentence. Write a program that reads in either a text file or text from standard input, builds a string vector for each sentence, and passes each vector to count(). Display the sentences in order of complexity. An interesting way to do that is to store each sentence as one large string in a second string vector and then pass that vector to sort() with a function object providing less-than semantics based on

the smaller string. (To read a more detailed description of a particular generic algorithm or to see a further example of its use, refer to the Appendix, where the algorithms are listed in alphabetical order.)

We create the class `Sentences`, an abbreviated version of the `TextQuery` class in Chapter 6.

```cpp
typedef vector<string>  *sentence;

class Sentences {
  public:
    ~Sentences();
    void getSentences();
    void displaySentences();
    void sort();

  private:
    void handle_word(vector<string> *&, string);

  private:
    vector<sentence>        sentences;
    static string           _punctuation;
};

string Sentences::_punctuation(".!?");
```

The new class provides four public methods. The first method is the destructor (`~Sentences()`). The second method, `getSentences()`, reads lines and picks the words out of each input line to build each sentence. For each word, we scan for punctuation characters that indicate the end of the sentence. A private auxiliary method `handle_word()` simplifies the handling of each word.

```cpp
void Sentences::getSentences()
{
    string file_name;

    cout << "please enter file name: ";
    cin  >> file_name;

    ifstream infile(file_name.c_str(), ios::in);
    if (!infile) {
        cerr << "oops! unable to open file "
             << file_name << " -- bailing out!\n";
        exit(-1);
    } else
        cout << "\n";
```

```
        string textline, word;
        vector<string> *words = new vector<string>;

        while (getline(infile, textline, '\n')) {
            string::size_type pos = 0, prev_pos = 0;

            while ((pos = textline.find_first_of(' ', pos)) !=
                                                    string::npos) {
                handle_word(words, textline.substr(prev_pos, pos - prev_pos));
                prev_pos = ++pos;
            }
            handle_word(words, textline.substr(prev_pos, pos - prev_pos));
        }
        sentences.push_back(words);
    }

    void Sentences::handle_word(vector<string> *& words, string word)
    {
        words->push_back(word);
        if (word.find_first_of(Sentences::_punctuation, 0) !=
                                            string::npos) {
            sentences.push_back(words);
            words = new vector<string>;
        }
    }
```

The third method displays the sentences.

```
    void Sentences::displaySentences()
    {
        vector<sentence>::iterator ss;
        vector<string>::iterator    s;

        for (ss = sentences.begin(); ss != sentences.end(); ++ss) {
            for (s = (*ss)->begin(); s != (*ss)->end(); ++s)
                cout << *s << " ";
            cout << "\n\n";
        }
    }
```

The fourth method sorts the sentences:

```
    void Sentences::sort()
    {
        stable_sort(sentences.begin(), sentences.end(), LessThan());
    }
```

We use `stable_sort()` to sort the sentences. That requires a function object to perform the comparisons. We create the function object `LessThan`, which is similar to L&L's (page 583):

```
class LessThan {
  public:
    bool operator()(const sentence &a, const sentence &b)
    {
        return a->size() < b->size();
    }
};
```

The `main()` program is, consequently, short and simple.

```
int main()
{
    Sentences s;
    s.getSentences();
    s.displaySentences();

    s.sort();
    s.displaySentences();

    return 0;
}
```

Exercise 12.3

A more reliable test of the difficulty level of a piece of text is the structural complexity of its sentences. Let each comma count as 1 point, each semicolon or colon as 2 points, and each dash as 3 points. Modify the program of Exercise 12.2 to calculate the complexity of each sentence. Use `count_if()` to determine the presence of each punctuation character in the sentence vector. Display the sentences in order of complexity.

We modify the function object `LessThan` in Exercise 12.2. The `operator()` compares the number of punctuation characters (`,`, `;`, `:`, and `-`) in the two incoming arguments. To simplify the method we added a private method, `count_punctuation()`, that counts the occurrences of each punctuation character.

```
class LessThan {
  public:
    bool operator ()(const sentence &a, const sentence &b)
    {
        return count_punctuation(a) < count_punctuation(b);
    }
```

```
    private:
      int count_punctuation(const sentence &s)
      {
          int total = 0;

          total += count_if(s->begin(), s->end(), Counter(','));
          total += count_if(s->begin(), s->end(), Counter(';')) * 2;
          total += count_if(s->begin(), s->end(), Counter(':')) * 2;
          total += count_if(s->begin(), s->end(), Counter('-')) * 3;
          return total;

      }
  };
```

The `count_punctuation()` method uses `count_if()` as this exercise requires, and `count_if()` uses a function object `Counter()` to return 1 if the punctuation character appears in the word. We created a constructor for `Counter` to remember the character that it should look for. Of course, `Counter` implements `operator()`.

```
  class Counter {
    public:
      Counter(char c) : _c(c) { }
      bool operator ()(const string &s)
      {
          return s.find_first_of(_c, 0) != string::npos;
      }
    private:
      char _c;
  };
```

No other changes were required in Exercise 12.2 to complete this exercise.

Exercise 12.4

Using the predefined function objects and function adaptors, create a function object to do the following:

(a) Find all values that are greater than 1024.
(b) Find all strings that are not equal to "pooh".
(c) Multiply all values by 2.

(a) Find all values that are greater than 1024.

We use bind2nd(greater<int>(), 1024):

```
          int a[] = { 4023, 1025, 1024, 4028, 1023, 4029 };
          int *iter = a;
```

```
      while((iter = find_if(iter, a+6, bind2nd(greater<int>(), 1024)))
              != a+6) {
          cout << *iter << " ";
          iter++;
      }
      cout << endl;
```

(b) Find all strings that are not equal to "pooh".

We use bind2nd(not_equal_to<string>(), "pooh"):

```
      string s[] = { "pooh", "paah", "peeh", "piih", "pooh", "puuh" };
      string *iter = s;

      while ((iter = find_if(iter, s+6, bind2nd(not_equal_to<string>(),
                          "pooh"))) != s+6) {
          cout << *iter << " ";
          iter++;
      }
      cout << endl;
```

(c) Multiply all values by 2.

We use bind2nd(multiplies<int>(), 2) and transform():

```
      int a[] = { 10, 20, 30, 40, 50, 60 };
      int i;

      for (i = 0; i < 6; i++)
          cout << a[i] << " ";
      cout << endl;

      transform(a, a+6, a, bind2nd(multiplies<int>(), 2));

      for (i = 0; i < 6; i++)
          cout << a[i] << " ";
      cout << endl;
```

Exercise 12.5

Define a function object to evaluate three objects and return the middle value. Define a function to do the same operation. Show examples of using each object directly and by passing each to a function. Compare and contrast the behavior of each.

We create a template for a function object that handles any number of odd objects. We use sort() and return an iterator to the middle of the object — that's the middle value.

```
template <typename Iterator>
class Middle {
  public:
    Middle(Iterator first, Iterator last) :
        _first(first), _last(last) { }
    Iterator operator ()()
    {
        sort(_first, _last);
        Iterator mid = _first + (_last - _first)/2;
        return mid;
    }
  private:
    Iterator _first, _last;
};
```

First, let's use the function object directly.

```
int ai[] = { 20, 30, 10 };
vector<int> vi(ai, ai+3);
string as[] = { "this", "is", "only", "a", "test" };
vector<string> vs(as, as+5);

cout << "answer should be 20:\t"
     << *Middle<int *>(ai, ai+3)() << endl;
cout << "answer should be 20:\t"
     << *Middle<vector<int>::iterator>(vi.begin(), vi.end())()
     << endl;
cout << "answer should be only:\t"
     << *Middle<string *>(as, as+5)() << endl;
cout << "answer should be only:\t"
     << *Middle<vector<string>::iterator>(vs.begin(), vs.end())()
     << endl;
```

Second, let's pass a function object to another function. To do that, we create a new template function getMiddle().

```
template <typename F>
void getMiddle(F func)
{
    cout << *func() << endl;
}
```

We pass a function object to getMiddle(), obtaining the same results as when we used the function object directly:

```
getMiddle(Middle< int * >(ai, ai+3));
getMiddle(Middle< vector<int>::iterator >(vi.begin(), vi.end()));
getMiddle(Middle< string * >(as, as+5));
getMiddle(Middle< vector<string>::iterator >(vs.begin(), vs.end()));
```

In the next case, when we create a template function, we have a more readable program. The template function is similar to the function object `operator()`.

First, let's use the template function directly.

```
template <typename Iterator>
Iterator f(Iterator first, Iterator last)
{
    sort(first, last);
    Iterator mid = first + (last - first)/2;
    return mid;
}
```

The `main()` program is easier to read.

```
int ai[] = { 20, 30, 10 };
vector<int> vi(ai, ai+3);
string as[] = { "this", "is", "only", "a", "test" };
vector<string> vs(as, as+5);

cout << "answer should be 20:\t"
     << *f(ai, ai+3) << endl;
cout << "answer should be 20:\t"
     << *f(vi.begin(), vi.end()) << endl;
cout << "answer should be only:\t"
     << *f(as, as+5) << endl;
cout << "answer should be only:\t"
     << *f(vs.begin(), vs.end()) << endl;
```

Second, let's pass the template function to another function. To do that, we create a new template function `getMiddle()`.

```
template <typename F>
void getMiddle(F func)
{
    cout << *func() << endl;
}
```

We pass the template function `f()` to `getMiddle()`, obtaining the same results as when we used the function object directly:

```
getMiddle(Middle< int * >(ai, ai+3));
getMiddle(Middle< vector<int>::iterator >(vi.begin(), vi.end()));
getMiddle(Middle< string * >(as, as+5));
getMiddle(Middle< vector<string>::iterator >(vs.begin(), vs.end()));
```

Notice that we must specify the instance of the template function we wish to pass to `getMiddle()`.

Exercise 12.6

Explain why each of the following is incorrect. Identify which errors are caught during compilation.

```
(a) const vector<string> file_names(sa, sa+6);
    vector<string>::iterator it = file_names.begin()+2;

(b) const vector<int> ivec;
    fill(ivec.begin(), ivec.end(), ival);

(c) sort(ivec.begin(), ivec.rend());

(d) list<int> ilist(ia, ia+6);
    binary_search(ilist.begin(), ilist.end());

(e) sort(ivec1.begin(), ivec2.end());
```

We know that all of them are incorrect. Here are the details.

```
(a) const vector<string> file_names(sa, sa+6);
    vector<string>::iterator it = file_names.begin()+2;
```

`file_names` is a const vector of strings that is properly initialized.

The second line is incorrect. The line attempts to initialize the nonconstant iterator `it` with a const vector. It is caught during compilation.

```
(b) const vector<int> ivec;
    fill(ivec.begin(), ivec.end(), ival);
```

It is incorrect because `ivec` is an empty const vector that cannot be modified, and `ivec.begin()` is equal to `ivec.end()`. The compiler should complain that `fill()` is receiving a const vector.

```
(c) sort(ivec.begin(), ivec.rend());
```

The function `sort()` has two problems.

1. It is attempting to sort a const vector, and the compiler will flag the error stating that "l-value specifies a const object." An l-value means the address of an object of some type. We cannot pass the address of a const of some type to a function that expects to modify that l-value.

2. The second problem is `rend()`; it is incompatible with `begin()` because `rend()` returns a reverse iterator positioned immediately before the first item. This error is not caught during compilation.

```
(d) list<int> ilist(ia, ia+6);
    binary_search(ilist.begin(), ilist.end());
```

The third required argument, the target, is missing in `binary_search()`. This is a compile-time error.

```
(e) sort(ivec1.begin(), ivec2.end());
```

When we invoke `sort` on a vector, we should have iterators indicating the starting and ending points in the same vector. `begin()` refers to `ivec1`, and `end()` refers to `ivec2`. This will cause problems at run-time.

Exercise 12.7

Write a program to read a sequence of integer numbers from standard input using an `istream_iterator`. **Write the odd numbers into one file using an** `ostream_iterator`. **Each value should be separated by a space. Write the even numbers into a second file also using an** `ostream_iterator`. **Each of these values should be placed on a separate line.**

To select the odd numbers, we use the binder adaptor bind2nd (L&L, page 592):

```
bind2nd(modulus<int>(), 2)
```

The result will be true when it is not zero; the number is not a multiple of 2.

To select the even numbers, we use the binder adaptor `bind2nd` with the predefined negator adaptor `not1`:

```
not1(bind2nd(modulus<int>(), 2))
```

The `main()` program is similar to the code in L&L, Section 12.4.

```
int main()
{
    cout << "please enter a few integers:" << endl;

    istream_iterator<int> input(cin), eos;
    ofstream efile("evenfile");
    ostream_iterator<int> evenfile(efile, "\n");
    ofstream ofile("oddfile");
    ostream_iterator<int> oddfile(ofile, "\n");

    vector<int> vi;

    // read integers into vector vi
    copy(input, eos, back_inserter(vi));
```

```
        vector<int>::iterator iter = vi.begin();

        // copy odd numbers to ofile
        while ((iter = find_if(iter, vi.end(),
                                bind2nd(modulus<int>(), 2)))
                != vi.end()) {
            copy(iter, iter+1, oddfile);
            iter++;
        }

        iter = vi.begin();

        // copy even numbers to efile
        while ((iter = find_if(iter, vi.end(),
                                not1(bind2nd(modulus<int>(), 2))))
                != vi.end()) {
            copy(iter, iter+1, evenfile);
            iter++;
        }
        cout << "results in 'evenfile' and 'oddfile'\n";

        return 0;
    }
```

Exercise 12.8

Reimplement the program of Section 12.2 using a list instead of a vector.

We use the code that begins on page 582 in L&L. The changes are straightforward and usually involve only replacing vector with list and changing the parameters for count() to avoid the obsolete form (as the authors indicated).

```
    typedef list<string> textwords;
    void process_vocab(list<textwords> *plist)
    {
        if (!plist)
            return;

        list<string> texts;

        list<textwords>::iterator iter;
        for(iter = plist->begin(); iter != plist->end(); ++iter)
            copy((*iter).begin(), (*iter).end(), back_inserter(texts));
```

```
// sort the elements of texts
sort(texts.begin(), texts.end());

// ok, let's see what we have
for_each(texts.begin(), texts.end(), PrintElem());
cout << "\n\n";

// delete all duplicate elements
list<string>::iterator it;
it = unique(texts.begin(), texts.end());
texts.erase(it, texts.end());

// ok, let's see what we have now
for_each(texts.begin(), texts.end(), PrintElem());
cout << "\n\n";

// sort the elements based on default length of 6
// stable_sort() preserves ordering of equal elements ...
stable_sort(texts.begin(), texts.end(), LessThan());

for_each(texts.begin(), texts.end(), PrintElem());
cout << "\n\n";

// count number of strings greater than length 6
int cnt = count_if(texts.begin(), texts.end(), GreaterThan());

cout << "Number of words greater than length 6 are "
     << cnt << endl;

static string rw[] = { "and", "if", "or", "but", "the" };
list<string> remove_words(rw, rw+5);

list<string>::iterator it2 = remove_words.begin();

for ( ; it2 != remove_words.end(); ++it2) {
    int cnt = count(texts.begin(), texts.end(), *it2);

    cout << cnt << " instances remove: " << (*it2) << endl;

    texts.erase(remove(texts.begin(), texts.end(), *it2), texts.end());
}
cout << "\n\n";
for_each(texts.begin(), texts.end(), PrintElem());
}
```

```
#include    <fstream>

int main()
{
    list<textwords> sample;
    list<string> t1, t2;
    string t1fn, t2fn;

    // request input files from user ...
    cout << "text file #1: "; cin >> t1fn;
    cout << "text file #2: "; cin >> t2fn;

    // open the files
    ifstream infile1(t1fn.c_str());
    if (!infile1) {
        cerr << "could not open file " << t1fn << endl;
    }
    ifstream infile2(t2fn.c_str());
    if (!infile2) {
        cerr << "could not open file " << t2fn << endl;
    }

    istream_iterator<string> input_set1(infile1), eos;
    istream_iterator<string> input_set2(infile2);

    copy(input_set1, eos, back_inserter(t1));
    copy(input_set2, eos, back_inserter(t2));

    sample.push_back(t1);
    sample.push_back(t2);
    process_vocab(&sample);

    return 0;
}
```

chapter thirteen

Classes

Exercise 13.1

Given a class named `Person`, **with the following two data members**

```
string _name;
string _address;
```

and the following member functions

```
Person(const string &n, const string &a)
      : _name(n), _address(a) {}
string name() { return _name; }
string address() { return _address; }
```

which members would you declare in the public section of the class and which members in the private section of the class? Explain your choice.

We want to use information hiding, so we declare the data members in the private section of the class and the member functions in the public section of the class. In general, we want to protect data members from direct access by nonmember functions. By declaring them in the private section and providing public member functions to access them, we achieve this. The member functions `name()` and `address()` are declared in the public section along with the constructor. The constructor is usually a public member so that programs can create objects of type `Person`.

Here is our declaration.

```
class Person {
  public:
    Person(const string &n, const string &a)
          : _name(n), _address(a) {}
    string name() { return _name; }
    string address() { return _address; }
    // ...
```

```
    private:
      string _name;
      string _address;
      // ...
  }
```

Exercise 13.2

Explain the difference between a class declaration and a class definition. When would you use a class declaration? A class definition?

A class declaration does not provide the class body. The class name is introduced into the program but has limited uses. Pointers and references to the class type are the only declarations allowed following a class declaration. Because the size of the class is not known, objects of the class type cannot be defined. A class declaration is most often used when another class needs to declare a pointer to the class but the class is not yet or cannot yet be defined. This occurs, for example, in the case of two classes that each contain a pointer to the other.

A class definition provides the class body and thus all the class member declarations. Objects of the class type can be defined because the size of the class is now known. A class definition is generally placed in a header file that is included whenever an object of that class type must be defined.

Exercise 13.3

Explain the behavior of copy() **in the following invocation:**

```
    Screen myScreen;
    myScreen.copy(myScreen);
```

The first statement in copy()

```
    if ( this != &sobj )
```

checks whether a copy is necessary. In this example, this refers to myScreen and the inbound parameter sobj also refers to myScreen. No copy is performed.

Exercise 13.4

Additional cursor movements might include moving forward or backward one character at a time. On reaching the bottom right corner or top left corner of the screen, the cursor wraps around. Implement the forward() **and** backward() **functions.**

We add the declarations

```
inline void forward();
inline void backward();
```

in the public section of the class definition. Because the functions are inline, the definitions for forward() and backward() are placed in the header file where the definition of class Screen appears.

The member function definitions are as follows:

```
void Screen::forward()
{
    ++_cursor;
    if (_cursor == _screen.size())
        home();
}
void Screen::backward()
{
    if (_cursor == 0)
        _cursor = _screen.size() - 1;
    else
        --_cursor;
}
```

forward() increments the cursor and checks whether the cursor is 1 past the bottom right corner position. If it is, the member function home() is called to wrap the cursor around to the top left corner of the screen.

backward() checks whether the cursor has reached the top left corner of the screen. If it has, the cursor is set to the bottom right corner of the screen. Otherwise, the cursor is decremented.

Exercise 13.5

Another useful capability might include moving the cursor up or down one row of the screen. On reaching the top or bottom row of the screen, the cursor does not wrap around; it sounds a bell and remains where it is. Implement the up() and down() functions, knowing that writing the character '\007' to cout will sound the bell.

The declarations

```
inline void up();
inline void down();
```

are added to the public section of the class definition. Because the functions are inline, the definitions for up() and down() are placed in the header file where the definition of class Screen appears.

A const char is defined for the bell character, and the member functions definitions are as follows:

```
const char BELL = '\007';

void Screen::up()
{
    if (row() == 1)
        cout << BELL << flush;
    else
        _cursor -= _width;
}

void Screen::down()
{
    if (row() == _height)
        cout << BELL << flush;
    else
        _cursor += _width;
}
```

We also add a private member function:

```
int row() { return (_cursor + _width) / _width; }
```

The functions up() and down() check whether the cursor is at the top or the bottom of the screen and, if it is, sound the bell and return without moving the cursor. If the cursor is not at a boundary, the cursor is adjusted by the width of the screen to either increment or decrement the row position while maintaining the same column position.

Exercise 13.6

Revisit the Screen member functions introduced thus far and change the member functions to const member functions where appropriate. Explain your decision.

Almost all the member functions can be changed to const member functions. The class constructor and the member functions set() and copy() modify the data members and thus remain non-const. The remaining member functions either do not modify the data members or modify only the mutable data member _cursor and thus can be declared const. (Recall that a mutable data member is never const even when it is the data member of a const object.)

Here is the modified Screen.h:

```
class Screen {
  public:
    Screen(int hi = 8, int wid = 40, char bkground = '#');
    void home() const { _cursor = 0; }
    inline void forward() const;
    inline void backward() const;
```

```
        inline void up() const;
        inline void down() const;
        inline void move(int, int) const;
        char get() const { return _screen[_cursor]; }
        int height() const { return _height; }
        int width() const { return _width; }
        inline char get(int, int) const;
        bool checkRange(int, int) const;
        void set(const string &s);
        void set(char ch);
        void copy(const Screen &sobj);
        bool isEqual(char ch) const;
        void display() const;
    private:
        inline int remainingSpace() const;
        int row() const { return (_cursor + _width) / _width; }
        mutable string::size_type    _cursor;
        string              _screen;
        short               _height;
        short               _width;
};

void Screen::move(int r, int c) const
{
    if (checkRange(r,c)) {
        int row = (r-1) * _width;
        _cursor = row + c - 1;
    }
}

char Screen::get(int r, int c) const
{
    move(r,c);
    return get();
}

int Screen::remainingSpace() const
{
    int sz = _width * _height;
    return (sz-_cursor);
}
```

```
void Screen::forward() const
{
    ++_cursor;
    if (_cursor == _screen.size())
        home();
}
void Screen::backward() const
{
    if (_cursor == 0)
        _cursor = _width * _height - 1;
    else
        --_cursor;
}
const char BELL = '\007';
void Screen::up() const
{
    if (row() == 1)
        cout << BELL << endl;
    else
        _cursor -= _width;
}
void Screen::down() const
{
    if (row() == _height)
        cout << BELL << endl;
    else
        _cursor += _width;
}
```

Exercise 13.7

The this **pointer can be used to modify the class object to which it refers as well as to override the object with a new object of the same type. For example, here is the member function** assign() **of the class** classType. **Can you explain what it does?**

```
classType& classType::assign(const classType& source)
{
    if (this != &source) {
        this->~classType();
        new (this) classType(source);
    }
    return *this;
}
```

Recall that ~classType() is the name of the destructor. The new expression may look a little bit funny, but we have seen this new expression called placement new expression in Section 8.4.

What is your opinion on this kind of coding style? Do you believe this is a safe operation? Why or why not?

The if statement checks that source is different from the object being assigned. If they are the same, nothing needs to be done and the object is returned. Otherwise, the current object's destructor is invoked and a new object put in its place and initialized with source. Because the new object uses the same memory as the old object, any existing references to the old object are now valid references to the new object.

The copy constructor of the class classType must be implemented appropriately, ensuring that the data members that cannot be memberwise copied are created appropriately. The destructor must also be implemented appropriately to delete memory created by the constructor, if necessary. This means that it is OK to destroy a class object and then create a new object in its place using the placement new expression.

Exercise 13.8

Given the following class Y, with two static data members and two static member functions,

```
class X {
  public:
    X(int i) { _val = i; }
    int val() { return _val; }
  private:
    int _val;
};

class Y {
  public:
    Y(int i);
    static X xval();
    static int callsXval();
  private:
    static X _xval;
    static int _callsXval;
};
```

initialize _xval to 20 and _callsXval to 0.

Because neither data member is const, both of them must be initialized outside the class body as follows:

```
X Y::_xval(20);
int Y::_callsXval = 0;
```

Recall that only one definition of a static data member can be provided in a program. If the class definitions for X and Y are in a header file, the definitions for _xval and _callsXval should be placed in a separate file.

Exercise 13.9

Using the classes in Exercise 13.8, implement the two static member access functions for class Y. callsXval() simply keeps count of how many times xval() **is called.**

The functions are small enough to declare inline. class Y's definition is now as follows:

```
class Y {
  public:
    Y(int i);
    static X xval() { ++_callsXval; return _xval; }
    static int callsXval() { return _callsXval; }
  private:
    static X _xval;
    static int _callsXval;
};
```

Exercise 13.10

Which ones, if any, of the following static data member declarations and definitions are errors? Explain why.

```
// example.h
class Example {
  public:
    static double rate = 6.5;

    static const int vecSize = 20;
    static vector<double> vec(vecSize);
};

// example.C
double Example::rate;
vector<double> Example::vec;
```

Only the declaration for vecSize is correct.

The declaration for rate

```
static double rate = 6.5;
```

is an error because it is not const and is not an integral type. Non-const, non-integral static data members cannot be initialized within the class body.

The declaration for vec

```
static vector<double> vec(vecSize);
```

is an error because specifying an explicit size for vector causes every element to be initialized with the associated default value for its type, in this case double. Because vec is non-const or non-integral, the initialization must occur outside the class body.

The corrected code is as follows:

```
// example.h
class Example {
  public:
    static double rate;

    static const int vecSize = 20;
    static vector<double> vec;
};

// example.C
double Example::rate = 6.5;
vector<double> Example::vec(vecSize);
```

Exercise 13.11

What is the type of the Screen class members _screen and _cursor?

The type of _screen is "member of class Screen of type string."
The type of _cursor is "member of class Screen of type string::size_type."

Exercise 13.12

Define and initialize a pointer to member with the value of Screen::_screen. Define and assign a pointer to member the value of Screen::_cursor.

The definitions are straightforward:

```
string Screen::*ps = &Screen::_screen;
string::size_type Screen::*pc = &Screen::_cursor;
```

Recall that a "member of class Screen of type string" is written as string Screen::. Thus, a pointer to such a type is written as string Screen::*.

Exercise 13.13

Define a typedef for each distinct type of Screen member function.

We have already seen the `typedef` for the cursor movement functions in Section 13.6.1 of L&L:

```
typedef Screen& (Screen::*pfcm)();
```

`move()` is overloaded and takes either two `int` arguments or a `CursorMovements` argument and returns a reference to `Screen`.

```
typedef Screen& (Screen::*pfm)(int, int);
typedef Screen& (Screen::*pfm2)(CursorMovements);
```

`get()` is overloaded and takes either two `int` arguments or no arguments and returns a char.

```
typedef char (Screen::*pfg)();
typedef char (Screen::*pfg2)(int, int);
```

`checkRange()` takes two `int` arguments and returns a `bool`.

```
typedef bool (Screen::*pfcr)(int, int);
```

`height()`, `width()`, `remainingSpace()`, and `row()` take no arguments and return an `int`.

```
typedef int (Screen::*pfi)();
```

`set()` is overloaded and takes either `string&` or char as an argument and returns a `Screen&`.

```
typedef Screen& (Screen::*pfs)(string&);
typedef Screen& (Screen::*pfs2)(char);
```

`repeat()` is overloaded and takes either an `Action` or a `CursorMovements` as a first argument, takes an `int` as its second argument, and returns a `Screen&`.

```
typedef Screen& (Screen::*pfr)(Action, int);
typedef Screen& (Screen::*pfr2)(CursorMovements, int);
```

Pointers to `copy()`, `isEqual()`, `reSize()`, and `clear()` take the following form:

```
typedef void (Screen::*pfc)(Screen&);
typedef bool (Screen::*pfe)(char);
typedef Screen& (Screen::*pfrS)(int, int, char);
typedef Screen& (Screen::*pfclear)(char);
```

Exercise 13.14

Pointers to members may also be declared as class data members. Modify the Screen class definition to contain a pointer to a Screen member function of the same type as `home()` and `end()`.

`home()` and `end()` take no arguments and return `Screen&`. We define a `typedef` for clarity and also use it in the next exercise.

```
typedef Screen&(Screen::*pfhe_type)();
```

Our new data member is

```
pfhe_type _pfhe;
```

Exercise 13.15

Modify the existing Screen constructor (or introduce a new constructor) to take a parameter of type pointer to Screen member function whose parameter list and return type are the same as those for the member functions home() and end(). Provide a default argument for this parameter. Use this parameter to initialize the data member introduced in Exercise 13.14. Provide a Screen member function to allow the user to set this member.

We modify the existing constructor and introduce the new member function setfunc().

```
class Screen {
  public:

    // ...
    typedef Screen&(Screen::*pfhe_type)();
    Screen(int hi = 8, int wid = 40, char bkground = '#',
           pfhe_type f = &Screen::home);
    inline Screen& setfunc(pfhe_type f) { _pfhe = f; return *this; }

  private:
    pfhe_type            _pfhe;
    // ...

Screen::Screen(int hi, int wid, char bk, pfhe_type f):
    _height(hi), _width(wid), _cursor(0), _screen(hi*wid, bk),
    _pfhe(f) {}
```

Exercise 13.16

Define an overloaded instance of repeat() that takes a parameter of type cursorMovements.

```
Screen& Screen::repeat(CursorMovements cm, int times)
{
    for (int i = 0; i < times; ++i)
        (this->*Menu[cm])();
    return *this;
}
```

Exercise 13.17

Rewrite the examples in this section such that the class File **uses the bitset class and its operators described in Section 4.12 instead of declaring and manipulating bit-field data members directly.**

Each of the bit-fields is replaced with a bitset of the appropriate size. The set() and test() member functions are used to manipulate the bits. Recall that the bits are numbered starting from zero.

```cpp
#include <iostream>
#include <bitset>
using namespace std;

enum { READ, WRITE };

class File {
  public:
    inline int isRead() { return mode.test(READ); }
    inline int isWrite() { return mode.test(WRITE); }
    void write();
    void close();

    bitset< 2 > mode;
    bitset< 1 > modified;
    bitset< 3 > prot_owner;
    bitset< 3 > prot_group;
    bitset< 3 > prot_world;
    // ...
};

void File::write()
{
    modified.set(0);
    // ...
}

void File::close()
{
    if (modified.test(0)) {
        // ... save contents
    }
}
```

```
int main()
{
    File myFile;

    myFile.mode.set(READ);
    if (myFile.isRead())
        cout << "myFile.mode is set to READ\n";
}
```

Exercise 13.18

Name the portions of program text that are considered in class scope.

The portions of the program text that are considered in class scope are as follows:

- The definition of the class itself

- If the definition of a class member appears outside the class body, the text that follows the name of the member being defined until the end of the member definition

- In static data member definitions, the text that follows the name of the static member being defined

Exercise 13.19

Name the portions of program text that are in class scope and for which the completed scope of the class is considered (that is, for which all the members declared in the class body are considered).

The portions of the program text that are in class scope and for which the completed scope of the class is considered are as follows:

- The definition of inline member functions

- The names used in default arguments to member functions

Exercise 13.20

To which declarations does the name `Type` refer when used in the body of class `Exercise` and in the definition of its member function `setVal()`? (Remember, different uses may refer to different declarations.) To which declarations does the name `initVal` refer when used in the definition of the member function `setVal()`?

```
typedef int Type;
Type initVal();

class Exercise {
  public:
    // ...
    typedef double Type;
    Type setVal(Type);
    Type initVal();
  private:
    int val;
};

Type Exercise::setVal(Type parm) {
    val = parm + initVal();
}
```

The definition of the member function setVal() **is in error. Can you see why? Apply the necessary changes so that the class Exercise uses the global typedef** Type **and the global function** initVal().

In the declaration for setVal()

```
Type setVal(Type);
```

both the return type and the argument type refer to the typedef within class Exercise — that is, double.

The same applies to the declaration for initVal(): the return type is equivalent to double.

The definition of setVal(), however, uses both Types. The return value is that of the global typedef, whereas the argument is that of the typedef in Exercise. This causes an error because the function signatures are not identical.

The use of initVal() in the definition of setVal() refers to the declaration within the body of Exercise.

Here are the corrections so that Exercise uses the global typedef Type and the global function initVal().

```
typedef int Type;
Type initVal();

class Exercise {
  public:
    // ...
    typedef double Type;
    ::Type setVal(::Type);
    Type initVal();
```

```
   private:
      int val;
};

Type Exercise::setVal(::Type parm) {
    val = parm + ::initVal();
}
```

Exercise 13.21

Chapter 11 has a running example using the class iStack. **Change this example to declare the exception classes** pushOnFull **and** popOnEmpty **as public nested classes of class** iStack. **Modify the definition of class** iStack **and the definitions of its member functions and the definition of** main() **presented in Chapter 11 to refer to these nested classes.**

Here is the modified iStack.h and main():

```
#include <iostream>
#include <vector>
using namespace std;

class iStack {
  public:
    iStack(int capacity)
        : _stack(capacity), _top(0) { }

    class popOnEmpty { };
    class pushOnFull {
      public:
        pushOnFull(int i) : _value(i) { }
        int value() { return _value; }
      private:
        int _value;
    };

    void pop(int &value) throw(popOnEmpty);
    void push(int value) throw(pushOnFull);

    bool full() { return _top >= _stack.size(); }
    bool empty() { return _top <= 0; }
    void display() { cout << "Stack: " << _top; }

    int size() { return _top; }
```

```cpp
  private:
    int _top;
    vector< int > _stack;
};

inline void iStack::pop(int &value) throw (popOnEmpty)
{
    if (empty())
        throw popOnEmpty();

    value = _stack[--_top];
    cout << "iStack::pop(): " << value << endl;
}

inline void iStack::push(int value) throw (pushOnFull)
{
    cout << "iStack::push(): " << value << endl;

    if (full())
        throw pushOnFull(value);

    _stack[_top++] = value;
}

#include "iStack.h"

int main()
{
    iStack stack(32);

    try {
        stack.display();
        for (int ix = 1; ix < 51; ++ix) {
            if (ix % 3 == 0)
                stack.push(ix);
            if (ix % 4 == 0)
                stack.display();
            if (ix % 10 == 0) {
                int dummy;
                stack.pop(dummy);
                stack.display();
            }
        }
    }
```

```
        catch(iStack::pushOnFull eObj) {
            cerr << "trying to push the value " << eObj.value()
                 << " on a full stack\n";
        }
        catch(iStack::popOnEmpty) {
            cerr << "trying to pop a value on an empty stack\n";
        }

        return 0;
    }
```

Exercise 13.22

Using the class iStack defined in Exercise 13.21, now declare the exception classes
pushOnFull and popOnEmpty as members of namespace LibException as follows,

```
    namespace LibException {
        class pushOnFull{};
        class popOnEmpty{};
    }
```

and declare the class iStack as a member of the namespace Container. **Modify the
definition of class** iStack **and the definitions of its member functions and the definition
of** main() **to refer to these classes as namespace members.**

Here is the modified iStack.h and main():

```
    #include <iostream>
    #include <vector>
    using namespace std;

    namespace LibException {
        class popOnEmpty { };
        class pushOnFull {
          public:
            pushOnFull(int i) : _value(i) { }
            int value() { return _value; }
          private:
            int _value;
        };
    }
```

```cpp
namespace Container {

    class iStack {
      public:
        iStack(int capacity)
            : _stack(capacity), _top(0) { }

        void pop(int &value) throw(LibException::popOnEmpty);
        void push(int value) throw(LibException::pushOnFull);

        bool full() { return _top >= _stack.size(); }
        bool empty() { return _top <= 0; }
        void display() { cout << "Stack: " << _top; }

        int size() { return _top; }

      private:
        int _top;
        vector< int > _stack;
    };

    inline void iStack::pop(int &value)
        throw(LibException::popOnEmpty)
    {
        if (empty())
            throw LibException::popOnEmpty();

        value = _stack[--_top];
        cout << "iStack::pop(): " << value << endl;
    }

    inline void iStack::push(int value)
        throw(LibException::pushOnFull)
    {
        cout << "iStack::push(): " << value << endl;

        if (full())
            throw LibException::pushOnFull(value);

        _stack[_top++] = value;
    }

}
```

```cpp
#include "iStack.h"

int main()
{
    Container::iStack stack(32);

    try {
        stack.display();
        for (int ix = 1; ix < 51; ++ix) {
            if (ix % 3 == 0)
                stack.push(ix);
            if (ix % 4 == 0)
                stack.display();
            if (ix % 10 == 0) {
                int dummy;
                stack.pop(dummy);
                stack.display();
            }
        }
    }
    catch(LibException::pushOnFull eObj) {
        cerr << "trying to push the value " << eObj.value()
            << " on a full stack\n";
    }
    catch(LibException::popOnEmpty) {
        cerr << "trying to pop a value on an empty stack\n";
    }

    return 0;
}
```

chapter fourteen

Class Initialization, Assignment, and Destruction

Exercise 14.1

Which, if any, of the following statements are untrue? Why?

(a) A class must provide at least one constructor.

(b) A default constructor is a constructor with no parameters for its parameter list.

(c) If there are no meaningful default values for a class, the class should not provide a default constructor.

(d) If a class does not provide a default constructor explicitly, the compiler generates one automatically, initializing each data member to the default value of its associated type.

(a) A class must provide at least one constructor.

Untrue. A class does not have to provide a constructor. If the class has data members, it is advisable to provide one or more constructors to initialize its data members.

(b) A default constructor is a constructor with no parameters for its parameter list.

Untrue. A default constructor is a constructor that does not require any parameters. We could create a constructor that takes, say, three parameters but we supply default values for each parameter. So this constructor does not require any parameters when it is invoked because of the default values.

Constructors with no parameters or constructors with parameters that have default values are known as default constructors.

(c)   If there are no meaningful default values for a class, the class should not provide a default constructor.

Untrue. A constructor could initialize an object to indicate that it is not yet initialized with a valid set of values. Because other methods would have to explicitly recognize and treat such an indication, it would then act as a "valid" value. This is a debatable issue.

(d)   If a class does not explicitly provide a default constructor, the compiler automatically generates one, initializing each data member to the default value of its associated type.

Untrue. The compiler does not, by default, generate a default constructor unless one of the following conditions holds: (a) a member class object defines a default constructor, (b) a base class subobject defines a default constructor, (c) a virtual function is either inherited or declared, or (d) a virtual base class is either derived from or inherited.

The point is that, even should the compiler generate a default constructor for one of these reasons, it does so only to do internal bookkeeping and not to provide initial values for any built-in types. See L&L, page 699.

Exercise 14.2

Provide one or a set of constructors for the following set of data members. Explain your choices.

```
class NoName {
  public:
    // constructor(s) go here . . .
    // . . .
  protected:
    char   *pstring;
    int     ival;
    double dval;
};
```

We provide five constructors:

```
class NoName {
  public:
    NoName();
    explicit NoName(char *);
    NoName(char *, int);
    NoName(char *, int, double);
    NoName(const NoName &);
  private:
    void initName(const char *);
```

```
    protected:
       char  *pstring;
       int    ival;
       double dval;
    };
```

The first constructor is a default constructor:

```
    NoName();
```

It can provide reasonable initial values for the data members so that an object of type NoName will be usable as soon as it is created. The default constructor will also be used when allocating arrays of NoName objects.

```
    NoName::NoName()
    {
        pstring  = new char[1];
        *pstring = '\0';
        ival     = 0;
        dval     = 0;
    }
```

The next three constructors are similar: they invoke initNoName() (which initializes pstring) and then initialize ival and dval.

```
    void NoName::initNoName(const char *ps)
    {
        if (ps) {
            pstring = new char[strlen(ps) + 1];
            strcpy(pstring, ps);
        } else {
            pstring = new char[1];
            *pstring = '\0';
        }
    }
```

Here's the second constructor:

```
    NoName::NoName(const char *ps)
    {
        initNoName(ps);
        ival = 0;
        dval = 0;
    }
```

The third constructor accepts arguments to initialize pstring and ival. The fourth constructor, in addition, accepts an argument to initialize dval as well.

The fifth constructor is a copy constructor: it takes one argument that is a const reference to another object of type NoName.

```
NoName::NoName(const NoName &nn)
{
    initNoName(nn.pstring);
    ival = nn.ival;
    dval = nn.dval;
}
```

An alternative is to supply one default constructor with suitable default values and one copy constructor.

```
class NoName {
  public:
    explicit NoName(char *ps = 0, int iv = 0, double dv = 0.);
    NoName(const NoName &);
  private:
    void initName(const char *);
  protected:
    char   *pstring;
    int     ival;
    double dval;
};
```

Because we are providing default values, missing right-hand side arguments will take the default values:

```
NoName::NoName(char *ps, int iv, double dv)
{
    initNoName(ps);
    ival = iv;
    dval = dv;
}
```

We could, then, create objects of type NoName and rely on the one constructor available:

```
NoName a;                    // NoName   a(0,      0, 0.);
NoName b("abc");             // NoName   b("abc", 0, 0.);
NoName c("abc", 1);          // NoName   c("abc", 1, 0.);
NoName d("abc", 1, 3.5);     // NoName   d("abc", 1, 3.5);
NoName e(d);                 // copy constructor
```

Exercise 14.3

Choose one of the following abstractions (or choose your own). Determine what data (that can be set by users) is appropriate for the class. Provide an appropriate set of constructors. Explain your decisions.

(a)   **Book**

(b)   **Date**

(c)   **Employee**

(d)   **Vehicle**

(e)   **Object**

(f)   **Tree**

We chose two abstractions to illustrate two different requirements.
First, we use the same class Date we created in Chapter 2.

```
class Date {
  public:
                                 // default constructor
    Date(int = 0, int = 0, int = 0);
    int   day() const;          // get day
    void day( int );            // set day
    int   month() const;
    void month( int );
    int   year() const;
    void year( int );

    friend ostream &operator <<(ostream &, const Date &);
  private:
    int _day, _month, _year;
};
```

The class Date allows the user to get or set day, month, and year, and it has a default
constructor. A possible implementation for the default constructor is

```
Date::Date(int d, int m, int y)
{
    _day = d;
    _month = m;
    _year = y;
}
```

This is a simple constructor that initializes the data members of an object of type Date. We
do not need to supply a copy constructor for this class because there are no pointers that
refer to memory allocated in the heap.

Second, we use the abstraction Book.

```
class Book {
  public:

    Book();
    Book(const string &, const string &, const string &, int);

    const string &author() const;          // get author
    void          author(const string &);  // set author
    const string &title() const;
    void          title(const string &);
    const string &publisher() const;
    void          publisher(const string &);
    int           pubdate() const;
    void          pubdate(int);

    friend ostream &operator <<(ostream &, const Book &);
  private:
    string _author;
    string _title;
    string _publisher;
    int    _pubdate;
};
```

The class Book allows the user to get or set author, title, publisher, and publication year. The default constructor must initialize _pubdate only. (The string members are initialized by the default constructor for the string class.)

```
Book::Book()
{
    _pubdate = 0;
}
```

L&L covers friend functions in Chapter 16.

Exercise 14.4

Using the following Account **class definition**

```
class Account {
  public:
    Account();
    explicit Account(const char*, double = 0.0);
    // ...
};
```

explain what happens with the following definitions:
```
(a) Account acct;
(b) Account acct2 = acct;
(c) Account acct3 = "Rena Stern";
(d) Account acct4("Anna Engel", 400.00);
(e) Account acct5 = Account(acct3);
```

```
(a) Account acct;
```

This definition creates the object acct of type class Account and invokes a default constructor to initialize acct.

```
(b) Account acct2 = acct;
```

This definition creates the object acct2; then the compiler uses memberwise initialization to set acct2 with a copy of acct.

```
(c) Account acct3 = "Rena Stern";
```

This definition is equivalent to
```
    Account acct3("Rena Stern", 0.0);
```
That is, it invokes the constructor that takes a const pointer to char and uses the default value 0.0 for the second argument.

```
(d) Account acct4("Anna Engel", 400.00);
```

This definition is similar to (c).

```
(e) Account acct5 = Account(acct3);
```

This definition creates the object acct5 and initializes it with a copy of acct3. (e) is equivalent to (b).

Exercise 14.5

The parameter of the copy constructor does not strictly need to be const, but it does strictly need to be a reference. Why is the following wrong?
```
    Account::Account(const Account rhs);
```

It is wrong because it is attempting to pass an argument by value to a copy constructor. Whenever we pass an argument by value, we invoke a copy constructor. Thus, to use this "copy constructor" that uses pass-by-value, we must use a copy constructor that does not use pass-by-value. An infinite recursion loop occurs if the copy constructor accepts an object of the class type rather than a reference. That's the reason we must pass arguments to a copy constructor by reference:
```
    Account::Account(const Account &rhs);
```

Exercise 14.6

Given the following set of class data members, in which `pstring` addresses a dynamic character array, write an appropriate destructor.

```
class NoName {
  public:
    ~NoName();
    // ...
  private:
    char  *pstring;
    int    ival;
    double dval;
};
```

The destructor must deallocate the space that `pstring` points to (which, presumably, was allocated within the constructor). The members `ival` and `dval` do not require any handling within the destructor.

```
NoName::~NoName()
{
    delete [] pstring;
}
```

Exercise 14.7

For the class chosen in Exercise 14.3 of Section 14.2, determine if a destructor is necessary. If not, explain why. Otherwise, provide its implementation.

The primary role of a class destructor is to give back any resources taken by the class in the course of the object's lifetime. This is most commonly a pointer addressing heap memory allocated within the constructor that the destructor then deallocates.

We do not need a destructor for the class `Date` because the class does not have members that are pointers and refer to space allocated in the heap. The same is true for class `Book`.

Exercise 14.8

How many destructor invocations occur in the following code fragment?

```
void mumble(const char *name, double balance, char acc_type)
{
    Account acct;

    if (!name)
        return;

    if (balance <= 99)
        return;

    switch(acct_type) {
    case 'z':  return;
    case 'a':
    case 'b':  return;
    }

    // ...
}
```

acct's destructor is the only one invoked. We mark the places with a comment where the destructors are invoked.

```
void mumble(const char *name, double balance, char acc_type)
{
    Account acct;

    if (!name)
        return;                    // 1

    if (balance <= 99)
        return;                    // 2

    switch(acct_type) {
    case 'z':  return;             // 3
    case 'a':
    case 'b':  return;             // 4
    }

    // ...
}                                  // 5
```

The destructor is invoked "at each exit point within a function for each active local class object" (L&L, page 707). If the destructor is an inline destructor, at each exit point we will have a copy of the destructor inserted in the code. See L&L, Section 14.3.2, Potential for Program Code Bloat, for details on how to eliminate the code bloat.

Exercise 14.9

Which of the following, if any, are incorrect? Correct each instance that you identify as incorrect.

```
(a) Account *parray[10] = new Account[10];
(b) Account iA[1024] = {
        "Nhi", "Le", "Jon", "Mike", "Greg", "Brent", "Hank",
        "Roy", "Elena" };
(c) string *ps = string[5]("Tina", "Tim", "Chyuan", "Mira", "Mike");
(d) string as[] = *ps;
```

```
(a) Account *parray[10] = new Account[10];
```

Incorrect. The object parray is an array of pointers to Account. The right-hand side of the = should contain a list of objects in curly braces. If the right-hand side of the = is correct because we wish to allocate an array of objects of type Account, we should modify the object:

```
Account *parray = new Account[10];
```

```
(b) Account iA[1024] = {
        "Nhi", "Le", "Jon", "Mike", "Greg", "Brent", "Hank", "Roy", "Elena" };
```

Correct. We can specify a list of values when the data members are public or when we have a constructor, as we have in Account, that takes each value as an argument. The remaining elements of the array iA will be initialized with the default constructor for Account.

```
(c) string *ps = string[5]("Tina", "Tim", "Chyuan", "Mira", "Mike");
```

Incorrect. We could create an array of strings by writing

```
string *ps = new string[5];
```

Because the language uses a default constructor to initialize the elements of the array, we cannot provide initial values for the array of strings that we create with new.

```
(d) string as[] = *ps;
```

Incorrect. We cannot specify initializers for an array, and we cannot copy the elements through a single copy/initialization. We must allocate an array of 10 strings and then copy each in turn.

Exercise 14.10

In each of the following situations, which is the more appropriate, if any: a static array, such as Account pA[10]; a dynamic array; or a vector? Explain why.

(a) A collection of 256 elements are needed to store class Color objects within a function named Lut(). The values are constant.

(b) An unknown collection of Account elements is needed. Data for each account is stored in a file to be read.

(c) A collection of elem_size strings are to be generated and passed back to a text manager by the function gen_words(elem_size).

Information about the use of the data helps determine which construct is more appropriate. For example, if we have a fixed collection of elements, a static array is appropriate. If we must read an unknown number of elements, a vector manages the memory automatically, growing dynamically as needed.

(a) A static array is appropriate because having constant value initialization means that the curly brace initialization of a fixed size is all done before run-time and is significantly more efficient.

(b) A vector is appropriate because we do not know the length of the collection at compile time; vector will expand as necessary.

(c) If the collection's size will be known at run-time, a dynamic array is appropriate because we want to allocate space for a collection of elements. Otherwise, a vector, which expands as necessary, is the better choice.

Exercise 14.11

A potential pitfall in the use of dynamic class arrays is to forget to place the bracket pair to indicate the pointer addresses an array; that is, to write

```
// oops: no check if parray addresses an array
delete parray;
```

rather than

```
// ok: retrieve size of array parray addresses
delete [] parray;
```

The presence of the bracket pair causes the compiler to retrieve the size of the array. The destructor is then applied size times to each element of the array in turn. Otherwise, a single element is destructed. The full space allocated is returned to the free store in either case.

In the original language design, extensive discussion took place on whether to require the bracket pair to initiate a search, on one hand, or whether to retain the original language requirement for the programmer to provide the explicit array size within the bracket pair:

```
// original language design required explicit size
delete [10] parray;
```

Why do you think the language was changed so as not to require the user to provide the explicit size of the array, requiring storage and retrieval of the size, but was not changed to omit the bracket pair on the delete expression, requiring that the implementation remember whether the pointer addresses a single object or an array? How would you have designed the language?

The original requirement that the user provide the explicit size of the array turned out to be a common source of errors. Users tended to provide incorrect numbers — that is, numbers that did not match the original allocation. For example:

```
Array *parray = new Array[10];
// ...
delete [5] parray;
```

would deallocate 5 Arrays when 10 had been allocated. Users could also write the opposite:

```
Array *parray = new Array[5];
// ...
delete [10] parray;
```

producing similar disastrous results.

In the case of an array of objects, the compiler must perform a hash lookup for the size of the array. "Concern over the impact of searching for the array dimension on the performance of delete operator led to the following compromise. The compiler searches for a dimension size only if the bracket is present. Otherwise, it assumes a single object is being deleted" (*Inside the C++ Object Model,* Stanley B. Lippman, Addison-Wesley, 1996, page 220). The omission of the bracket still is a common source of errors even for experienced programmers.

Exercise 14.12

What, if anything, is wrong with the following constructor definitions? How would you fix those identified as wrong?

```
(a) Word::Word(char *ps, int count = 1)
        : _ps(new char[strlen(ps) + 1]),
          _count(count)
    {
```

```
                if (ps)
                    strcpy(_ps, ps);
                else {
                    _ps = 0;
                    _count = 0;
                }
        }

(b) class CL1 {
        public:
          CL1() {c.real(0.0); c.imag(0.0); s = "not set"; }
          // ...
        private:
          complex<double> c;
          string s;
    };

(c) class CL2 {
        public:
          CL2(map<string, location> *pmap, string key)
              : _text(key), _loc((*pmap)[key]) { }
          // ...
        private:
          location _loc;
          string   _text;
    };
```

All the items have problems.

The problem in (a) is that the constructor tests ps in the body of method after ps was already used in the initialization list as the argument to strlen(). If strlen() receives a pointer with the value zero, the behavior of the function is undefined.

We could defer setting _ps until after testing ps in the body of the constructor:

```
    Word::Word(char *ps, int count = 1)
        : _count(count)
    {
        if (ps)
            _ps = new char[strlen(ps) + 1];
            strcpy(_ps, ps);
        else {
            _ps = 0;
            _count = 0;
        }
    }
```

Part (b) is correct but inefficient. Because s is an object of type string, the constructor for s is called before the body of CL1's constructor is executed. Then CL1() resets s. Something similar happens to the data member c. We could avoid the double initializations by using an initialization list:

```
class CL1 {
  public:
    CL1() : s("not set")
    { }
    // ...
  private:
    complex<double> c;
    string s;
};
```

Part (c) is incorrect because pmap, as a pointer, can be 0.

Exercise 14.13

Which class definition is likely to need a copy constructor?

(a)   **A `Point3w` representation containing four float members**

(b)   **A `matrix` class in which the actual matrix is allocated dynamically within the constructor and is deleted within its destructor**

(c)   **A payroll class in which each object is provided with a unique ID**

(d)   **A word class containing a `string` object and `vector` object of line and column location pairs**

As a heuristic, a class needs a copy constructor if it has at least one pointer.

(a)   A `Point3w` representation containing four float members

A copy constructor is not required for `Point3w`. The default copy constructor the compiler provides is sufficient because there are no data members that are pointers.

(b)   A `matrix` class in which the actual matrix is allocated dynamically within the constructor and is deleted within its destructor

A copy constructor is required to allocate the space for a copy of the matrix because pointers and dynamic memory allocation are involved.

(c)   A payroll class in which each object is provided with a unique ID

A copy constructor will be necessary for this class to provide a unique ID for a copy of an existing object.

(d)   A word class containing a `string` object and `vector` object of line and column location pairs

A copy constructor is not required because the compiler will invoke the copy constructors for the data members of type `string` and `vector`.

Exercise 14.14

Given the following classes, implement a copy constructor for each, as well as a default constructor, and a destructor.

```
(a) class BinStrTreeNode {
    public:
        // ...
    private:
        string _value;
        int    _count;
        BinStrTreeNode *_leftchild;
        BinStrTreeNode *_rightchild;
    };

(b) class BinStrTree {
    public:
        // ...
    private:
        BinStrTreeNode *_root;
    };

(c) class iMatrix {
    public:
        // ...
    private:
        int  _rows;
        int  _cols;
        int *_matrix;
    };

(d) class theBigMix {
    public:
        // ...
```

```
    private:
      BinStrTree     _bst;
      iMatrix        _im;
      string         _name;
      vector<float> *_pvec;
  };
```

(a) class BinStrTreeNode

```
  BinStrTreeNode::BinStrTreeNode() :
                  _count(0), _leftchild(0), _rightchild(0)
  { }

  BinStrTreeNode::BinStrTreeNode(const BinStrTreeNode &rhs) :
                  _value(rhs._value)
  {
      _count = rhs._count;
      if (rhs._leftchild)
          _leftchild = new BinStrTreeNode(*rhs._leftchild);
      else
          _leftchild = 0;
      if (rhs._rightchild)
          _rightchild = new BinStrTreeNode(*rhs._rightchild);
      else
          _rightchild = 0;
  }

  BinStrTreeNode::~BinStrTreeNode()
  {
      delete _leftchild;
      delete _rightchild;
  }
```

(b) class BinStrTree

```
  BinStrTree::BinStrTree() : _root(0)
  { }

  BinStrTree::BinStrTree(const BinStrTree &rhs)
  {
      if (rhs._root)
          _root = new BinStrTree(*rhs._root);
```

```
        else
            _root = 0;
    }

    BinStrTree::~BinStrTree()
    {
        delete _root;
    }
```

(c) class iMatrix

```
    iMatrix::iMatrix() : _matrix(0)
    {
        _rows = _cols = 0;
    }

    iMatrix::iMatrix(const iMatrix &rhs)
    {
        _rows = rhs._rows;
        _cols = rhs._cols;
        _matrix = new int[_rows * _cols];
        // now copy rhs._matrix into _matrix...
    }

    iMatrix::~iMatrix()
    {
        delete [] _matrix;
    }
```

(d) class theBigMix

```
    theBigMix::theBigMix() : _pvec(0)
    { }

    theBigMix::theBigMix(const theBigMix &rhs) :
                    _bst(rhs._bst), _im(rhs._im), _name(rhs._name)
    {
        _pvec = new vector<float>;
        // copy the contents of rhs._pvec into _pvec...
    }
```

```
theBigMix::~theBigMix()
{
    delete _pvec;
}
```

Exercise 14.15

For the class chosen in Exercise 14.3 of Section 14.2, determine if a copy constructor is necessary. If not, explain why. Otherwise, provide its implementation.

It is not necessary to implement a copy constructor for the class Date in Exercise 14.3. The reason is that the class does not have pointers to objects in the heap or references to objects of another class type.

The class Book does not require a copy constructor.

Exercise 14.16

Identify each instance of memberwise initialization in this program fragment:

```
Point global;

Point foo_bar(Point arg)
{
    Point local = arg;
    Point *heap = new Point(global);
    *heap = global;
    Point pa[4] = { local, *heap };
    return *heap;
}
```

```
Point foo_bar(Point arg)
```

The function foo_bar receives arg by value. If we do not provide a copy constructor, the compiler provides memberwise initialization to make a copy of the incoming argument. This is instance 1.

```
Point local = arg;              // instance 2
*heap = new Point(global);      // instance 3
Point pa[4] = { local, *heap }; // instances 4 and 5
return *heap;                   // instance 6
```

Exercise 14.17

Provide a copy assignment operator for each of the classes defined in Exercise 14.14 of Section 14.6.

(a) class BinStrTreeNode

```
BinStrTreeNode &BinStrTreeNode::operator =(const BinStrTreeNode &rhs)
{
    if (this != &rhs) {
        _value = rhs._value;
        _count = rhs._count;
        delete _leftchild;
        if (rhs._leftchild)
            _leftchild = new BinStrTreeNode(*rhs._leftchild);
        else
            _leftchild = 0;
        delete _rightchild;
        if (rhs._rightchild)
            _rightchild  = new BinStrTreeNode(*rhs._rightchild);
        else
            _rightchild  = 0;
    }
    return *this;
}
```

(b) class BinStrTree

```
BinStrTree &BinStrTree::operator =(const BinStrTree &rhs)
{
    if (this != &rhs) {
        delete _root;
        if (rhs._root)
            _root = new BinStrTree(*rhs._root);
        else
            _root = 0;
    }
    return *this;
}
```

(c) class iMatrix

```
iMatrix &iMatrix::operator =(const iMatrix &rhs)
{
    if (this != &rhs) {
        _rows = rhs._rows;
        _cols = rhs._cols;
        delete _matrix;
        _matrix = new int[_rows * _cols];
        // now copy rhs._matrix into _matrix...
    }
    return *this;
}
```

(d) class theBigMix

```
theBigMix &theBigMix::operator =(const theBigMix &rhs)
{
    if (this != &rhs) {
        _bst   = rhs._bst;
        _im    = rhs._im;
        _name  = rhs._name;
        delete _pvec;
        _pvec = new vector<float>;
        // now copy the contents of rhs._pvec into _pvec...
    }
    return *this;
}
```

We set _leftchild in (a) using an if statement:

```
if (rhs._leftchild)
    _leftchild = new BinStrTreeNode(*rhs._leftchild);
else
    _leftchild = 0;
```

A less verbose way to set _leftchild is to use the conditional operator:

```
_leftchild = rhs._leftchild ?
             new BinStrTreeNode(*rhs._leftchild) : 0;
```

See L&L, page 159.

Exercise 14.18

For the class chosen in Exercise 14.3 of Section 14.2, determine if a copy assignment operator is necessary. If it is, provide it. Otherwise, explain why it is unnecessary.

It is not necessary to implement a copy assignment operator for the class Date in Exercise 14.3. In general, if a copy constructor is needed, a copy assignment operator is needed and vice versa. The default memberwise copy that the compiler provides will suffice.

The class Book does not require a copy assignment operator either.

chapter fifteen

Overloaded Operators and
User-Defined Conversions

Exercise 15.1

Why does the following *not* **invoke the overloaded** `operator==(const String&, const String&)`?

```
"cobble" == "stone"
```

Because neither operand is a `String` object, the overload resolution process chooses the built-in operator `==` as the best match. In this case the built-in operator is applied to two operands of type `const char *`. This results in a comparison of the two pointers and not the character strings.

Exercise 15.2

Provide overloaded inequality operators that can handle the following three cases:

```
String != String
String != C-style string
C-style string != String
```

Explain why you chose to implement one or multiple operators.

We chose to implement three operators, one for each of the three cases. Having all three should result in faster run-times. Because the functions are very small, code space is not a concern.

Here are the operators:

```
bool operator!=(const String &str1, const String &str2)
{
    if (str1.size() != str2.size())
        return true;
    return strcmp(str1.c_str(), str2.c_str()) ? true : false;
}

bool operator!=(const String &str, const char *s)
{
    return strcmp(str.c_str(), s) ? true : false;
}

bool operator!=(const char *s, const String &str)
{
    return strcmp(s, str.c_str()) ? true : false;
}
```

Exercise 15.3

Identify which member function of the Screen **class implemented in Chapter 13, in Sections 13.3, 13.4, and 13.6, are candidates for operator overloading.**

Several of the Screen member functions are good candidates for operator overloading.

Function	Operator
forward()	++
back()	--
get()	[]
set()	=, []
copy()	=
isEqual()	==

Exercise 15.4

Explain why the overloaded input and output operators defined for class String **in Section 3.15 are declared as global functions and not as member functions.**

The input and output operators are not defined as member functions because the left operand for each operator is a stream instead of an object of class String. Why not define input and output operators as istream and ostream member functions? It is because we cannot modify those classes.

Exercise 15.5

Implement the overloaded input and output operators for the class Screen **defined in Chapter 13.**

The implementation of the operators is straightforward. The output operator displays the size of the Screen followed by each element using the access function get(). The input operator, for each element of the Screen object, reads a character, moves to the appropriate screen position, and sets the element.

The input and output operators are declared as global functions as follows:

```cpp
ostream& operator<<(ostream& os, Screen& s)
{
    os << "(" << s.height() << "," << s.width() << ")\n\n";
    for (int ix = 1; ix <= s.height(); ++ix) {
        for (int iy = 1; iy <= s.width(); ++iy)
            os << s.get(ix, iy);
        os << "\n";
    }
    return os;
}

istream& operator>>(istream& is, Screen& s)
{
    char ch;

    for (int ix = 1; ix <= s.height(); ++ix)
        for (int iy = 1; iy <= s.width(); ++iy) {
            is >> ch;
            s.move(ix, iy);
            s.set(ch);
        }
    return is;
}
```

Exercise 15.6

Reimplement the input and output operators defined for class Screen **in Exercise 15.5 as friend functions and modify their definition to access the class private members directly. Which implementation is preferable? Explain why?**

Here are our new implementations.

```
ostream& operator<<(ostream& os, Screen& s)
{
    os << "(" << s._height << "," << s._width << ")\n\n";
    for (int ix = 1; ix <= s._height; ++ix) {
        int row = (ix - 1) * s._width;
        for (int iy = 1; iy <= s._width; ++iy)
            os << s._screen[row + iy - 1];
        os << "\n";
    }
    return os;
}

istream& operator>>(istream& is, Screen& s)
{
    for (int ix = 1; ix <= s._height; ++ix) {
        int row = (ix - 1) * s._width;
        for (int iy = 1; iy <= s._width; ++iy)
            is >> s._screen[row + iy - 1];
    }
    return is;
}
```

The friend implementations are preferable. Because we can access the private members directly, we can avoid using the get(), move(), and set() member functions. By reading or modifying _screen directly, we end up with a faster implementation.

Exercise 15.7

Provide the definitions for the overloaded increment and decrement operators of class ScreenPtr when they are declared as friend functions.

Because the operators are not member functions, we must reference data members through the ScreenPtr argument. The definitions are as follows:

```
Screen& operator++(ScreenPtr &ps)
{
    if (ps.size == 0) {
        cerr << "cannot increment pointer to single object\n";
        return *ps.ptr;
    }
    if (ps.offset >= ps.size-1) {
        cerr << "already at the end of the array\n";
        return *ps.ptr;
    }
```

```
        ++ps.offset;
        return *++ps.ptr;
    }
    Screen& operator--(ScreenPtr &ps)
    {
        if (ps.size == 0) {
            cerr << "cannot decrement pointer to single object\n";
            return *ps.ptr;
        }
        if (ps.offset <= 0) {
            cerr << "already at the beginning of the array\n";
            return *ps.ptr;
        }
        --ps.offset;
        return *--ps.ptr;
    }
    Screen& operator++(ScreenPtr &ps,int)
    {
        if (ps.size == 0) {
            cerr << "cannot increment pointer to single object\n";
            return *ps.ptr;
        }
        if (ps.offset == ps.size) {
            cerr << "already one past the end of the array\n";
            return *ps.ptr;
        }
        ++ps.offset;
        return *ps.ptr++;
    }
    Screen& operator--(ScreenPtr &ps,int)
    {
        if (ps.size == 0) {
            cerr << "cannot decrement pointer to single object\n";
            return *ps.ptr;
        }
        if (ps.offset == -1) {
            cerr << "already one before the beginning of the array\n";
            return *ps.ptr;
        }
        --ps.offset;
        return *ps.ptr--;
    }
```

Exercise 15.8

The class `ScreenPtr` **can now represent a pointer that points into an array of** `Screen`
classes. Modify the overloaded `operator*()` **and overloaded** `operator->()` **(defined in**
Section 15.6) to ensure that if the `ScreenPtr` **object refers to an array element, the pointer**
does not refer to one before the beginning of the array or one past the end of the array.
Hint: These overloaded operators should use the new data members `size` **and** `offset`.

If `size == 0`, the `ScreenPtr` object does not refer to an array and the operators return the
appropriate value as before.

If the `ScreenPtr` object does refer to an array, we use the C library function `assert()` to
perform the bounds check.

```
Screen& ScreenPtr::operator*()
{
    if (size == 0)
        return *ptr;
    assert(offset >= 0 && offset < size);
    return *ptr;
}

Screen* ScreenPtr::operator->()
{
    if (size == 0)
        return ptr;
    assert(offset >= 0 && offset < size);
    return ptr;
}
```

Exercise 15.9

Explain which, if any, of the following initializations are errors. Explain why.

```
class iStack {
  public:
    iStack(int capacity)
            : _stack(capacity), _top(0) {}
    // ...
  private:
    int _top;
    vector< int > _stack;
};
```

```
(a) iStack *ps = new iStack(20);
(b) iStack *ps2 = new const iStack(15);
(c) iStack *ps3 = new iStack[100];
```

Both (b) and (c) are errors.

(b) iStack *ps2 = new const iStack(15);
   The const modifier means that ps2 must be declared as a pointer to const iStack.

(c) iStack *ps3 = new iStack[100];
   Because iStack has a constructor but no default constructor, this initialization is an error. To allocate an array of iStack objects with new, we must declare a default constructor.

Exercise 15.10

Explain what happens in the following new and delete expressions:

```
class Exercise {
  public:
    Exercise();
    ~Exercise();
};

Exercise *pe = new Exercise[20];
delete [] pe;
```
Change the new and delete expressions to call the global operators new() and delete().

The new expression first calls the class operator new[]() to allocate storage for 20 Exercise objects. The default constructor is then called to iteratively initialize each of the array elements.

The delete expression first calls the class destructor to iteratively destroy each of the array elements. The class operator delete[]() is then called to deallocate the storage.

If the class operators are not defined, the global operators are called.

Here are the expressions changed to call the global operators.

```
Exercise *pe = ::new Exercise[20];
::delete [] pe;
```

Exercise 15.11

Explain why a class designer should provide a class placement operator delete()?

If a class allocates memory by calling a class placement operator new(), the class designer should provide a class placement operator delete(). If an exception occurs during the construction of the class, the implementation automatically calls this operator delete() to deallocate storage. If this operator is not provided, a memory leak occurs.

Exercise 15.12

There are no conversion functions defined for the classes in the C++ standard library, and many of the constructors taking one argument are declared to be explicit. However, many overloaded operators are defined for the classes in the C++ standard library. Why do you think this design decision was chosen?

The C++ standard library was designed to be used by a wide variety of programs in a wide variety of situations, so its behavior must be as consistent and predictable as possible. If conversion functions were defined for the classes in the library, the possible implicit conversions that would result might lead to surprising and unexpected results. By using overloaded operators, the C++ standard library allows for flexibility in its use without the hidden surprises of implicit conversions.

Exercise 15.13

Why is the overloaded input operator for class SmallInt defined at the beginning of this section not implemented in the following manner?

```
istream& operator>>(istream& is, SmallInt& si)
{
    return (is >> si.value);
}
```

This implementation assigns the private data member value directly. By avoiding SmallInt::operator=(), it bypasses the call to rangeCheck() and may result in an invalid value being assigned.

Exercise 15.14

Show the possible user-defined conversion sequences for each of the following initializations. What is the outcome of each initialization?

```
class LongDouble {
    operator double();
    operator float();
};

extern LongDouble ldObj;
```

```
(a) int ex1 = ldObj;
(b) float ex2 = ldObj;
```

We have only two user-defined conversions and the standard conversions to consider.

(a) `int ex1 = ldObj;`

The two possible sequences are as follows:

1. `operator double()` -> standard conversion (`double->int`)

2. `operator float()` -> standard conversion (`float->int`)

This initialization is ambiguous because the two standard conversions have equal precedence. The programmer can disambiguate the expression using an explicit call to the desired operator or using an explicit cast.

(b) `float ex2 = ldObj;`

The two possible sequences are as follows:

1. `operator double()` -> standard conversion (`double->float`)

2. `operator float()` -> exact match

It is a choice between a user-defined conversion followed by a standard conversion (1) and user-defined conversion (2). The second sequence is better, and it is the sequence applied.

Exercise 15.15

Name the three sets of candidate functions considered during function overload resolution if a function argument has class type.

The three sets of candidate functions considered are as follows:

1. The functions visible at the point of call

2. The functions declared within the namespace where the class type is defined

3. The functions that are declared as friends within the class member list

Exercise 15.16

Which `calc()` **function, if any, is selected as the best viable function for the following call? Show the conversion sequences needed to call each function and explain why the best viable function is selected.**

```
class LongDouble {
  public:
    LongDouble(double);
    // ...
};

extern void calc(int);
extern void calc(LongDouble);
double dval;

int main() {
    calc(dval);     // which function?
}
```

Here, the function `calc(LongDouble)` is chosen as the best viable function. The two conversion sequences are as follows:

1. Standard conversion (`double->int`)

2. User-defined conversion (`double` to `LongDouble`)

A standard conversion is better than a user-defined conversion, so the first conversion is selected. See L&L, Section 15.10.4.

Exercise 15.17

Name the five sets of candidate functions considered during function overload resolution if an operator is used with an operand of class type.

The five sets of candidate functions considered are as follows:

1. The set of operators visible at the point of the call

2. The set of operators declared within the namespace where the type of an operand is defined

3. The set of operators that are declared as friends of an operand's class type

4.   The set of member operators declared in the class of the left-hand operand

5.   The set of built-in operators

Exercise 15.18

Which `operator+()`, if any, is selected as the best viable function for the addition operation in `main()`? List the candidate functions, the viable functions, and the type conversions on the arguments for each viable function.

```
namespace NS {
    class complex {
        complex(double);
        // ...
    };
    class LongDouble {
        friend LongDouble operator+(LongDouble &, int) { /*...*/ }
      public:
        LongDouble(int);
        operator double();
        LongDouble operator+(const complex &);
        // ...
    };
    LongDouble operator+(const LongDouble&, double);
}

int main() {
    // the type of si is class SmallInt;
    // the class is declared in namespace NS
    NS::LongDouble ld(16.08);

    double res = ld + 15.05;     // which operator+?
    return 0;
}
```

The best viable function is
`NS::LongDouble NS::LongDouble::operator+ (const LongDouble&, double)`.
The candidate functions are as follows:

1.   `NS::LongDouble NS::operator+(LongDouble &, int)`

2.   `NS::LongDouble NS::operator+(const complex &)`

3.   `NS::LongDouble NS::LongDouble::operator+(const LongDouble &, double)`

4. `int operator+(int, int)`

5. `double operator+(double, double)`

6. `T* operator+(T*, I)`

7. `T* operator+(I, T*)`

The viable functions are as follows:

1. `NS::LongDouble NS::operator+(LongDouble &, int)`

2. `NS::LongDouble NS::operator+(const complex &)`

3. `NS::LongDouble NS::LongDouble::operator+(const LongDouble &, double)`

4. `int operator+(int, int)`

5. `double operator+(double, double)`

The type conversions necessary for each of the viable functions are as follows:

1. The left operand is an exact match. The right operand can be converted with a standard conversion (`double` to `int`).

2. The left operand is the same type (`LongDouble`) as the class type in which the overloaded operator is defined as a member function. The right operand is a user-defined conversion sequence. It uses the constructor as a conversion function to convert the operand from type `double` to type `complex`. The result of this conversion is an exact match for the operator's reference parameter.

3. The left operand is an exact match as an initializer for the reference parameter. The right operand is an exact match.

4. The left operand goes through a user-defined conversion sequence: operator `double()` is called to convert the operand from type `LongDouble` to type `double`, followed by a standard conversion (`double` to `int`) to convert the result of the first conversion to type `int`. The right operand requires only the `double` to `int` standard conversion.

5. The left operand goes through a user-defined conversion sequence: operator `double()` is called to convert the operand from type `LongDouble` to type `double`. The right operand is an exact match.

As you can see, the third viable function is the best one because both operands are exact matches.

chapter sixteen

Class Templates

Exercise 16.1

Identify which, if any, of the following template class declarations (or declaration pairs) are illegal.

```
(a) template <class Type>
        class Container1;

    template <class Type, int size>
        class Container1;

(b) template <class T, U, class V>
        class Container2;

(c) template <class C1, typename C2>
        class Container3{ };

(d) template <typename myT, class myT>
        class Container4{ };

(e) template <class Type, int *ptr>
        class Container5;

    template <class T, int *pi>
        class Container5;

(f) template <class Type, int val = 0>
        class Container6;

    template <class T = complex<double>, int v>
        class Container6;
```

Only (c), (e), and (f) are legal.

```
(a) template <class Type>
        class Container1;

    template <class Type, int size>
        class Container1;
```

This declaration pair is illegal because the two declarations have different template parameters.

```
(b) template <class T, U, class V>
        class Container2;
```

This declaration is illegal because each template parameter must be preceded by the keyword class or the keyword typename, or it can be a nontype parameter. See (e). It should read

```
    template <class T, class U, class V>
        class Container2;
```

or

```
    template <class T, typename U, class V>
        class Container2;
```

```
(c) template <class C1, typename C2>
        class Container3{ };
```

This is a legal template definition. "The name of a template parameter can be used after it has been declared as a template parameter and until the end of the template declaration or definition" (L&L, page 815). Container3 does not use any of its template parameters.

```
(d) template <typename myT, class myT>
        class Container4{ };
```

This is illegal because the name of the template parameter myT can be introduced only once within the template parameter list.

```
(e) template <class Type, int *ptr>
        class Container5;

    template <class T, int *pi>
        class Container5;
```

This is a legal template declaration. The second parameter is "a nontype parameter [that] consists of an ordinary parameter declaration. A nontype parameter indicates that the parameter name represents a potential value" (L&L, page 815). The names of the template parameters are allowed to be different in different declarations of the same template (L&L, page 816).

```
(f) template <class Type, int val = 0>
       class Container5;

    template <class T = complex<double>, int v>
       class Container5;
```

This is a legal template declaration. "Subsequent declarations of the class template can provide additional default arguments for the template parameters. As it is the case with default arguments for function parameters, the rightmost uninitialized parameter must be supplied with a default argument before any default argument for a parameter to its left may be supplied" (L&L, page 817).

Exercise 16.2

The following definition of List is incorrect. How would you fix it?

```
template <class elemType>
class ListItem;

template <class elemType>
class List {
  public:
    List<elemType>()
          : _at_front(0), _at_end(0), _current(0),
            _size(0) { }
    List<elemType>(const List<elemType>&);
    List<elemType>& operator=(const List<elemType>&);
    ~List();

    void insert(ListItem *ptr, elemType value);
    int remove(elemType value);

    ListItem *find(elemType value);

    void display(ostream &os = cout);
    int size() { return _size; }

  private:
    ListItem *_at_front;
    ListItem *_at_end;
    ListItem *_current;
    int _size;
};
```

All uses of ListItem are incorrect because ListItem is a class template that is defined outside the class template List, and explicit parameters are required for it. See the template class QueueItem defined on page 817, L&L.

```
    template <class Type>
    class QueueItem {
      public:
        QueueItem(const Type &);
      private:
        Type item;
QueueItem *next;
    };
```

"Each occurrence of the QueueItem class template name within the class template definition is a shorthand notation for QueueItem<Type>.... When QueueItem is used a type specifier in another template definition, the full template parameter list must be specified" (L&L, page 817).

The correct definition of List could read as follows:

```
    template <class elemType>
    class ListItem;

    template <class elemType>
    class List {
      public:
        List<elemType>()
              : _at_front(0), _at_end(0), _current(0),
                _size(0) { }
        List<elemType>(const List<elemType>&);
        List<elemType>& operator=(const List<elemType>&);
        ~List();

        void insert(ListItem<elemType> *ptr, elemType value);
        int remove(elemType value);

        ListItem<elemType> *find(elemType value);

        void display(ostream &os = cout);
        int size() { return _size; }

      private:
        ListItem<elemType> *_at_front;
        ListItem<elemType> *_at_end;
        ListItem<elemType> *_current;
        int _size;
    };
```

Exercise 16.3

Identify which, if any, of the following uses of a template instantiation causes the template to be instantiated.

```
template <class Type>
    class Stack{ };

void fl(Stack<char>);        // (a)

class Exercise {
    // ...
    Stack<double> &rsd;      // (b)
    Stack<int>     si;       // (c)
};

int main() {
    Stack<char> *sc;         // (d)
    fl(*sc);                 // (e)

    int iObj = sizeof(Stack<string>);  // (f)
}
```

"A class template is instantiated only when the name of an instantiation is used in a context that requires a class definition to exist" (L&L, page 822). A class definition is not required before pointers and references to a class can be declared.

So,

```
void fl(Stack<char>);  // (a)
```

is a declaration. It does not require that the template be instantiated.

```
Stack<double> &rsd;     // (b)
```

(b) does not require that the template be instantiated because the object being defined is a reference.

```
Stack<int>     si;      // (c)
```

(c) requires that the template be instantiated because si is an object of the Stack type.

```
Stack<char> *sc;        // (d)
```

(d) does not require that the template be instantiated because sc is a pointer.

```
fl(*sc);                // (e)
```

(e) requires that the template be instantiated because the argument we are passing to fl() is an object of the Stack type.

```
int iObj = sizeof(Stack<string>);  // (f)
```

(f) requires that the template be instantiated because sizeof() computes the size of an object of type Stack<string>. To compute the size, the compiler must create the type and therefore must use the class definition.

Exercise 16.4

Identify which, if any, of the following template instantiations are valid. Explain why.

```
template <int *ptr> class Ptr { ... };
template <class Type, int size> class Fixed_Array{ ... };
template <int hi, int wid> class Screen { ... };
```

(a) `const int size = 1024;`
    `Ptr <&size> bp1;`

(b) `int arr[10];`
    `Ptr <arr> bp2;`

(c) `Ptr <0> bp3;`

(d) `const int hi = 40;`
    `const int wi = 80;`
    `Screen <hi, wi+32> sObj;`

(e) `const int size_val = 1024;`
    `Fixed_Array<string, size_val> fa1;`

(f) `unsigned int fasize = 255;`
    `Fixed_Array<string, fasize> fa2;`

(g) `const double db = 3.1415;`
    `Fixed_Array<double, db> fa3;`

The template instantiations (b), (d), and (e) are valid.

(a) `const int size = 1024;`
    `Ptr <&size> bp1;`

(a) is incorrect because the compiler will not convert the address of a const int into int *.

(b) `int arr[10];`
    `Ptr <arr> bp2;`

(b) is correct because Ptr expects a pointer to int. The name of an array of ints is a synonym for int *.

(c) `Ptr <0> bp3;`

(c) is incorrect because 0 is of type int, and that requires an implicit conversion to a null pointer to obtain int *.

(d) ```
const int hi = 40;
const int wi = 80;
Screen <hi, wi+32> sObj;
```

(d) is correct because Screen expects two ints.

(e) ```
const int size_val = 1024;
Fixed_Array<string, size_val> fa1;
```

(e) is correct because Screen expects two ints.

(f) ```
unsigned int fasize = 255;
Fixed_Array<string, fasize> fa2;
```

(f) is incorrect because "the expression to which a nontype parameter is bound must be a constant expression. That is, it must be possible to evaluate it at compile-time" (L&L, page 825). If we made fasize a const, (f) would be correct:
```
const unsigned int fasize = 255;
Fixed_Array<string, fasize> fa2;
```

(g) ```
const double db = 3.1415;
Fixed_Array<double, db> fa3;
```

(g) is incorrect because the compiler will not convert const double to int. "The type float [or double] cannot represent with as much precision all the values that can be represented by the type int" (L&L, page 468).

Exercise 16.5

Using the class template Screen defined in Section 16.2, reimplement the member functions of the class Screen implemented in Chapter 13, Sections 13.3, 13.4, and 13.6, as template member functions.

First, we reimplement the functions of the class Screen, using a template, for Section 13.3. The template for Screen is the one from L&L, Section 16.2.1, with the member functions from Section 13.3:
```
template <int hi, int wid>
class Screen {
  public:
    Screen() : _cursor(0), _screen(hi * wid, '#')
        { }
    void home()     { _cursor = 0;                }
    void move(int, int);
    char get()      { return _screen[_cursor];  }
```

```
        char get(int, int);
        bool checkRange(int, int);
        void copy(const Screen &sobj);
        void set(char c){ _screen = string(hi * wid,
                                           c);        }
        void set(const string &);

    private:
      string              _screen;
      string::size_type   _cursor;
};
```

We have five member functions that are defined outside the template. checkRange(), move(), get(), and copy() are like the functions in Section 13.3. We need only convert them to template form.

```
template <int hi, int wid>
bool Screen<hi, wid>::checkRange(int row, int col)
{
    // validate coordinates
    if (row < 1 || row > hi ||
        col < 1 || col > wid) {
            cerr << "System coordinate ( "
                << row << ", " << col
                << " ) out of bounds.\n";
            return false;
        }
        return true;
}
template<int hi, int wid>
void Screen<hi, wid>::move(int r, int c)
{
    // move _cursor to absolute position
    if (checkRange(r, c)) {              // valid screen position?
        int row = (r - 1) * wid;         // row location
        _cursor = row + c - 1;
    }
}
template<int hi, int wid>
char Screen<hi, wid>::get(int r, int c)
{
    move(r, c);       // position _cursor
    return get();     // the other get() template function
}
```

```
template<int hi, int wid>
void Screen<hi, wid>::copy(const Screen &sobj)
{
    // if this Screen object and sobj are the same object,
    // no copy is necessary
    // we look at the 'this' pointer in Section 13.4
    if ( this != &sobj) {
        _cursor = 0;

        // creates a new string
        // its content is the same as sobj._screen
        _screen = sobj._screen;
    }
}
```

We also write two set() member functions: the first one appears in the class definition
itself and sets all characters in _screen to the character that we pass to it; the second set()
function takes a string argument and copies it to the _screen.

```
template<int hi, int wid>
void Screen<hi, wid>::set(const string &s)
{
    for (int r = 1; r <= hi; r++)
        for (int c = 1; c <= wid; c++) {
            move(r, c);
            _screen[_cursor] = s[_cursor];
        }
}
```

The main() is similar to the examples in Section 13.3.

```
int main()
{
    Screen<2, 3> s1;
    display<2, 3>(s1);

    Screen<2, 3> s2;
    display<2, 3>(s2);

    s2.set('*');
    display<2, 3>(s2);

    s1.copy(s2);
    display<2, 3>(s1);
    display<2, 3>(s2);
```

```
    Screen<3, 3> s3;
    string init("abcdefghi");
    display<3, 3>(s3);
    s3.set(init);
    display<3, 3>(s3);


    return 0;
}
```

We write a display() template function to display the various screens we created in main():

```
template <int hi, int wid>
void display(Screen<hi, wid> s)
{
    for (int r = 1; r <= hi; r++) {
        for (int c = 1; c <= wid; c++)
            cout << s.get(r, c);
        cout << '\n';
    }
    cout << '\n';
}
```

Second, we reimplement the functions of the class Screen, using a template, for Section 13.4.

There are two additions to the template:

```
Screen<hi, wid> &clear(char bkground = '$');
Screen<hi, wid> &reSize(int h, int w, char bkground = '$');
```

clear() clears the _screen, sets each character to be the same as the bkground character, and returns a reference to the Screen template object.

```
template<int hi, int wid>
Screen<hi, wid> &Screen<hi, wid>::clear(char bkground)
{
    // reset the cursor and clear the screen
    _cursor = 0;
    _screen.assign(              // assign the string
        _screen.size(),          // with size() characters
        bkground);               // of value bkground
    return *this;
}
```

reSize() is similar to the original member function in L&L:

```
template<int hi, int wid>
Screen<hi, wid> &Screen<hi, wid>::reSize(int h, int w, char bkground)
{
    // remember the content of the screen
    string local(_screen);
    // replace the string to which _screen refers
    _screen.assign(h*w, bkground);

    typedef string::size_type idx_type;
    idx_type local_pos = 0;

    // copy content of old screen into the new one
    for (idx_type ix = 0; ix < hi; ++ix) {
        // for each row
        idx_type offset = wid * ix;         // row position

        for (idx_type iy = 0; iy < wid; ++iy)
            // for each column, assign the old value
            _screen[offset + iy] = local[local_pos++];
    }
    // cursor remains unchanged

    return *this;
}
```

We added a few statements to the main() we used for Section 13.3 to test the two new functions:

```
s2.clear();
display<2, 3>(s2);

s3.reSize(4, 5, '%');
display<3, 3>(s3);
```

Third, we reimplement two of the functions of the class Screen, using a template, for Section 13.6: forward() and back().

The reimplementations are straightforward. The function forward() becomes

```
template<int hi, int wid>
Screen<hi, wid> &Screen<hi, wid>::forward()
{
    // advance _cursor one screen element
    ++_cursor;
    // check for end of screen; wraparound
    if (_cursor == _screen.size())
        home();
    return *this;
}
```

And back() becomes

```
template<int hi, int wid>
Screen<hi, wid> &Screen<hi, wid>::back()
{
    // move _cursor backward one screen element

    // check for top of screen; wraparound
    if (_cursor == 0)
        ends();
    else
        --_cursor;
    return *this;
}
```

We modify a copy of main() to test both functions:

```
Screen<2, 2> s4;
string numbers("0123");
s4.set(numbers);
s4.home();
cout << "char at 0 should be 0, it is " << s4.get() << "\n";
s4.forward();
cout << "char at 1 should be 1, it is " << s4.get() << "\n";
s4.forward();
cout << "char at 2 should be 2, it is " << s4.get() << "\n";
s4.forward();
cout << "char at 3 should be 3, it is " << s4.get() << "\n";
cout << "after advancing past the end, wraparound\n";
s4.forward();
cout << "char at 0 should be 0, it is " << s4.get() << "\n";
s4.back();
cout << "char at 3 should be 3, it is " << s4.get() << "\n";
s4.back();
cout << "char at 2 should be 2, it is " << s4.get() << "\n";
```

Exercise 16.6

Using the Screen class template defined in Exercise 16.5, reimplement the input and output operators defined for class Screen in Exercise 15.6 of Section 15.2 as templates. Explain your reason behind the kind of friend declarations you choose to add to the class template Screen.

The operator <<() and operator >>() could be implemented as global functions and use public interface to access the data. We implement the operator <<() and `operator >>()` as `friend` functions (because the exercise asked for it) so that they have access to the private data in an object of type `Screen`. We define them inside the template class because our compiler does not let us create a `friend` function to a template class outside the template class itself.

```
template <int hi, int wid>
class Screen {
  public:
    // ...

    friend ostream &operator <<(ostream &out, const Screen<hi, wid> &s)
    {
        int i = 0;
        for (int r = 1; r <= hi; r++) {
            for (int c = 1; c <= wid; c++)
                out << s.get(r, c);
            out << '\n';
        }
        out << '\n';
        return out;
    }

    friend istream &operator >>(istream &in, Screen<hi, wid> &s)
    {

        s.home();
        for (int r = 1; r <= hi; r++) {
            for (int c = 1; c <= wid; c++)
                in >> s._screen[s._cursor++];
        }
        s.home();
        return in;
    }

  private:
    string              _screen;
    string::size_type   _cursor;
};
```

The two `friend` functions make the I/O for an object of type `Screen` rather easy:

```
int main()
{
    Screen<2, 3> s1;
    cout << s1;
```

```
    cout << "please enter a string (6 chars): ";
    cin  >> s1;
    cout << s1;

    return 0;
}
```

There are three kinds of friend function declarations (L&L, page 833):

1.   A nontemplate function declaration

2.   A bound friend function template

3.   An unbound friend function template

We used a bound friend function template to gain access to the template arguments.

Exercise 16.7

Using operator new(), operator delete(), and their associated static members screenChunk **and** freeStore **defined in Section 15.8, implement these operators and static members for the class template** Screen **defined in Exercise 16.6.**

We add two public method declarations to Screen:
```
    void *operator new(size_t);
    void operator delete(void *, size_t);
```

We add one private member:
```
    Screen              *next;
```

and two private static members:
```
    static Screen       *freeStore;
    static const int    screenChunk;
```

The static members must be defined before main(). We write a small main() to test the allocation and deallocation of a Screen object.
```
    template <int hi, int wid>
        Screen<hi, wid> *Screen<hi, wid>::freeStore = 0;
    template <int hi, int wid>
        const int Screen<hi, wid>::screenChunk = 10;

    int main()
    {
        Screen<2, 3> *p1 = new Screen<2, 3>;
        display<2, 3>(*p1);
        delete p1;
```

```
        return 0;
    }
```

The `operator new` looks like the one from Section 15.8 with the proper template modifications:

```
    template<int hi, int wid>
    void *Screen<hi, wid>::operator new(size_t size)
    {
        Screen<hi, wid> *p;

        if (!freeStore) {
            // linked list empty; grab a chunk
            // this call is to the global new
            size_t chunk = screenChunk * size;
            freeStore = p = reinterpret_cast<Screen *>(new char[chunk]);

            // now thread the memory allocated
            for ( ; p != &freeStore[screenChunk - 1]; ++p)
                p->next = p + 1;
            p->next = 0;
        }
        p = freeStore;
        freeStore = freeStore->next;
        return p;
    }
```

`operator delete` is similar to the original definition in Section 15.8:

```
    template<int hi, int wid>
    void Screen<hi, wid>::operator delete(void *p, size_t)
    {
        // insert the 'deleted' object back
        // into the free list
        (static_cast<Screen *>(p))->next = freeStore;
        freeStore = static_cast<Screen *>(p);
    }
```

Exercise 16.8

**Define the class `List` and its nested class `ListItem` defined in Section 13.10 as class
templates. Also provide the template definitions for the associated class members.**

The template class `List` with a nested template class `ListItem` is similar to the original
nested classes in Section 13.10:

```
template <class Type>
class List {
  public:
    List() : list(0), at_end(0) { }
    ~List();
    void add(const Type &);
    void display() const;
    // ...
  private:
    class ListItem {
      public:
        ListItem(const Type &v) : value(v), next(0) { }
        ListItem    *next;
        Type          value;
    };
    ListItem    *list;
    ListItem    *at_end;
};
```

The destructor must traverse the list to deallocate it:

```
template <class Type>
List<Type>::~List()
{
    for (ListItem *p = list; p; ) {
        ListItem *tmp = p;
        p = p->next;
        cout << "deleting " << tmp->value << "\n";
        delete tmp;
    }
}
```

We use an add() member function to add a new element at the end of the list:

```
template <class Type>
void List<Type>::add(const Type &v)
{
    ListItem *p = new ListItem(v);
    if (at_end)
        at_end->next = p;
    else
        list = p;
    at_end = p;
}
```

And we use a `display()` member function to verify that the list is correct:

```
template <class Type>
void List<Type>::display() const
{
    for (ListItem *p = list; p; p = p->next)
        cout << p->value << " ";
    cout << "\n";
}
```

The `main()` routine creates a list of `int`s, adds three integers to the list, and then displays it:

```
#include    "List.h"

int main()
{
    List<int> a;

    a.add(10);
    a.add(20);
    a.add(30);
    a.display();

    return 0;
}
```

See L&L, page 848, to define the nested type `ListItem` outside its class template definition.

Exercise 16.9

Where would you place the definitions for the member functions and static data members of your class templates if the implementation you use supports the separation compilation model? Explain why.

"With the separation compilation model, the class template definition and the definitions of its inline member functions are placed in a header file, whereas the definitions of the non-inline member functions and static data members are placed in a program text file" (L&L, page 851).

The compiler must see each inline function before it can expand it inline. The definitions of the non-inline member functions that either the user does not want to see or we do not want the user to see will be placed in a text file. We simply `export` the class template.

Exercise 16.10

Given the class template Screen you developed in the exercises of the previous sections (in particular, the member functions you defined in Exercise 16.5 of Section 16.3, and the static members you defined in Exercise 16.7 of Section 16.5), organize these definitions to take advantage of the template separation compilation model.

We keep the inline template functions in Screen.h.

```cpp
template <int hi, int wid>
class Screen {
  public:
    Screen() : _cursor(0), _screen(hi * wid, '#')
        { }
    void home()         { _cursor = 0;                }
    void ends()         { _cursor = _screen.size() -1;  }
    void move(int, int);
    char get() const    { return _screen[_cursor];     }
    char get(int, int);
    bool checkRange(int, int);
    void copy(const Screen &sobj);
    void set(char c)    { _screen = string(hi * wid, c);}
    void set(const string &);
    Screen<hi, wid> &clear(char bkground = '$');
    Screen<hi, wid> &reSize(int h, int w, char bkground = '$');
    Screen &forward();
    Screen &back();
    void *operator new(size_t);
    void operator delete(void *, size_t);

    friend ostream &operator <<(ostream &out, Screen<hi, wid> &s)
    {
        for (int r = 1; r <= hi; r++) {
            for (int c = 1; c <= wid; c++)
                out << s.get(r, c);
            out << '\n';
        }
        out << '\n';
        return out;
    }
    friend istream &operator >>(istream &in, Screen<hi, wid> &s)
    {
```

```
            s.home();
            for (int r = 1; r <= hi; r++) {
                for (int c = 1; c <= wid; c++)
                    in >> s._screen[s._cursor++];
            }
            s.home();
            return in;
        }

    private:
        string             _screen;
        string::size_type  _cursor;
        Screen             *next;
        static Screen      *freeStore;
        static const int   screenChunk;
};
```

We use the template separation compilation model to keep the remaining template methods in a separate file that contains the exported functions. Each method must be preceded by the keyword export. Consequently, the file contains each definition as in the first part of Exercise 16.5, this time preceded by export. Here's move():

```
export template<int hi, int wid>
void Screen<hi, wid>::move(int r, int c)
{
    // move _cursor to absolute position
    if (checkRange(r, c)) {              // valid screen position?
        int row = (r - 1) * wid;         // row location
        _cursor = row + c - 1;
    }
}
```

The remaining functions are modified similarly.

Exercise 16.11

Change the Array class template defined in this section to remove the member functions sort(), find(), max(), min(), and swap(), and change the function template try_array() to use the generic algorithms (defined in Chapter 12) instead.

We create the template Iterator:

```
template <class elemType>
class Iterator {
  public:
    Iterator()                 { _loc = 0;        }
```

```
    Iterator(elemType *p)   { _loc = p;              }
    Iterator &operator ++() {
        _loc++;
        return *this;
    }
    const elemType &operator *() {
        if (!_loc)
            throw "Iterator: pointer not initialized";
        return *_loc;
    }
    bool operator ==(const Iterator &b) {
        return _loc == b._loc;
    }
    bool operator !=(const Iterator &b) {
        return _loc != b._loc;
    }
  private:
    elemType *_loc;
};
```

Iterator provides the methods operator *, operator ++, operator ==, and operator !=, which the regular iterators support.

We remove sort(), find(), max(), min(), and swap() from Array.h, and we add two methods to support Iterator:

```
    Iterator<elemType> begin() {
        return Iterator<elemType>(_ia);
    }
    Iterator<elemType> end() {
        return Iterator<elemType>(_ia + _size);
    }
```

Here's the new template Array:

```
    template <class elemType>
    class Array {
      public:
        explicit Array(int sz = DefaultArraySize) {
            init(0, sz);
        }
        Array(const elemType *ar, int sz) {
            init(ar, sz);
        }
        Array(const Array &iA) {
            init(iA._ia, iA._size);
        }
```

```
        ~Array() {
            delete [] _ia;
        }

        Array &operator =(const Array &);
        int size() {
            return _size;
        }
        elemType &operator [](int ix) const {
            return _ia[ix];
        }

        void print(ostream &os = cout) const;
        void grow();

        Iterator<elemType> begin() {
            return Iterator<elemType>(_ia);
        }
        Iterator<elemType> end() {
            return Iterator<elemType>(_ia + _size);
        }

    private:
        void init(const elemType *, int);

        static int DefaultArraySize;

        int         _size;
        elemType    *_ia;
};
```

To find the minimum value, in try_array(), instead of using

```
    iA[iA.size() - 1] = iA.min();
```

we use the generic algorithm min_element(), which takes two iterators and returns an iterator to the minimum element in iA:

```
    Iterator<elemType> iter     = iA.begin();
    Iterator<elemType> iter_end = iA.end();
    iA[iA.size() - 1] = *min_element(iter, iter_end);
```

To find the largest element, we change the code similarly, from

```
    iA[0] = iA.max();
```

to

```
    iA[0] = *max_element(iter, iter_end);
```

To replace `find()` we have a bit more work. The original code read

```
int index = iA.find(find_val);
```

We use the generic algorithm `find()`, which takes two iterators (starting and ending addresses) and the value to be found. It returns an iterator to the first matching value or returns `iter_end` if the element searched for does not exist. Consequently, the code becomes

```
Iterator<elemType> ip = find(iter, iter_end, find_val);
if (ip == iter_end)
    cout << "value not found\n";
else
    cout << "value found: " << *ip << endl;
```

chapter seventeen

Class Inheritance and Subtyping

Exercise 17.1

A library supports the following categories of lending materials, each with its own check-out and check-in policy. **Organize these into an inheritance hierarchy:**

book	audio book
record	children's puppet
video	sega video game
rental book	sony playstation video game
cdrom book	nintendo video game

Figure 17.1 shows the hierarchy.

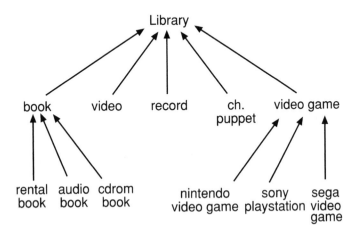

Figure 17.1   Exercise 17.1

Exercise 17.2

Choose one of the following general abstractions containing a family of types (or choose one of your own). Organize the types into an inheritance hierarchy:

(1) Graphical file formats (such as gif, tiff, jpeg, bmp)
(2) Geometric primitives (such as box, circle, sphere, cone)
(3) C++ language types (such as class, function, member function)

Figure 17.2 shows one possible hierarchy for
(2) Geometric primitives (such as box, circle, sphere, cone)

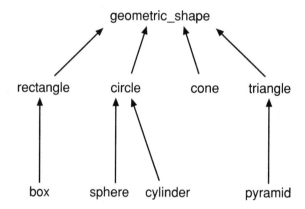

Figure 17.2   Exercise 17.2

Exercise 17.3

Consider the following members of the library class hierarchy of Exercise 17.1 at the end of Section 17.1. Identify which instances are likely virtual function candidates, and which, if any, are likely to be common among all library materials and therefore able to be fully represented within the base class. (Note: LibMember is the abstraction representing a member of the library able to borrow library materials. Date is a class representing a calendar day of a particular year.)

```
class Library {
  public:
    bool check_out(LibMember *);
    bool check_in (LibMember *);
    bool is_late(const Date &today);
```

```
      double apply_fine();
      ostream &print(ostream & = cout);

      Date *due_date() const;
      Date *date_borrowed() const;

      string title() const;
      const LibMember *member() const;
   };
```

The following member functions are likely virtual function candidates (assuming that different lending materials have different check-out and check-in procedures):

```
   bool check_out(LibMember *);
   bool check_in (LibMember *);
   ostream &print(ostream & = cout);
```

The following member functions are likely to be common among all library materials and therefore able to be fully represented within the base class:

```
   bool is_late(const Date &today);
   double apply_fine();

   Date *due_date() const;
   Date *date_borrowed() const;

   string title() const;
   const LibMember *member() const;
```

Exercise 17.4

Identify the base and derived class members for the chosen class hierarchy of Exercise 17.2 at the end of Section 17.1. Identify virtual functions as well as public and protected members.

```
   class Geometric_Shape {
     public:
       Geometric_Shape();
       virtual ~Geometric_Shape();

       virtual void draw();
       virtual double area();
       virtual double volume();
```

```cpp
    private:
      // ...
  };

  class Box : public Rectangle {
    public:
      Box();
      ~Box();

      void draw();
      double  volume();
    private:
      // ...
  };

  class Circle : public Geometric_Shape {
    public:
      Circle();
      ~Circle();

      void draw();
      double  area();
    private:
      // ...
  };

  class Sphere : public Circle {
    public:
      Sphere();
      ~Sphere();

      void draw();
      double  volume();
    private:
      // ...
  };

  class Cone : public Geometric_Shape {
    public:
      Cone();
      ~Cone();
```

```
      void draw();
      double  area();
      double  volume();
   private:
      // ...
};
```

Exercise 17.5

Which of the following, if any, are incorrect?

```
class Base { ... };

(a) class Derived : public Derived { ... };
(b) class Derived : Base { ... };
(c) class Derived : private Base { ... };
(d) class Derived : public Base;
(e) class Derived inherits Base { ... };
```

Items (a), (d), and (e) are incorrect.

(a) class Derived : public Derived { ... };

This is incorrect because a class cannot be the target of its own derivation. The class specified in the derivation list must be defined before being specified as a base class, and a class cannot be a specialization or subtype of itself.

(d) class Derived : public Base;

This is incorrect because a forward declaration of a derived class, showing the base class derivation, is not allowed.

(e) class Derived inherits Base { ... };

This is incorrect because C++ indicates inheritance with a colon instead of a keyword.

Exercise 17.6

Given the following base and derived class definitions

```
class Base {
  public:
    foo(int);
    // ...
```

```
    protected:
      int _bar;
      double _foo_bar;
    };

    class Derived : public Base {
      public:
        foo(string);
        bool bar(Base *pb);
        void foobar();
        // ...
      protected:
        string _bar;
    };
```

identify what is wrong with each of the following code fragments and how each might be fixed:

```
    (a) Derived d; d.foo(1024);
    (b) void Derived::foobar() { _bar = 1024; }
    (c) bool Derived::bar(Base *pb)
            { return _foo_bar == pb->_foo_bar; }
```

Here are the details.
(a) Derived d; d.foo(1024);

The function foo(int) is a member of the class Base. We could explicitly invoke foo() that belongs to Base:

```
    d.Base::foo(1024);
```

Or we could modify the class Derived to have a using declaration:

```
    using Base::foo;
```

to enter foo(int) from Base into the scope of Derived.
(b) void Derived::foobar() { _bar = 1024; }

In this case we must explicitly qualify _bar to access the int variable in Base:

```
    void Derived::foobar() { Base::_bar = 1024; }
```

(c) bool Derived::bar(Base *pb)
        { return _foo_bar == pb->_foo_bar; }

The derived class Derived has access to the protected _foo_bar data member of *its* base class subobject. The derived class does not have access to the protected members of an independent base class object. See L&L, page 904. The solution is for Base to provide a member function f_b() that returns the value of the member _foo_bar:

```
    double f_b() { return _foo_bar; }
```

Then we could rewrite bar():

```
    bool Derived::bar(Base *pb)
            { return _foo_bar == pb->f_b(); }
```

Exercise 17.7

Identify the base and derived class constructors and destructors for the chosen class hierarchy of Exercise 17.2 at the end of Section 17.1.

Because we did not specify the data members for the classes in the solution for Exercise 17.4, the constructors are all default constructors. The destructor for the base class `Geometric_Shape` is a virtual destructor, so the destructors in all derived classes will be virtual by default.

Exercise 17.8

Reimplement the `OrQuery` class to derive it from an abstract `UnaryQuery` class.

Let's use the `Query` class from page 911 in L&L. The `UnaryQuery` class could look like this:

```
class UnaryQuery : public Query {
  public:
    const Query *op() { return _op; }

  protected:
    UnaryQuery() : _op(0) {}
    UnaryQuery(Query *op) : _op(op) {}
    Query *_op;
};
```

The problem is that `UnaryQuery` has one operand. The `OrQuery` should have two operands. If we must implement `OrQuery` as a class derived from `UnaryQuery`, we arrange for `OrQuery` to have one operand of its own — let's say the right operand — and we use the operand in `UnaryQuery` as the left operand.

```
class OrQuery : public UnaryQuery {
  public:
    OrQuery() : _rop(0) {}
    OrQuery(Query *lop, Query *rop) : UnaryQuery(lop), _rop(rop) {}
    ~OrQuery() { delete _rop; }
    virtual void eval();

  private:
    Query *_rop;
};
```

The solution may not be as graceful as the one in L&L that uses a `BinaryQuery` class, but it solves this exercise.

Exercise 17.9

What is wrong with the following class definition?

```
class Object {
  public:
    virtual ~Object();
    virtual string isA();
  protected:
    string _isA;
  private:
    Object(string s) : _isA(s) {}
};
```

The problem is that the constructor for `Object` is private. The constructor `Object(string)` cannot be called to instantiate any object of type `Object`.

Sometimes we make a constructor protected: it can be called only by derived classes. This technique allows derived class types to initialize the base class subobject while preventing independent objects of the base class from being created. But we never make a constructor private when we expect the users of the class `Object` to call it to instantiate an object. (See L&L, page 911, for a `private` constructor that is used by a `friend` class.)

Exercise 17.10

Given the following base class definition,

```
class ConcreteBase {
  public:
    explicit ConcreteBase(int);
    virtual ostream &print(ostream &);
    virtual ~ConcreteBase();

    static int object_count();
  protected:
    int _id;
    static int _object_count;
};
```

What is wrong with the following?

```
// (a)
class C1 : public ConcreteBase {
  public:
    C1(int val)
        : _id(_object_count++) {}
```

```
      // ...
   };

   // (b)
   class C2 : public C1 {
     public:
       C2(int val)
         : ConcreteBase(val), C1(val) {}
       // ...
   };

   // (c)
   class C3 : public C2 {
     public:
       C3(int val)
         : C2(val), _object_count(val) {}
       // ...
   };

   // (d)
   class C4 : public ConcreteBase {
     public:
       C4(int val)
         : ConcreteBase(_id+val) {}
       // ...
   };
```

Here are some answers and alternatives.

```
   // (a)
   class C1 : public ConcreteBase {
     public:
       C1(int val)
         : ConcreteBase(val) {}
       // ...
   };
```

We modified (a) to explicitly invoke the constructor ConcreteBase(int) from the initialization list. Also, it is the responsibility of ConcreteBase(int) to initialize _id.

```
   // (b)
   class C2 : public C1 {
     public:
       C2(int val)
         : C1(val) {}
```

```
      // ...
    };
```

The constructor C2(int) should not explicitly invoke the constructor for the base class of C1; that's C1(int)'s problem.

```
    // (c)
    class C3 : public C2 {
      public:
        C3(int val)
          : C2(val) {}
        // ...
    };
```

The constructor C2(int) should not attempt to access _object_count; that's the responsibility of ConcreteBase(int).

```
    // (d)
    class C4 : public ConcreteBase {
      public:
        C4(int val)
          : ConcreteBase(_id+val) {}
        // ...
    };
```

The invocation of ConcreteBase() is dangerous because it uses _id before it is initialized.

Exercise 17.11

In the original definition of C++, the order of initialization within the member initialization list determined the order of constructor invocation. This was changed to the current language rule back around 1986. Why do you think the original language rule was changed?

This change lets the user take a look at class definition and know the order in which the elements will be initialized. For example:

```
    class X {
      public:
        X(int size)
            : _str(new char[_size]),
              _size(size) {}
        // ...
      private:
        int    _size;
        char *_str;
    };
```

We swapped the natural order of _size and _str in the initialization list. Still, _size will be initialized before the compiler attempts to allocate space for _str.

Another consideration is that multiple constructors within the class would provide alternative orders of member initialization. There was no way to know which constructor was used to initialize a particular object.

Exercise 17.12

Within the NameQuery object, the most straightforward internal representation of the location vector is a pointer initialized with the pointer stored within the text location map. This is also the most efficient because we'd be copying a single address rather than each location pair within the vector. The AndQuery, OrQuery, and NotQuery classes must construct their location vectors based on the evaluation of their operands. When the lifetime of one of these class objects ends, the associated location vector must be deleted. When the lifetime of a NameQuery object ends, the location vector must *not* be deleted. How might we store the location vector as a pointer within the Query base class, delete the instances associated with the AndQuery, OrQuery, and NotQuery class objects but not that of the NameQuery class objects? (Note that we are not permitted to add a flag to the Query class indicating whether or not to delete the pointer to the location vector!)

We can declare the destructor in the Query base class as a virtual function. The destructors for the AndQuery, OrQuery, and NotQuery classes delete the associated location vector, whereas the destructor for the NameQuery class does not delete it. Recall that destructors are not inherited and that a destructor in a derived class overrides a base class destructor that is declared virtual. That is, the derived class destructor is invoked before the base class destructor.

Exercise 17.13

What is wrong with the following class definition?

```
class AbstractObject {
  public:
    ~AbstractObject();
    virtual void doit() = 0;
    // ...
};
```

"As a general rule of thumb, we recommend that the root base class hierarchy declaring one or more virtual functions declare its destructor virtual as well" (L&L, page 933). The class should read:

```
class AbstractObject {
  public:
    virtual ~AbstractObject();
    virtual void doit() = 0;
    // ...
};
```

Exercise 17.14

Why is it that, given

```
NameQuery nq("Sneezy");
Query q(nq);
Query *pq = &nq;
```

the invocation

```
pq->eval();
```

invokes the NameQuery **instance of** eval(), **whereas**

```
q.eval();
```

invokes the Query **instance?**

See Query and NameQuery in L&L, pages 933 and 934.

"When a member function is virtual, the function invoked is the one defined in the dynamic type of the class object (or pointer or reference) through which it is invoked.... The virtual function mechanism works only as we expect when used with pointers and references " (L&L, page 919).

pq points to an object of type NameQuery. The virtual mechanism works as expected because pq is a pointer.

The object q is an instance of the Query part of the object nq of type NameQuery. Because q is only a Query object, polymorphism is not supported and eval() always evaluates to Query::eval(). The virtual mechanism does not work as expected because q is neither a pointer nor a reference.

Exercise 17.15

Which virtual function redeclarations of the Derived **class are in error?**

```
(a) Base *Base::copy(Base *);
    Base *Derived::copy(Derived *);

(b) Base *Base::copy(Base *);
    Derived *Derived::copy(Base *);
```

```
(c) ostream &Base::print(int, ostream & = cout);
    ostream &Derived::print(int, ostream &);

(d) void Base::eval() const;
    void Derived::eval();
```

The redeclarations in (a), (c), and (d) are in error.

```
(a) Base *Base::copy(Base *);
    Base *Derived::copy(Derived *);
```

The derived instance has a different parameter type and does not overload the base class copy(). Recall that the signature must be exact so that the derived copy() represents an alternative version and not an overriding instance.

```
(c) ostream &Base::print(int, ostream & = cout);
    ostream &Derived::print(int, ostream &);
```

It is dangerous to provide a default value to one print() method and not the other.

```
(d) void Base::eval() const;
    void Derived::eval();
```

It is dangerous to have the eval() methods differ by const. Base's eval() can be invoked for const and non-const objects, but Derived's eval() can be invoked only for non-const objects.

Exercise 17.16

In practice, our programs are unlikely to run correctly the first time we exercise them and the first time we exercise them against real data. It is often useful to incorporate a debugging strategy into the design of our classes. Implement a debug() **virtual function for our** Query **class hierarchy that displays the data members of the respective classes. Support a level of detail control as (a) an argument to the** debug() **function and (b) as a class data member. (The latter allows individual class objects to turn on or turn off the display of debugging information.)**

Part (a) takes an argument level. We want a lower value to display less detail than a higher value, so the switch labels are arranged in descending order. Each case falls through to the next one, so the higher-valued levels display at least as much information as the levels below them.

```
void
Query::
debug(short level, ostream &os)
{
```

```
      switch (level) {
        case 3:
          display_solution(os);
        case 2:
          display_location( &_loc );
        case 1:
          os << "_lparen: " << _lparen
             << "\t_rparen: " << _rparen;
          os << endl;
      }
}

void
NameQuery::
debug(short level, ostream &os)
{
      switch (level) {
        case 3:
          display_solution(os);
        case 2:
          display_location( &_loc );
        case 1:
          os << "_name: " << _name;
          os << endl;
      }
}

void
NotQuery::
debug(short level, ostream &os)
{
      switch (level) {
        case 3:
          display_solution(os);
        case 2:
          display_location( &_loc );
        case 1:
          os << "_op: " << _op
             << "\t_all_locs: " << _all_locs;
          os << endl;
      }
}
```

```
    void
    OrQuery::
    debug(short level, ostream &os)
    {
        switch (level) {
          case 3:
            display_solution(os);
          case 2:
            display_location( &_loc );
          case 1:
            os << "_lop: " << _lop
               << "\t_rop: " << _rop;
            os << endl;
        }
    }

    void
    AndQuery::
    debug(short level, ostream &os)
    {
        switch (level) {
          case 3:
            display_solution(os);
          case 2:
            display_location( &_loc );
          case 1:
            os << "_lop: " << _lop
               << "\t_rop: " << _rop
               << "\t_max_col: " << _max_col;
            os << endl;
        }
    }
```

Part (b) is similar to part (a), but it uses the class data member _level to control the amount of detail displayed. The function level() is provided to set the value of _level, and the constructor sets it to the default value of 0.

```
    class Query {
    public:
        ...
        void level(short lvl) { _level = lvl; }
        ...
```

```
protected:
    Query() : _lparen( 0 ), _rparen( 0 ), _solution( 0 ), _level ( 0 )
    {}
    ...
    short    _level;
};
void
Query::
debug(ostream &os)
{
    switch (_level) {
      case 3:
        display_solution(os);
      case 2:
        display_location( &_loc );
      case 1:
        os << "_lparen: " << _lparen
            << "\t_rparen: " << _rparen;
        os << endl;
    }
}

void
NameQuery::
debug(ostream &os)
{
    switch (_level) {
      case 3:
        display_solution(os);
      case 2:
        display_location( &_loc );
      case 1:
        os << "_name: " << _name;
        os << endl;
    }
}
```

(The remaining functions are similar.)

Exercise 17.17

What are likely errors in the following inheritance hierarchy?

```
class Object {
  public:
    virtual void doit() = 0;
    // ...
  protected:
    virtual ~Object();
};
class MyObject : public Object {
  public:
    MyObject(string isA);
    string isA() const;
  protected:
    string _isA;
};
```

Here are some likely errors.

- `doit()` is a pure virtual function in `Object`, and it is not defined in `MyObject`; we cannot instantiate an object of type `MyObject` unless all the pure virtual functions in the parent class(es) are defined.

- The virtual destructor in `Object` should be `public` instead of `protected`; for example, with the current implementation of `Object`,

```
Object *p = new MyObject("some string");
// ...
delete p;   // illegal: destructor is protected
```

Here is the inheritance hierarchy rewritten to resolve these problems:

```
class Object {
  public:
    virtual void doit() = 0;
    virtual ~Object();
    // ...
  protected:
    // ...
};
class MyObject : public Object {
  public:
    MyObject(const string &isA);
    string isA() const;
    void doit();
```

```
   protected:
     string _isA;
};
```

Exercise 17.18

Implement the `AndQuery` **and** `OrQuery` **copy constructors.**

The copy constructors are similar. The `Query` copy constructor is invoked and the two data members `_lop` and `_rop` are copied using the virtual function `clone()`.

```
AndQuery(const AndQuery &rhs) : Query(rhs)
    { _lop = rhs._lop->clone(); _rop = rhs._rop->clone(); }

OrQuery(const OrQuery &rhs) : Query(rhs)
    { _lop = rhs._lop->clone(); _rop = rhs._rop->clone(); }
```

Exercise 17.19

Implement the `AndQuery` **and** `OrQuery` **copy assignment operators.**

Again, the two operators are similar. We test the addresses of the operands to prevent self-assignment. Then we invoke the `Query` copy assignment operator and copy the operands.

```
AndQuery& AndQuery::operator=(const AndQuery &rhs)
{
    // prevent self-assignment
    if (&rhs != this) {
        // invoke Query copy assignment operator
        this->Query::operator=(rhs);

        // copy the operands
        _lop = rhs._lop->clone();
        _rop = rhs._rop->clone();
    }
    return *this;
}

OrQuery& OrQuery::operator=(const OrQuery &rhs)
{
    // prevent self-assignment
    if (&rhs != this) {
        // invoke Query copy assignment operator
        this->Query::operator=(rhs);
```

```
            // copy the operands
            _lop = rhs._lop->clone();
            _rop = rhs._rop->clone();
        }
        return *this;
    }
```

Exercise 17.20

What are the likely indications that a class requires an explicit instance of a copy constructor and copy assignment operator?

A class needs an instance of a copy constructor and copy assignment operator if the class has at least one pointer that addresses heap memory allocated during the lifetime of the object and that must be freed by the destructor.

Exercise 17.21

Provide a destructor, copy constructor, and copy assignment operator for the UserQuery **class.**

The destructor and copy constructor are straightforward. The copy constructor must invoke clone() to copy _eval and must iterate over _query to copy the vector of strings.

```
// destructor
~UserQuery() { delete _eval; delete _query; }

// copy constructor
UserQuery(const UserQuery &rhs)
    : _paren(rhs._paren), _query_stack(rhs._query_stack),
      _current_op(rhs._current_op) {

    _eval = rhs._eval->clone();
    _query = new vector< string >;
    vector< string >::iterator
        it = rhs._query->begin(), end_it = rhs._query->end();

    for ( ; it != end_it; ++it )
        _query->push_back( *it );
}

UserQuery& operator=(const UserQuery &rhs);
```

The copy assignment operator performs the familiar check for self-assignment and copies the data members.

```
// copy assignment operator
UserQuery& UserQuery::operator=(const UserQuery &rhs)
{
    if (&rhs != this) {
        _paren = rhs._paren;
        _query_stack = rhs._query_stack;
        _current_op = rhs._current_op;
        _eval = rhs._eval->clone();

        _query = new vector< string >;
        vector< string >::iterator
            it = rhs._query->begin(), end_it = rhs._query->end();

        for ( ; it != end_it; ++it )
            _query->push_back( *it );
    }
    return *this;
}
```

Exercise 17.22

Provide a `print()` **function for** `UserQuery`. **Explain what you chose for it to display.**

Because we already have `displayQuery()` to print the string vector `_query`, we chose to display the `Query` hierarchy. The function first checks whether a valid object exists and, if it does, invokes `Query::print()`. We chose not to display the details of other class members because that level of detail is better suited for a `debug()` routine.

```
inline ostream& UserQuery::print( ostream &os ) const
{
    if (_eval)
        _eval->print( os );
    else
        os << "Query hierarchy not built";

    os << endl;

    return os;
}
```

Exercise 17.23

Our handling of the user query fails currently in that it does not apply the same preprocessing to each word as the front end does in building up the text; see Sections 6.9 and 6.10. Thus, for example, a user wishing to find maps discovers that only map is recognized in our representation of the text. Modify query_text() to provide equivalent preprocessing.

query_text() must perform three types of preprocessing on the user query to match the front end. As each word is read, query_text() removes punctuation, capitalization, and suffixes. Because some of our operators are also considered punctuation, we filter only punctuation from text that is greater than two characters in length.

```
void
TextQuery::
query_text()
{
    string text;
    string caps( "ABCDEFGHIJKLMNOPQRSTUVWXYZ" );

    vector<string> query_text;

    UserQuery user_query;
    init_query_statics();

    do {
        query_text.clear();

        cout << "Enter a query -- please separate each item "
             << "by a space.\n"
             << "Terminate query (or session) with a dot( . ).\n\n"
             << "==> ";

        while( cin >> text )
        {
            if ( text == "." )
                break;

            string::size_type pos = 0;

            // filter ...
            if ( text.size() > 2 && !filt_elems.empty() )
                while (( pos = text.find_first_of( filt_elems, pos ))
                         != string::npos )
                    text.erase(pos,1);
```

```
            // process suffixes ...
            if ( text.size() > 3 )
                if ( text[ text.size()-1 ] == 's' )
                    suffix_s( text );

            // remove all capitalization ...
            pos = 0;
            while (( pos = text.find_first_of( caps, pos ))
                        != string::npos )
                text[pos] = tolower( text[pos] );

            query_text.push_back( text );
        }

        if ( ! query_text.empty() )
        {
            user_query.query( &query_text );
            query = user_query.eval();
            query->eval();
            display_solution();
                cout << endl;
        }
    } while ( ! query_text.empty() );
        cout << "Ok, bye!\n";
}
```

Exercise 17.24

The query system would be enhanced by a second InclusiveAndQuery, perhaps represented by a single &. It would evaluate as true if both words were on the same line, rather than having both words be adjacent. For example, given the line

```
We were her pride of ten, she named us
```

the InclusiveAndQuery

```
pride & ten
```

evaluates as true, whereas our original AndQuery

```
pride && ten
```

evaluates as false. Provide the necessary support for an InclusiveAndQuery.

The implementation of InclusiveAndQuery is very similar to that of AndQuery. The primary difference occurs in eval().

Here is our definition of our InclusiveAndQuery class and its supporting methods.

```
class InclusiveAndQuery : public Query {
public:
    InclusiveAndQuery( Query *lop = 0, Query *rop = 0 )
        : _lop( lop ), _rop( rop ) {}
    ~InclusiveAndQuery() { delete _lop; delete _rop; }

    InclusiveAndQuery( const InclusiveAndQuery& );
    InclusiveAndQuery& operator=( const InclusiveAndQuery& );

    virtual void eval();
    virtual ostream& print( ostream &os ) const;
    virtual bool add_op( Query* );
    virtual void display_solution( ostream &os=cout, int tabcnt=0 );
    virtual Query* clone() const;

    const Query *rop() const { return _rop; }
    const Query *lop() const { return _lop; }

    static void max_col( const vector< int > *pcol )
            { if ( !_max_col ) _max_col = pcol; }

protected:
    Query *_lop;
    Query *_rop;
    static const vector< int > *_max_col;
};

inline InclusiveAndQuery&
InclusiveAndQuery::
operator=( const InclusiveAndQuery &rhs )
{
        if ( &rhs != this )
        {
                this->Query::operator=( rhs );
                _lop = rhs._lop->clone();
                _rop = rhs._rop->clone();
        }

        return *this;
};
```

```
inline
InclusiveAndQuery::
InclusiveAndQuery( const InclusiveAndQuery &rhs )
        : Query( rhs )
{
        _lop = rhs._lop->clone();
        _rop = rhs._rop->clone();
};

inline bool
InclusiveAndQuery::
add_op( Query *op )
{
    bool status = false;
    if ( !_lop ) {
        _lop = op; status = true;
    }
    else
    if ( ! _rop ) {
        _rop = op; status = true;
    }
    return status;
}

inline void
InclusiveAndQuery::
display_solution( ostream &os, int tabcnt )
{
    handle_tab( os, tabcnt );
    os << "& solution line set: ";
    Query::display_solution( os, 0 );
    _lop->display_solution( os, tabcnt+1 );
    _rop->display_solution( os, tabcnt+1 );
}

inline ostream&
InclusiveAndQuery::
print( ostream &os ) const
{
    if ( _lparen )
        print_lparen( _lparen, os );

    _lop->print( os );
    os << " & ";
    _rop->print( os );
```

```
        if ( _rparen )
            print_rparen( _rparen, os );


        return os;
    }
```

   `InclusiveAndQuery::eval()` is similar to `AndQuery::eval()` except for the third nested while loop. For an `AndQuery` the two operands (words) must be adjacent on the same line. `InclusiveAndQuery` does not require adjacent words; it determines a match based solely on their presence on the same line.

```
    void InclusiveAndQuery::eval()
    {
        if ( ! _lop || ! _rop ) {
            cerr << "Internal error: InclusiveAndQuery: \n"
                 << "no "
                 << ( _lop ? "right " : "left " )
                 << "operand -- bailing out... \n";
            return;
        }


        _lop->eval();
        _rop->eval();


        vector< location>::const_iterator
            riter = _rop->locations()->begin(),
            liter = _lop->locations()->begin(),
            riter_end = _rop->locations()->end(),
            liter_end = _lop->locations()->end();


        while ( liter != liter_end && riter != riter_end ) {

            // while left line number is greater than right
            while ( (*liter).first > (*riter).first ) {
                ++riter;
                if ( riter == riter_end ) {
                    display_partial_solution();
                    display_location( &_loc );
                    return;
                }
            }
```

```
        // while left line number is less than right
        while ( (*liter).first < (*riter).first ) {
            if (((*liter).first == (*riter).first-1 ) &&
                ((*riter).second == 0 ) &&
                ((*liter).second == (*_max_col)[ (*liter).first ] )) {
                _loc.push_back( *liter );
                _loc.push_back( *riter );
                ++riter;
                if ( riter == riter_end ) {
                    display_partial_solution();
                    display_location( &_loc );
                    return;
                }
            }
            ++liter;
            if ( liter == liter_end ) {
                display_partial_solution();
                display_location( &_loc );
                return;
            }
        }

        // while both are on the same line
        while ( (*liter).first == (*riter).first ) {
            _loc.push_back( *liter );
            _loc.push_back( *riter );
            ++riter;
            ++liter;

            if ( liter == liter_end || riter == riter_end ) {
                display_partial_solution();
                display_location( &_loc );
                return;
            }
        }
    }
}

Query* InclusiveAndQuery::clone() const
{
        return new InclusiveAndQuery( *this );
}
```

In class UserQuery we add a new QueryType.

```
enum QueryType {
    WORD = 1, AND, INCLUSIVEAND, OR, NOT, RPAREN, LPAREN
};

void        evalInclusiveAnd();
```

We also add an evaluation function.

```
inline void UserQuery::evalInclusiveAnd()
{
    Query *pop = _query_stack.top(); _query_stack.pop();
    InclusiveAndQuery *paq = new InclusiveAndQuery( pop );

    if ( _lparenOn ) { paq->lparen( _lparenOn ); _lparenOn = 0; }
    if ( _rparenOn ) { paq->rparen( _rparenOn ); _rparenOn = 0; }

    _current_op.push( paq );
}
```

The appropriate changes are made to eval_query() and evalQueryString() to recognize the new operator.

```
Query*
UserQuery::
eval_query()
{
    vector<string>::iterator
        it = _query->begin(), end_it = _query->end();

    for ( ; it != end_it; ++it )
    {
        switch( evalQueryString( *it ))
        {
        case WORD:
            evalWord( *it );
            break;
        case AND:
            evalAnd();
            break;
        case INCLUSIVEAND:
            evalInclusiveAnd();
            break;
        case OR:
            evalOr();
            break;
```

```
            case NOT:
                evalNot();
                break;
            case LPAREN:
                ++_paren;
                ++_lparenOn;
                break;
            case RPAREN:
                --_paren;
                ++_rparenOn;
                evalRParen();
                break;
        }
        cout << " lparenOn: " << _lparenOn << endl;
        cout << " rparenOn: " << _rparenOn << endl;
    }

    if ( integrity_check() ) {
        _eval = _query_stack.top(); _query_stack.pop();

        if ( _rparenOn )
            { _eval->rparen( _rparenOn ); _rparenOn = 0; }

        return _eval;
    }
    else return _eval = 0;
}

UserQuery::QueryType
UserQuery::
evalQueryString( const string &query )
{
    if ( query == "&&" )
        return AND;

    if ( query == "&" )
        return INCLUSIVEAND;

    if ( query == "||" )
        return OR;

    if ( query == "!" )
        return NOT;
```

```
        if ( query == "(" )
            return LPAREN;
        if ( query == ")" )
            return RPAREN;

        return WORD;
    }
```

Here is an example showing the different results between the original AndQuery and the new InclusiveAndQuery.

```
==> long && hair .

    long ( 1 ) lines match

display_location vector:
    first: 0      second: 3

    hair ( 2 ) lines match

display_location vector:
    first: 0      second: 6
    first: 1      second: 6

    long && hair ( 0 ) lines match

display_location vector:

Requested query: long && hair

    Sorry, no matching lines were found in text.

==> long & hair .

    long ( 1 ) lines match

display_location vector:
    first: 0      second: 3

    hair ( 2 ) lines match

display_location vector:
    first: 0      second: 6
    first: 1      second: 6

    long & hair ( 1 ) lines match

display_location vector:
    first: 0      second: 3
    first: 0      second: 6

Requested query: long & hair

( 1 ) Alice Emma has long flowing red hair.   Her Daddy says
```

Exercise 17.25

Our current implementation of `display_solution()`, included here, only prints to standard output. A more reasonable implementation would allow the user to indicate an ostream with which to direct the display. Modify `display_solution()` to allow a user-specified ostream object. What other changes are necessary within the `TextQuery` class definition?

```
void TextQuery::
display_solution()
{
    cout << "\n"
         << "Requested query: "
         << *query << "\n\n";

    const set<short> *solution = query->solution();
    if (!solution->size()) {
        cout << "\n\tSorry, "
             << "no matching lines were found in text.\n"
             << endl;
        return;
    }

    set<short>::const_iterator
        it = solution->begin(),
        end_it = solution->end();

    for (; it != end_it; ++it) {
        int line = *it;

        // don't confound user with text lines starting at 0 ...
        cout << "( " << line+1 << " ) "
             << (*lines_of_text)[line] << '\n';
    }
    cout << endl;
}
```

The changes to `display_solution()` are simple. We substitute an `ostream` data member, `_os`, in place of `cout`.

```
void TextQuery::
display_solution()
{
    _os << "\n"
        << "Requested query:\n ";
    _os << *query << "\n\n";
```

```
        const set<short> *solution = query->solution();

    if ( ! solution->size() ) {
        _os << "\n\tSorry, "
            << "no matching lines were found in text.\n"
            << endl;
        return;
    }

    set<short>::const_iterator
        it = solution->begin(),
        end_it = solution->end();

    for ( ; it != end_it; ++it ) {
        int line = *it;

        // don't confound user with text lines starting at 0 ...
        _os << "( " << line+1 << " ) "
            << (*lines_of_text)[line] << '\n';
    }

    _os << endl;
}
```

class TextQuery must be changed to include the ostream data member and to provide a function to set the member to an ostream that the user specifies.

```
    class TextQuery {
    public:
        TextQuery() { memset( this, 0, sizeof( TextQuery )); }

        static void filter_elements( string felems )
        { filt_elems = felems; }

        void query_text();
        void display_map_text();
        void display_text_locations();
        void build_up_text() {
                retrieve_text();
                separate_words();
                filter_text();
                suffix_text();
                strip_caps();
                build_word_map();
        }
```

```
private:
    void retrieve_text();
    void separate_words();
    void filter_text();
    void strip_caps();
    void suffix_text();
    void suffix_s( string& );
    void build_word_map();
    void init_query_statics();
    void display_solution(ostream &os = cout);


private:
    vector<string>                      *lines_of_text;
    text_loc                            *text_locations;
    map<string,loc*,less<string> >      *word_map;
    Query                          *query;
    static string                  filt_elems;
    vector<int>                    line_cnt;
};
```

Exercise 17.26

What our TextQuery **class really needs is the ability to accept command line arguments from the user.**

(a)   **Identify a possible command line syntax for our text query system.**

(b)   **Indicate the additional data members and member functions that are necessary.**

(c)   **Sketch out a command line facility implementation (see Section 7.8 for an example).**

The command line syntax is the same as our interactive syntax. If we limit the command line version to one query per invocation, we need not require the trailing period to indicate the end of the query. Otherwise, the period can be used as a query separator.

class TextQuery must be modified to parse the command line and store the arguments (the query) in a vector of strings. query_text() will take its input not from cin but rather from this vector of strings. Processing of the query does not change.

Exercise 17.27

As a possible programming project, consider one of the following enhancements to the query system:

(a)   Introduce support for representing an AndQuery as a string, as in "Motion Picture Screen Cartoonists."

(b)   Introduce support for evaluating words based on their presence within the same sentence rather than the same line.

(c)   Introduce a history system in which the user can refer to a previous query by number, possibly adding to it or combining it with another.

(d)   Rather than display the count of matches and all the matching lines, allow the user to indicate a range of lines to display, both for intermediate query evaluation and the final query. For example:

```
==> John && Jacob && Astor

(1)          john ( 3 ) lines match
(2)          jacob ( 3 ) lines match
(3)          john && jacob ( 3 ) lines match
(4)          astor ( 3 ) lines match
(5)          john && jacob && astor ( 5 ) lines match

// New facility: let user choose which query to display
// user types in number
==> display?   3

// System then asks how many lines to display
// return displays all, else user can enter single line number or range
==> how many( return displays all, else enter single line or range) 1-3
```

We present a solution for part (a). Here is an example of how the new query works.

```
==> "long flowing" || fiery .

    ( long ( 1 ) lines match

display_location vector:
    first: 0     second: 3

    flowing ( 1 ) lines match
```

```
display_location vector:
    first: 0      second: 4

    ( long && flowing ( 1 ) lines match

display_location vector:
    first: 0      second: 3
    first: 0      second: 4

    fiery ( 1 ) lines match

display_location vector:
    first: 2      second: 2
    first: 2      second: 9

    ( long && flowing || fiery ) ( 2 ) lines match

display_location vector:
    first: 0      second: 3
    first: 0      second: 4
    first: 2      second: 2
    first: 2      second: 9

Requested query: ( long && flowing || fiery )

( 1 ) Alice Emma has long flowing red hair.  Her Daddy says
( 3 ) like a fiery bird in flight. A beautiful fiery bird, he tells her,
```

One method for handling an `AndQuery` as a string is to process the string in `query_text()`. When the start of the string is found, we set the flag `AndString` and strip off the leading quote. After each word is processed, we inject an `&&` onto the stack. We check each word for a trailing double quote and, if it is found, set `AndString` to `false` to prevent an extra `&&` from being placed on the stack.

Here is the modified `query_text()`.

```cpp
void
TextQuery::
query_text()
{
    string text;
    string caps( "ABCDEFGHIJKLMNOPQRSTUVWXYZ" );
    bool AndString = false;

    vector<string> query_text;
```

```
        UserQuery user_query;
        init_query_statics();

do {
        query_text.clear();

        cout << "Enter a query -- please separate each item "
             << "by a space.\n"
             << "Terminate query (or session) with a dot( . ).\n\n"
             << "==> ";

        while( cin  >> text )
        {
            if ( text == "." )
                  break;

            if (AndString) {
                if (text[text.size()-1] == '"') {
                    text.erase(text.size()-1);
                    AndString = false;
                }
            }
            if ( text[0] == '"') {
                text.erase(0,1);
                AndString = true;
            }

            // remove all capitalization ...
            string::size_type pos = 0;
                while (( pos = text.find_first_of( caps, pos ))
                            != string::npos )
                    text[pos] = tolower( text[pos] );

            query_text.push_back( text );

            if (AndString)
                query_text.push_back( "&&" );
        }

        if ( ! query_text.empty() )
        {
            user_query.query( &query_text );
            query = user_query.eval();
            query->eval();
```

```
              display_solution();
                  cout << endl;
          }
      }
      while ( ! query_text.empty() );
          cout << "Ok, bye!\n";
  }
```

A better solution is to add a new QueryType, STRING, to UserQuery.

```
    enum QueryType {
        WORD = 1, STRING, AND, INCLUSIVEAND, OR, NOT, RPAREN, LPAREN
    };

    void      evalString( const string &query );
```

evalString() treats the string as a parenthesized AND query.

```
  inline void
  UserQuery::
  evalString( const string &query )
  {
  cout << "evalString() : " << query << endl;
      string text, textline = query;

      // treat string as parenthesized AND expression
      ++_paren;
      ++_lparenOn;

      string::size_type pos = 0, prev_pos = 0;

      textline.erase(0,1);    // remove leading quote
      while (( pos = textline.find_first_of( ' ', pos )) !=
                     string::npos ) {
         text = textline.substr( prev_pos, pos - prev_pos );
               pos++; prev_pos = pos;

         evalWord(text);
         evalAnd();
      }

      text = textline.substr( prev_pos, pos - prev_pos );
      text.erase(text.size()-1);  // skip trailing quote
      evalWord(text);
```

```
        --_paren;
        ++_rparenOn;
        evalRParen();
    }
```

The appropriate case must be added to the switch in UserQuery::eval_query().

```
        case STRING:
            evalString( *it );
            break;
```

evalQueryString() is modified to recognize a STRING.

```
UserQuery::QueryType
UserQuery::
evalQueryString( const string &query )
{
    if ( query == "&&" )
        return AND;

    if ( query == "&" )
        return INCLUSIVEAND;

    if ( query == "||" )
        return OR;

    if ( query == "!" )
        return NOT;

    if ( query == "(" )
        return LPAREN;

    if ( query == ")" )
        return RPAREN;

    if ( query[0] == '"' )
        return STRING;

    return WORD;
}
```

Finally, query_text() must recognize a complete string in the user's query. Because we rely on the presence of the quotes to recognize the STRING query, we must preserve the quotes when filtering the text for unwanted punctuation.

```
void
TextQuery::
query_text()
{
    string text;
    string caps( "ABCDEFGHIJKLMNOPQRSTUVWXYZ" );

    vector<string> query_text;

    UserQuery user_query;
    init_query_statics();

    do {
        query_text.clear();

            cout << "Enter a query -- please separate each item "
            << "by a space.\n"
            << "Terminate query (or session) with a dot( . ).\n\n"
            << "==> ";

        while( cin >> text )
        {
            if ( text == "." )
                break;

            // process the entire string as one entity
            if ( text[0] == '"') {
                char ch;
                text += ' ';
                while (cin >> ch) {
                    text += ch;
                    if (ch == '"')
                        break;
                }
            }

            string::size_type pos = 0;

            if (text[0] == '"') pos = 1;

            // filter ...
            if ( text.size() > 2 && !filt_elems.empty() )
                while (( pos = text.find_first_of( filt_elems, pos ))
                        != string::npos )
                    text.erase(pos,1);
```

```
            if (text[0] == '"') text += '"';

            // process suffixes ...
            if ( text.size() > 3 )
                if ( text[ text.size()-1 ] == 's' )
                    suffix_s( text );

            // remove all capitalization ...
            pos = 0;
            while (( pos = text.find_first_of( caps, pos ))
                    != string::npos )
                text[pos] = tolower( text[pos] );

            query_text.push_back( text );
        }

        if ( ! query_text.empty() )
        {
            user_query.query( &query_text );
            query = user_query.eval();
            query->eval();
            display_solution();
                cout << endl;
        }
    }
    while ( ! query_text.empty() );
        cout << "Ok, bye!\n";
}
```

chapter eighteen

Multiple and Virtual Inheritance

Exercise 18.1

Which, if any, of the following declarations are in error? Explain why.

```
(a) class CADVehicle : public CAD, Vehicle { ... };
(b) class DoublyLinkedList :
        public List, public List { ... };
(c) class iostream :
        private istream, private ostream { ... };
```

Only (b) is in error.

(a) class CADVehicle : public CAD, Vehicle { ... };

This is correct because, by default, if a base class does not specify an access level, it is treated as private. If we intended to inherit publicly from both CAD and Vehicle, we should write

```
class CADVehicle : public CAD, public Vehicle { ... };
```

(b) class DoublyLinkedList :
        public List, public List { ... };

This is incorrect because a class cannot be directly used as a base class more than once. List is used twice as a base class for DoublyLinkedList.

(c) class iostream :
        private istream, private ostream { ... };

This is correct because there is no requirement that a class be derived from one or more public classes.

Exercise 18.2

Given the following class hierarchy, each class of which defines a default constructor,

```
class A { ... };
class B : public A { ... };
class C : public B { ... };
class X { ... };
class Y { ... };
class Z : public X, public Y { ... };
class MI : public C, public Z { ... };
```

what is the order of constructor execution for the following definition?

```
MI mi;
```

The order of constructor execution is "the declaration order within the class derivation list" (L&L, page 971).

The rule is that the base class constructor is invoked before that of the derived class. In the case of multiple inheritance, the constructors of the base classes are invoked in the order the base classes appear in the class derivation list — in this case, first C and then Z.

When the base class is itself an object of derivation, the rule is recursively applied. Thus, because C is derived from B, B's constructor is invoked before C's constructor. Similarly, A's constructor is invoked before B's.

To make this clear, we picture the derivation hierarchy in Figure 18.1. We see that the order of constructor execution is A, B, C, X, Y, Z, and MI.

Exercise 18.3

Given the following class hierarchy, each class of which defines a default constructor,

```
class X { ... };
class A { ... };
class B : public  A { ... };
class C : private B { ... };
class D : public  X, public C { ... };
```

which, if any, of the following conversions are not permitted?

```
D *pd = new D;
```

(a) X *px = pd;   (c) B *pb = pd;
(b) A *pa = pd;   (d) C *pc = pd;

Conversions to private base classes are not permitted. B is a private base class in C. That precludes the conversion of pd, of type D, into B or A. The conversions in (b) and (c) are not permitted.

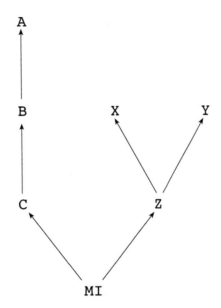

Figure 18.1 Class MI, Exercise 18.2

Exercise 18.4

Given the following class hierarchy, with the following collection of virtual functions,

```
class Base {
  public:
    virtual ~Base();
    virtual ostream &print();
    virtual void debug();
    virtual void readOn();
    virtual void writeOn();
    virtual void log();
    // ...
};

class Derived1 : virtual public Base {
  public:
    virtual ~Derived1();
    virtual void writeOn();
    // ...
};
```

```
class Derived2 : virtual public Base {
  public:
    virtual ~Derived2();
    virtual void readOn();
    // ...
};


class MI : public Derived1, public Derived2 {
  public:
    virtual ~MI();
    virtual ostream &print();
    virtual void debug();
    // ...
};
```

which instance of each function is invoked for the following?

```
    Base *pb = new MI;
(a) pb->print();        (c) pb->readOn();        (e) pb->log();
(b) pb->debug();        (d) pb->writeOn();       (f) delete pb;
```

Read Section 18.5, Virtual Inheritance, in L&L, before you proceed.
It is easier to visually depict the classes and their member functions (Figure 18.2).

(a) pb->print();

  We find MI::print().

(b) pb->debug();

  We find MI::debug().

(c) pb->readOn();

   The derived MI class inherits the members of its two base classes. Under nonvirtual
derivation we cannot access readOn() because "all unqualified references under a nonvirtual derivation are ambiguous" (L&L, page 1002). Under virtual derivation we find
readOn() in Derived2, instead of Base::readOn(), because of the dominance of Derived2
as being more derived than the Base instance inherited by Derived1.

(d) pb->writeOn();

  We find Derived1::writeOn() for the reasons in (c).

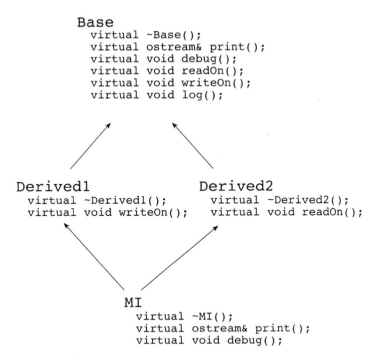

Base
```
    virtual ~Base();
    virtual ostream& print();
    virtual void debug();
    virtual void readOn();
    virtual void writeOn();
    virtual void log();
```

Derived1
```
    virtual ~Derived1();
    virtual void writeOn();
```

Derived2
```
    virtual ~Derived2();
    virtual void readOn();
```

MI
```
    virtual ~MI();
    virtual ostream& print();
    virtual void debug();
```

Figure 18.2   Class MI, Exercise 18.4

(e) pb->log();

We find `Base::log()`.

(f) delete pb;

See Section 18.5.3, Constructor and Destructor Order, L&L, page 1000.

`MI::~MI()` is invoked because pb addresses an MI object and the destructor is virtual.

"Virtual base classes are always constructed prior to nonvirtual base classes regardless of where they appear in the inheritance hierarchy" (L&L, page 1000). The class MI has one `virtual` base class (Base) and two nonvirtual base classes (Derived1 and Derived2). This means that when we create an MI object, the constructors are invoked in the following order: (1) the virtual base class constructors (one constructor for Base) and (2) the nonvirtual base class constructors in the order of declaration (Derived1, Derived2, and then MI). "The order of base class destructor calls is guaranteed to be the reverse order of constructor invocation" (L&L, page 1002). Consequently, the order of the destructors called is MI, ~Derived2(), ~Derived1(), and ~Base().

Exercise 18.5

Using the class hierarchy defined in Exercise 18.4, identify the virtual functions active when invoked through (a) pd1 **and (b)** d2**:**

```
(a) Derived1 *pd1 = new MI;
(b) MI obj;
    Derived2 d2 = obj;
```

Again we refer to Figure 18.2.

(a) Derived1 *pd1 = new MI;

Because pd1 points to an object of type MI, the virtual functions active are as follows:

```
pd1->print();        // MI's
pd1->debug();        // MI's
pd1->readOn();       // Derived2's
pd1->writeOn();      // Derived1's
pd1->log();          // Base's
```

```
(b) MI obj;
    Derived2 d2 = obj;
```

"When a member function is virtual, the function invoked is the one defined in the dynamic type of the class object (or pointer or reference) through which it is invoked. As it happens, however, the static and dynamic type of a class object is the same. The virtual function mechanism works only as we expect when used with pointers and references" (L&L, page 919).

The object d2 is an object of type Derived2 that receives a copy of the Derived2 part of obj that is of type MI. Consequently, the compiler can search for virtual functions starting at the level that Derived2 appears and then move upward toward the base class Base. The virtual functions active are as follows:

```
pd1->print();        // Base's
pd1->debug();        // Base's
pd1->readOn();       // Derived2's
pd1->writeOn();      // Base's
pd1->log();          // Base's
```

But we cannot call any virtual function directly using the object d2. We can invoke virtual functions through a pointer or a reference but not with an object (L&L, page 920).

Exercise 18.6

Identify which of the following are type inheritance and which are implementation inheritance.

(a) Queue : list
(b) EncryptedString : String
(c) Gif : FileFormat
(d) Circle : Point
(e) Dqueue : Queue, List
(f) DrawableGeom : Geom, Canvas

L&L, in Section 18.3, state that "a public derivation is referred to as *type inheritance*. The derived class is a subtype of the base class." The derived class in general reflects an *is-a* relationship; that is, it provides a specialization of its more general base class.

"A private derivation is referred to as *implementation inheritance*. The derived class does not support the public interface of the base class directly; rather, it wishes to reuse the implementation of the base class while providing its own public interface" (L&L, page 977).

The idea in this exercise is to analyze the relationship of the base class and derived classes based on the names of the two abstractions.

(a) Queue : list

This is implementation inheritance because a Queue has a very specific interface that a List is not subtype to.

(b) EncryptedString : String

This is type inheritance because an EncryptedString is a type of String.

(c) Gif : FileFormat

This is type inheritance because a Gif is a type of FileFormat.

(d) Circle : Point

This is implementation inheritance because Circle uses Point.

(e) Dqueue : Queue, List

Dqueue is mix-in. Queue is a public inheritance of interface, and List is a private inheritance of implementation.

(f) DrawableGeom : Geom, Canvas

This is implementation inheritance because DrawableGeom is a subtype of both Geom and Canvas, with a common interface to each. That is, there is a Geom hierarchy and a Canvas hierarchy.

Exercise 18.7

Replace our Array **member of** PeekbackStack **in Section 18.3.1 with the standard library** deque. **Write a small program to exercise it.**

The transformation is similar to the transformation of iStack in Section 6.18. The class PeekbackStack becomes simpler when we use the standard library deque instead of Array. Here are a few reasons.

- We do not need the member top because a deque keeps track of its size.

- It is unlikely that the stack will ever be full, but it could happen; see the vector implementation in L&L, page 326.

- We use deque's empty() to determine whether the stack is empty.

- We use deque's size() to determine the top index of the stack.

The new class PeekbackStack now looks like this:

```
class PeekbackStack {
  public:
    explicit PeekbackStack(int size) : stack(size) { }

    bool empty() const  { return stack.empty();                    }
    bool full()  const  { return stack.max_size() == stack.size(); }
    int  top()   const  { return stack.size() - 1;                 }

    int pop() {
        if (empty())
            throw "empty stack";

        int v = stack[top()];
        stack.pop_back();
        return v;
    }

    void push(int value) {
        if (full())
            throw "stack full";
        stack.push_back(value);
    }

    bool peekback(int index, int &value) const;
```

```
    private:
       deque<int> stack;
};
```

The method `peekback()` has minor changes:

```
inline bool
PeekbackStack::peekback(int index, int &value) const
{
    if (empty()) {
        return false;
    }
    if (index < 0 || index > top()) {
        value = stack[top()];
        return false;
    }
    value = stack[index];
    return true;
}
```

The `main()` program starts with an empty stack, pushes five integers, tests some boundaries, and then pops the stack.

```
int main()
{
    PeekbackStack s(0);      // preallocate an empty stack

    cout << "stack empty should be true; "
         << "it is " << s.empty() << "\n";
    cout << "stack full should be false; "
         << " it is " << s.full() << "\n";
    for (int i = 0; i < 5; i++)
        s.push(i+10);
    int v;
    s.peekback(0, v);
    cout << "s[0] should be 10; it is " << v << "\n";
    s.peekback(1, v);
    cout << "s[1] should be 11; it is " << v << "\n";
    s.peekback(2, v);
    cout << "s[2] should be 12; it is " << v << "\n";
    s.peekback(3, v);
    cout << "s[3] should be 13; it is " << v << "\n";
    s.peekback(4, v);
    cout << "s[4] should be 14; it is " << v << "\n";
    s.peekback(5, v);
    cout << "s[5] should be false; it is " << s.peekback(5, v) << "\n";
```

```
    s.peekback(s.top(), v);
    cout << "top of stack should be 14; it is " << v << "\n";
    cout << "pop entire stack: ";
    while (!s.empty())
        cout << s.pop() << " ";
    cout << "\n";

    return 0;
}
```

Here's the output for the preceding program.

```
stack empty should be true; it is 1
stack full should be false;  it is 0
s[0] should be 10; it is 10
s[1] should be 11; it is 11
s[2] should be 12; it is 12
s[3] should be 13; it is 13
s[4] should be 14; it is 14
s[5] should be false; it is 0
top of stack should be 14; it is 14
pop entire stack: 14 13 12 11 10
```

Exercise 18.8

Contrast composition by value with composition by reference. Give an example of each use to illustrate your discussion.

L&L discuss object composition in Section 18.3.4. In composition by value, the actual object is a member of the class; for example, in Exercise 18.7, the class PeekbackStack contains the member stack, which is an object of type deque<int>. "Composition by value provides automatic management of the object's lifetime and copy semantics, and provides more efficient, direct access of the object itself" (L&L, page 983). This means that we do not have to provide a copy constructor, a copy assignment operator, or a destructor for PeekbackStack.

In composition by reference, the actual object is indirectly addressed through either a reference or a pointer member to the class object. For example, we could modify the class PeekbackStack, which contains

```
    deque<int> stack;
```

to contain instead

```
    deque<int> *stack;
```

Now PeekbackStack has at least one pointer. This means that we must provide a copy constructor, a copy assignment operator, and a destructor for this class.

The advantage of composition by reference is that it allows for polymorphism and amortizes resource allocation because the object referred to may need not be present in all cases.

Exercise 18.9

Given the following class hierarchy, with the following collection of data members,

```
class Base1 {
  public:
    // ...
  protected:
    int    ival;
    double dval;
    char   cval;
    // ...
  private:
    int *id;
    // ...
};

class Base2 {
  public:
    // ...
  protected:
    float  fval;
    // ...
  private:
    double dval;
    // ...
};

class Derived : public Base1 {
  public:
    // ...
  protected:
    string sval;
    double dval;
    // ...
};

class MI : public Derived, public Base2 {
  public:
    void foo(double);
```

```
    // ...
  protected:
    int     *ival;
    complex<double> cval;
    // ...
};
```

and the following `MI::foo()` **member function skeleton,**

```
    int     ival;
    double  dval;

    void MI::foo(double dval)
    {
        int id;

        // ...
    }
```

(a) **Identify the set of members visible from within** `MI`**. Are there any visible from multiple base classes?**

(b) **Identify the set of members visible from within** `MI::foo()`**.**

In Section 18.4, page 985, L&L state that "each class maintains its own scope, within which the names of its members and any nested types are defined.... Under inheritance, the scope of the derived class is nested within the scope of its immediate base classes. If a name is unresolved within the scope of the derived class, the enclosing base class scope is searched for a definition of the name." If a name is resolved within the scope of the derived class, the name hides direct access of the base class member.

We use Figure 18.3 to see the parts accessible to `MI`.

(a) Identify the set of members visible from within `MI`. Are there any visible from multiple base classes?

"All the immediate base classes are searched simultaneously, giving rise to the possibility of an ambiguous reference if a member with the same name is inherited from two or more base classes" (L&L, page 988). The members visible from within `MI` are as follows:

```
        int     *MI::ival;              protected
        complex<double> MI::cval;       protected
        double  Derived::dval;          protected
        string  Derived::sval;          protected
        float   Base2::dval;            private
        float   Base2::fval;            protected
        float   *Base1::id;             private
```

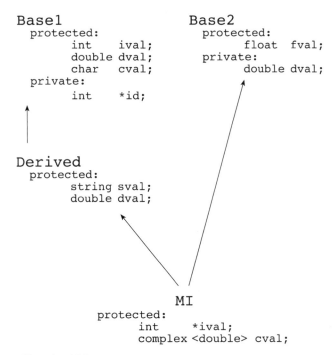

Figure 18.3 Class MI, Exercise 18.9

What happened to ival and cval from Base1? They are redefined in MI and, consequently, are hidden. Derived::dval hides Base1::dval.

The members that are visible from multiple base classes and, consequently, ambiguous (if they are referred to as plain dval), are

```
double   Derived::dval;        protected
float    Base2::dval;          private
```

After the compiler resolves which instance of a name it should use, it then checks to see whether access of that instance is legal. "The primary rationale governing resolving a member prior to considering its access level is to prevent possibly subtle changes in the program semantics based on a seemingly unrelated change in the access level of a member" (L&L, page 987). The member that is not accessible from MI is

```
float    *Base1::id;           private
```

because it is private to Base1.

(b)   Identify the set of members visible from within MI::foo().

The members visible from within foo() are as follows:

```
double    dval;                      foo() parameter
int       id;                        foo() local
int       *MI::ival;                 protected
complex<double> MI::cval;            protected
string    Derived::sval;             protected
float     Base2::fval;               protected
```

The parameter dval hides the other dvals; of course, Base2::dval and Base1::dval are still accessible in foo() with their class qualification. The local id in foo() hides the private id in Base1. See a good example in L&L, page 987.

Exercise 18.10

Using the class hierarchy defined in Exercise 18.9, identify which of the assignments, if any, are in error within the MI::bar() member function:

```
void MI::bar()
{
    int sval;
    // exercise questions occur here ...
}
```
(a) dval = 3.14159;   (d) fval = 0;
(b) cval = 'a';   (e) sval = *ival;
(c) id   = 1;

Only (a) and (c) are in error.

(a) dval = 3.14159;

This is an error for the reasons described in Exercise 18.9, part (a): dval is ambiguous.

(b) cval = 'a';

This is technically correct, but the cval that is used is of type complex<double> (that is because the cval in MI hides the char definition of cval in Base1). So the character constant 'a' is promoted to double.

(c) id = 1;

This is an error because id is a private member of Base1.

(d) fval = 0;

This is correct. fval is of type float and belongs to Base2.

(e) sval = *ival;

This is correct because sval is a local int that receives a copy of *ival.

Exercise 18.11

Using the class hierarchy defined in Exercise 18.9, and the following skeleton of the `MI::foobar()` **member function,**

```
int id;

void MI::foobar(float cval)
{
    int dval;
    // exercise question occurs here ...
}
```

(a) Assign the local instance of `dval` **the sum of the** `dval` **member of** `Base1` **added to the** `dval` **member of** `Derived`.

(b) Assign the real portion of the `cval` of `MI` to the `fval` member of `Base2`.

(c) Assign the `cval` member of `Base1` **to the first character of the** `sval` **member of** `Derived`.

Here are the answers.

(a) Assign the local instance of `dval` the sum of the `dval` member of `Base1` added to the `dval` member of `Derived`.

We must explicitly refer to `dval` in each class because they are hidden by the local `dval`:

```
dval = Base1::dval + Derived::dval;
```

(b) Assign the real portion of the `cval` of `MI` to the `fval` member of `Base2`.

We could qualify `fval` for the compiler to use the one in `Base2` (see the first line in the following code); or we could omit `Base2::` because there is only one `fval` visible in the inheritance tree (see the second line). We need to qualify `cval` with `MI::`; otherwise, the compiler will attempt to use the incoming parameter `cval`.

```
Base2::fval = MI::cval.real();
```

or

```
fval = MI::cval.real();
```

The second form is preferred because L&L do not qualify a member reference if it is not necessary.

(c) Assign the `cval` member of `Base1` to the first character of the `sval` member of `Derived`.

We could qualify sval for the compiler to use the one in Derived (see the first line of the following code); or we could omit Derived:: because there is only one sval visible in the inheritance tree (see the second line of code). We must qualify cval with Base1::; otherwise, the compiler will attempt to use the incoming parameter cval.

```
Derived::sval[0] = Base1::cval;
```

or

```
sval[0] = Base1::cval;
```

Exercise 18.12

Given the following class hierarchy, with the following collection of member functions named print(),

```
class Base {
  public:
    void print(string) const;
    // ...
};

class Derived1 : public Base {
  public:
    void print(int) const;
    // ...
};

class Derived2 : public Base {
  public:
    void print(double) const;
    // ...
};

class MI : public Derived1, public Derived2 {
  public:
    void print(complex<double>) const;
    // ...
};
```

(a)   Why does the following result in a compile-time error?

```
MI mi;
string dancer("Njinsky");
mi.print(dancer);
```

(b) How can we revise the definition of `MI` **to allow this to compile and execute correctly?**

First, let's address the reason for the error.

(a)   Why does the following result in a compile-time error?

The problem is that the `print()` method that is visible to the object `mi` of type `MI` is

```
void print(complex<double>) const;
```

The compiler reports that it cannot convert an object of type `string` into `complex<double>`. Keep in mind that the `print()` methods are not overloaded. The overload resolution limits candidates to those in the same scope (that is, the same class). See L&L, pages 448 and 903.

Second, let's look at how we can fix the error.

(b)   How can we revise the definition of `MI` to allow this to compile and execute correctly?

We need a `print(string)` method in `MI`:

```
void print(string) const;
```

This method would invoke the `print(string)` that belongs to `Base`. But we have another problem: because we are not yet using virtual inheritance, the compiler does not know whether we wish to invoke `print(string)` through the `Derived1` or the `Derived2` path. We then modify `Derived1` to provide its own `print(string)` to invoke `Base`'s `print(string)`:

```
void Derived1::print(string s) {
    Base::print(s);
}
```

The `print(string)` that belongs to `MI` could then read

```
void MI::print(string s) {
    Derived1::print(s);
}
```

Note that we cannot say

```
void MI::print(string s) {
    Derived1::Base::print(s);
}
```

`Derived1::Base::print(s)` cannot be used because the interpretation of this refers to a member function `print()` of class `Base` that is nested within `Derived1`. That is, the syntax does not refer to an inheritance relationship but rather to a nesting of one type within another. And

```
void MI::print(string s) {
    Base::print(s);
}
```

does not work either because Base is not an immediate base class of MI.

How about the using mechanism from L&L, page 904? Suppose we wrote

```
class MI : public Derived1, public Derived2 {
  public:
    void print(complex<double>) const;
    using Derived1::Base::print;   // error
    using Base::print;             // also an error
    // ...
};
```

That is an error again because Base is not a member of Derived1 and Base is not an immediate base class of MI.

Exercise 18.13

Given the following class hierarchy,

```
class Class { ... };
class Base : public Class { ... };
class Derived1 : virtual public Base { ... };
class Derived2 : virtual public Base { ... };
class MI : public Derived1, public Derived2 { ... };
class Final : public MI, public Class { ... };
```

(a)   **What is the order of constructor and destructor for the definition of a** Final **class object?**

(b)   **How many** Base **subobjects does a** Final **class object contain? How many** Class **subobjects?**

(c)   **Which of the following assignments is a compile-time error?**

```
        Base     *pb;
        MI       *pmi;
        Class    *pc;
        Derived2 *pd2;

    (i)  pb = new Class;      (iii) pmi = pb;
    (ii) pc = new Final;      (iv)  pd2 = pmi;
```

(a) What is the order of constructor and destructor for the definition of a `Final` class object?

A `Final` class object is made up of `MI` and `Class`. `MI` is made up of `Derived1` and `Derived2`; these two latter classes are derived from `Base`, which in turn is derived from `Class`. The first constructor to be called is the constructor for the virtual class `Base`; but `Base` has a base class (`Class`). So the order of constructors for the definition of a `Final` class object is

```
Class           // base class of Base
Base            // virtual base class of Derived1 and Derived2
Derived1        // base class of MI
Derived2        // base class of MI
MI              // base class of Final
Class           // base class of Final
Final           // constructor for Final
```

The order of destructors is guaranteed to be the reverse of the order of constructors (L&L, page 1002).

(b) How many `Base` subobjects does a `Final` class object contain? How many `Class` subobjects?

A `Final` class object has one `Base` subobject because `Base` is a virtual base class for `Derived1` and `Derived2`; but it has two `Class` subobjects: one because it is a base class for `Base` and a second one because it is a base class for `Final`.

(c) Which of the following assignments is a compile-time error?

```
Base      *pb;
MI        *pmi;
Class     *pc;
Derived2  *pd2;
```

(i) `pb = new Class;`   (iii) `pmi = pb;`
(ii) `pc = new Final;`   (iv) `pd2 = pmi;`

The assignments (i), (ii), and (iii) produce compile-time errors. The reason is the same for both (i) and (iii): we cannot assign an object or a pointer to a class higher in the inheritance tree (a more general class) to an object or a pointer lower in the inheritance tree (a more specialized class). (i) attempts to assign to pb, a pointer to `Base` (a more specialized class), a pointer to `Class` (a more general class). (iii) is similar because it involves `MI` and `Base`.

Item (ii) produces a compile-time error because `Final` contains two subobjects of type `Class`, so it is not possible to implicitly assign to pc.

Exercise 18.14

Given the following class hierarchy, with the following members,

```
class Base {
  public:
    bar(int);
    // ...
  protected:
    int ival;
    // ...
};

class Derived1 : virtual public Base {
  public:
    bar(char);
    foo(char);
    // ...
  protected:
    char cval;
    // ...
};

class Derived2 : virtual public Base {
  public:
    foo(int);
    // ...
  protected:
    int  ival;
    char cval;
    // ...
};

class VMI : public Derived1, public Derived2 { };
```

**which inherited members can be accessed without qualification from within the VMI
class? Which require qualification?**

The class VMI is derived from Derived1 and Derived2, which have one base virtual class
Base. There is one Base subobject in the inheritance tree. We also have access to members
in either Derived1 or Derived2. We have the following in these two classes:

```
Derived1                Derived2
    bar(char);              int ival;
    foo(char);              foo(int);
    char cval;              char cval;
```

From within the VMI class we can access bar(char) in Derived1 and ival in Derived2 without any qualification because "under a virtual derivation, the inheritance of a virtual base class member is given less weight than a subsequently redefined instance of that member" (L&L, page 1003).

There are two foo() methods at the same level of the hierarchy (although they have different signatures), so we cannot access them directly. We must qualify the two different accesses:

```
Derived1::foo('a');
Derived2::foo(3);
```

We also must qualify accesses to cval:

```
Derived1::cval = 'a';
Derived2::cval = 'b';
```

Base has ival and bar(int). We must qualify these two members to access them.

Exercise 18.15

Given the following Base class with the following three constructors,

```
class Base {
  public:
    Base();
    Base(string);
    Base(const Base&);
    // ...
  protected:
    string _name;
};
```

define the associated three constructors for the following:

(a) one of either

```
        class Derived1 : virtual public Base { ... };
        class Derived2 : virtual public Base { ... };
```

(b)   class VMI : public Derived1, public Derived2 { ... };

(c)   class Final : public VMI { ... };

(a)   one of either

```
        class Derived1 : virtual public Base { ... };
        class Derived2 : virtual public Base { ... };
```

We choose to provide three associated constructors for `Derived1`, each invoking the associated `Base` class constructor.

```
class Derived1 : virtual public Base {
  public:
    Derived1() {
        cout << "Derived1() : Base()\n";
    }
    Derived1(string s) : Base(s) {
        cout << "Derived1(string) : Base(" << s << ")\n";
    }
    Derived1(const Derived1 &d) : Base(d) {
        cout << "Derived1(const Derived1 &d) : Base(d)\n";
    }
};
```

(b)   `class VMI : public Derived1, public Derived2 { ... };`

Both `Derived1` and `Derived2` have a `virtual` base class. We know that the virtual base class constructors are invoked before the nonvirtual base class constructors. "The initialization of a virtual base class becomes the responsibility of the *most derived class* as determined by the declaration of each particular class object" (L&L, Section 18.5).

```
class VMI : public Derived1, public Derived2 {
  public:
    VMI() {
        cout << "VMI()\n";
    }
    VMI(string s) : Derived1(s), Derived2(s), Base(s) {
        cout << "VMI(string) s = " << s << "\n";
    }
    VMI(const VMI &v) : Base(v) {
        cout << "VMI(const VMI &)\n";
    }
};
```

(c)   `class Final : public VMI { ... };`

The class `Final` is similar to `VMI`:

```
class Final : public VMI {
  public:
    Final() {
        cout << "Final()\n";
    }
```

```
    Final(string s) : VMI(s) {
        cout << "Final(string) s = " << s << "\n";
    }
    Final(const Final &f) : Base(f) {
        cout << "Final(const Final &)\n";
    }
};
```

Exercise 18.16

Add an additional member function to Array: spy(). If invoked, it remembers the operations applied to the class object: (a) number of index accesses, (b) number of times each member function is invoked, (c) the element value searched for, when find() is invoked, and (d) number of successful element searches. Explain your design. Modify the entire collection of Array subtypes so that spy() works for them as well.

We modify Array.h to include a few counters:

```
int     _assign_cnt;
int     _find_cnt;
int     _find_success_cnt;
Type    *_find_last_arg;
int     _index_cnt;
int     _min_cnt;
int     _max_cnt;
int     _print_cnt;
int     _size_cnt;
int     _sort_cnt;
int     _spy_cnt;
```

The appropriate functions increment their own counters. For example, min() increments _min_cnt:

```
virtual Type min() {
    _min_cnt++;
    Type *ep_begin = getArray();
    Type *ep_end   = ep_begin + size();
    return *min_element(ep_begin, ep_end);
}
```

All counters are initialized in init():

```
template <class Type>
void Array<Type>::init(const Type *array, int sz)
{
    _size = sz;
    _ia   = new Type[_size];
```

```
            for (int ix = 0; ix < _size; ++ix)
                _ia[ix] = array[ix];


            _assign_cnt = _find_cnt  = _index_cnt
                        = _min_cnt   = _max_cnt
                        = _print_cnt = _size_cnt
                        = _sort_cnt  = _spy_cnt = 0;
            _find_success_cnt = 0;
            _find_last_arg    = 0;
        }
```

The new spy() method reports the value of the counters:

```
        template <class Type>
        void Array<Type>::spy()
        {
            _spy_cnt++;
            cout << "\t# operator =():\t\t" << _assign_cnt  << "\n";
            cout << "\t# find()       :\t\t" << _find_cnt    << "\n";
            if (_find_last_arg)
                cout << "\t# find() arg  :\t\t" << *_find_last_arg
                                               << "\n";
            cout << "\t# successful finds:\t"
                                          << _find_success_cnt
                                               << "\n";
            cout << "\t# operator []():\t"  << _index_cnt  << "\n";
            cout << "\t# min():\t\t"        << _min_cnt    << "\n";
            cout << "\t# max():\t\t"        << _max_cnt    << "\n";
            cout << "\t# print():\t\t"      << _print_cnt  << "\n";
            cout << "\t# size():\t\t"       << _size_cnt   << "\n";
            cout << "\t# sort():\t\t"       << _sort_cnt   << "\n";
            cout << "\t# spy():\t\t"        << _spy_cnt    << "\n";
        }
```

The method is straightforward. We add the counters in Array.h, modify the corresponding methods, and let spy() display the results.

Exercise 18.17

An associative array is another name for the standard library map due to its support of indexing based on a key value. Do you think an associative array makes a good candidate for subtyping of our Array class? Why or why not?

We could create a subtype `AssociativeArray` from the concrete base class `Array`:

```
class AssociativeArray : public Array {
    // ...
}
```

An associative array associates a non-int index with a value. The class `AssociativeArray` could map a non-index index to an `int` index that could then be used in `Array`. This new subtype would be a useful addition to the original class.

Exercise 18.18

Reimplement our `Array` hierarchy using the standard library template container class and as many of the generic algorithms as possible.

We choose to use a `vector` in the reimplementation of `Array`.

```
#ifndef     ARRAY_H
#define     ARRAY_H
#include    <iostream>
#include    <vector>
using namespace std;

template <class Type> class Array;
template <class Type> ostream &
    operator <<(ostream &, const Array<Type> &);

template <class Type>
class Array {
  public:
    explicit Array(int sz = 0) {
        init(0, sz);
    }
    Array(const Type *ar, int sz) {
        init(ar, sz);
    }
    Array(const Array &iA) {
        _ia = iA._ia;
    }

    Type &operator [](int ix) {
        return _ia[ix];
    }
    void print(ostream &os = cout) const;
```

```
        virtual int findit(const Type &find_val) {
            Type *ip = find(_ia.begin(), _ia.end(), find_val);
            if (ip == _ia.end())
                return -1;
            else
                return ip - _ia.begin();
        }
        virtual Type min() const {
            return *min_element(_ia.begin(), _ia.end());
        }
        virtual Type max() const {
            return *max_element(_ia.begin(), _ia.end());
        }
        int size() const {
            return _ia.size();
        }

    protected:
        void init(const Type *, int);

        vector<Type>    _ia;
};
#endif
```

The copy constructor and copy assignment operator are no longer necessary within the Array class. The shallow copy of the pointer member that previously resulted in a dangerous aliasing is not present because we are using a vector.

Where the generic algorithms are used

find()	in findit()
min_element()	in min()
max_element()	in max()

The method init() becomes

```
template <class Type>
void Array<Type>::init(const Type *array, int sz)
{
    for (int ix = 0; ix < sz; ++ix)
        _ia.push_back(array[ix]);
}
```

The main() is the same program we used in Exercise 16.11.

chapter nineteen

Uses of Inheritance in C++

Exercise 19.1

Given the following class hierarchy, in which each class defines a default constructor and a virtual destructor,

```
class X { ... };
class A { ... };
class B : public A { ... };
class C : public B { ... };
class D : public X, public C { ... };
```

which, if any, of the following dynamic_cast**s fail?**

```
(a) D *pd = new D;
    A *pa = dynamic_cast< A* >(pd);

(b) A *pa = new C;
    C *pc = dynamic_cast< C* >(pa);

(c) B *pb = new B;
    D *pd = dynamic_cast< D* >(pb);

(d) A *pa = new D;
    X *px = dynamic_cast< X* >(pa);
```

The dynamic_casts in (a), (b), and (d) succeed. (a) succeeds because it is always safe to cast *up* in the inheritance tree. (b) succeeds because pa, even though it is of type pointer to A, points to an object of type C. (d) succeeds because pa points to an object of type D, and D contains a subobject of type X, so the dynamic_cast succeeds and refers to the X subobject within D.

The dynamic_cast (c) fails because pb does not point to an object of type D.

Exercise 19.2

Explain when you would use `dynamic_cast` **instead of a virtual function.**

See the class employee on page 1023, L&L. The class provides two virtual functions: `salary()` and `bonus()`. When the pointer pe in payroll points to an object of type programmer and we invoke bonus(),

```
pe->bonus();
```

we invoke the function bonus() defined in the class programmer. If the pointer pe points to an object of type manager and we invoke bonus(), we invoke the function bonus() defined in the class employee because the class manager does not override the virtual function bonus().

Sometimes we want to add new functions in derived classes (such as programmer), but we do not have access to the source code to add new virtual functions such as bonus() in the base class (employee). We resort to adding a function bonus() only in programmer (page 1024, L&L). Now we cannot use the pointer pe in payroll to invoke the function bonus(); we must resort to a dynamic_cast to convert pe to a pointer to programmer to invoke bonus().

The moral of the answer is this: We use dynamic_cast when we cannot add virtual functions to a base class.

Exercise 19.3

Using the class hierarchy defined in Exercise 19.1, rewrite the following piece of code to perform a reference `dynamic_cast` **to convert the expression** *pa **to the type** D&:

```
if (D *pd = dynamic_cast< D* >(pa)) {
    // use D's members
} else {
    // use A's members
}
```

We must change the code a bit. When we use dynamic_cast on a reference, the cast succeeds only when the variable we are casting actually refers to an object that is of a type that has a base class or a derived class that is of the type Type:

```
if (D &pd = dynamic_cast< D& >(pa))
```

A reference is never null (unlike pointers, which may be null), so when a dynamic_cast fails it throws an exception. The modified code must be prepared to handle the exception:

```
try {
    D &pd = dynamic_cast< D& >(pa);
    // use D's members
}
catch (std::bad_cast) {
    // use A's members
}
```

Exercise 19.4

Given the following class hierarchy, in which each class defines a default constructor and a virtual destructor,

```
class X { ... };
class A { ... };
class B : public A { ... };
class C : public B { ... };
class D : public X, public C { ... };
```

which type name in each case is printed to standard output?

(a) `A *pa = new D;`
    `cout << typeid(pa).name() << endl;`

(b) `X *px = new D;`
    `cout << typeid(*px).name() << endl;`

(c) `C cobj;`
    `A &ra = cobj;`
    `cout << typeid(&ra).name() << endl;`

(d) `X *px = new D;`
    `A &ra = *px;`
    `cout << typeid(ra).name() << endl;`

The output for (a), (b), and (c) corresponds to

```
class A *
class D
class A *
```

(d) is incorrect because we cannot convert *px into a reference to A.

Exercise 19.5

Which exceptions might the following functions throw?

```
#include    <stdexcept>


(a) void operate() throw(logic_error);
(b) int  mathOper(int) throw(underflow_error, overflow_error);
(c) char manip(string) throw();
```

"Using an exception specification, a function declaration may specify the exceptions the function may throw directly or indirectly. An exception specification is a guarantee that the function will not throw any exception not listed in the exception specification" (L&L, page 1042). Toward the bottom of page 1044, L&L add, "If an exception specification specifies a class, then the function may throw exception objects of a class publicly derived from the class type in the exception specification."

This means that

```
(a) void operate() throw(logic_error);
```

can throw `logic_error` and any class derived from it (L&L, page 1048). So operate can throw exceptions of type `invalid_argument`, `out_of_range`, `length_error`, `domain_error`, or any other type defined in our program that uses `logic_error` as a base class.

```
(b) int  mathOper(int) throw(underflow_error, overflow_error);
```

can throw `underflow_error`, `overflow_error`, or any other type defined in our program that specifies one of these classes as base classes. If no other class in our program specifies one of these classes as base classes, then only these two classes can be thrown because the C++ standard library does not define classes further derived from these.

```
(c) char manip(string) throw();
```

cannot throw any exception because the exception list is empty.

Exercise 19.6

Explain how C++ exception handling supports the programming technique known as "resource acquisition is initialization; resource release is destruction."

C++ supports the technique "resource acquisition is initialization, resource release is destruction" because the destruction of objects of automatic storage duration is handled automatically; an object of class object with automatic storage duration is guaranteed to be destroyed even though the block in which it is defined exits with an exception. See L&L, page 1042.

Exercise 19.7

Why is the list of catch clauses following the try block incorrect? How would you fix it?

```cpp
#include <stdexcept>

int main()
{
    try {
        // use of the C++ standard library
    }
    catch(exception) {
    }
    catch(const runtime_error &re) {
    }
    catch(overflow_error eobj) {
    }
}
```

The programmer wrote the code by providing a catch clause for the base class first and for the most derived class last. The correct order is the reverse; the catch clause for the most derived (most specialized) class should always appear first, and the one for the base class should always appear last.

Here's a possible fix:

```cpp
#include <stdexcept>
using namespace std;

int main()
{
    try {
        // use of the C++ standard library
    }
    catch(const overflow_error &eobj) {
    }
    catch(const runtime_error &re) {
    }
    catch(exception) {
    }

    return 0;
}
```

Exercise 19.8

Given a basic C++ program,

```
int main() {
  // use the C++ standard library
}
```

modify `main()` to catch any exception thrown by functions in the C++ standard library. The handlers should print the error message associated with the exception before calling `abort()` (defined in the header `<cstdlib>`) to terminate `main()`.

```
#include    <iostream>
#include    <stdexcept>
#include    <cstdlib>
using namespace std;

int main()
{
    try {
        // use of the C++ standard library
    }
    catch (const exception &e) {
        cerr << "exception: " << e.what() << endl;
        abort();
    }
    return 0;
}
```

Exercise 19.9

Given the following class hierarchy, with the following collection of member functions,

```
class Base1 {
  public:
    ostream &print();
    void debug();
    void writeOn();
    void log(string);
    void reset(void *);
    // ...
};
```

```
class Base2 {
  public:
    void debug();
    void readOn();
    void log(double);
    // ...
};


class MI : public Base1, public Base2 {
  public:
    ostream &print();
    using Base1::reset;
    void reset(char *);
    using Base2::log;
    using Base1::log;
    // ...
};
```

which functions are in the set of candidate member functions for the following calls?

```
MI *pi = new MI;
(a) pi->print();     (c) pi->readOn();    (e) pi->log(num);
(b) pi->debug();     (d) pi->reset(0);    (f) pi->writeOn();
```

Call	Candidate Member Functions
(a) pi->print();	MI::print()
(b) pi->debug();	Base1::debug() Base2::debug() the call is ambiguous
(c) pi->readOn();	Base2::readOn()
(d) pi->reset(0);	MI::reset(char *)
(e) pi->log(num);	Base1::log(string) Base2::log(double)
(f) pi->writeOn();	Base1::writeOn()

In (e), the call is not ambiguous right away because both functions are introduced in class MI through using declarations (see L&L, page 1054).

Exercise 19.10

Given the following class hierarchy, with the following collection of conversion functions,

```
class Base {
  public:
    operator int();
    operator const char *();
    // ...
};

class Derived : public Base {
  public:
    operator double();
};
```

which function, if any, is selected as the best viable function for the following calls? List the candidate functions, the viable functions, and the type conversions on the argument for each viable function.

```
(a) void operate(double);
    void operate(string);
    void operate(const Base &);

    Derived *pd = new Derived;
    operate(*pd);

(b) void calc(int);
    void calc(double);
    void calc(const Derived &);

    Base *pb = new Derived;
    calc(*pb);
```

The candidate functions for (a) are

```
    void operate(double);
    void operate(string);
    void operate(const Base &);
```

The viable functions are

```
    void operate(double);
```

because there is a user-defined conversion sequence that uses Derived::operator double() to convert the argument from type Derived to type double, and

```
    void operate(const Base &);
```

See L&L, page 1057, which indicates that "initializing a reference to a base class type with an lvalue of a derived class type" is ranked as a standard conversion.

```
void operate(const Base &);
```

is the best viable function because a standard conversion sequence is always better than a user-defined conversion sequence.

Although there is a conversion function

```
Base::operator const char *();
```

the function

```
void operate(string);
```

is not a viable function because this would require the application of two user-defined conversions in a user-defined conversion sequence, something that is not allowed. That is,

```
Base::operator const char *();
```

would need to convert the object of type Derived to the type const char *, and the constructor for class string

```
string(const char *)
```

would be needed to convert the result of the first conversion to the type string.

The candidates for (b) are

```
void calc(int);
void calc(double);
void calc(const Derived &);
```

The viable function is

```
void calc(int);
```

Because the argument is of class type Base, only the conversion functions in class Base are considered, and there is a type conversion function from Base to int.

The best viable function is

```
void calc(int);
```

because when there is only one viable function, it automatically becomes the best viable function.

chapter twenty

The iostream Library

Exercise 20.1

Given the following object definitions,

```
string sa[4] = { "pooh", "tigger", "piglet", "eeyore" };
vector <string> svec(sa, sa+4);
string robin("christopher robin");
const  char *pc = robin.c_str();
int    ival = 1024;
double dval = 3.14159;
complex<double> purei(0, 7);
```

(a) Print out the value of each object on standard output.

(b) Print out the address value of pc.

(c) Print out the minimum value of ival and dval using the result of the conditional operator:

```
    ival < dval ? ival : dval
```

We write a small program to provide some alternatives.

(a)   Print out the value of each object on standard output.

To print the contents of svec we could use a loop and iterate through and output each individual element (L&L, page 1071).

```
vector<string>::iterator iter = svec.begin();
vector<string>::iterator iter_end = svec.end();
```

```
for ( ; iter != iter_end; iter++)
    cout << *iter << " ";
cout << endl;
```

An `ostream_iterator` can be used to effect the same behavior. We create `output_string` to print `strings` and invoke the standard library algorithm `copy()` with the beginning and ending addresses for sa:

```
ostream_iterator<string> output_string(cout, " ");
copy(sa, sa + 4, output_string);
cout << endl;
```

We print the vector `svec` in a similar manner. We must provide the iterators indicating the beginning and ending addresses for the vector. The `ostream_iterator` is the same as the one we used to print the array sa.

```
copy(svec.begin(), svec.end(), output_string);
cout << endl;
```

The built-in types and the `complex` object do not require special treatment. Note that `pc` is a pointer to char. So `<< pc` prints the array of characters that `pc` points to instead of the value of the pointer itself. See also (b).

```
cout << "robin:\t" << robin << endl;
cout << "pc:\t"    << pc << endl;
cout << "ival:\t"  << ival << endl;
cout << "dval:\t"  << dval << endl;
cout << "purei:\t" << purei << endl;
```

(b) Print out the address value of pc.

We must use a cast as L&L demonstrate in Section 20.1, page 1069: "To print out the address value that `pstr` contains, we must override the default handling of `const char *`. We do this in two steps: first cast the const away, then cast `pc` to type `void *`:"

```
cout << "pc:\t"   << static_cast<void *>(const_cast<char *>(pc))
        << endl;
```

(c) Print out the minimum value of ival and dval using the result of the conditional operator:

```
ival < dval ? ival : dval
```

We must use parentheses because the conditional operator `?:` has lower priority than the output operator `<<` (L&L, page 1070):

```
cout << (ival < dval ? ival : dval) << endl;
```

Exercise 20.2

Read from standard input a sequence of types: `string, double, string, int, string.`
Check whether an input error occurs.

There are many ways we can read the information from standard input and check for input errors. We show two ways.

The first solution reads all the elements from `cin` using one expression in a `while` loop. The advantage is that it is simple. The disadvantage is that we do not pinpoint precisely where the error occurred. We use `cin.eof()` to determine why the loop terminated (see L&L, Section 20.1):

```
string s1, s2, s3;
int    i;
double d;

while (cin >> s1 >> d >> s2 >> i >> s3)
    cout << s1 << "\t" << d << "\t"
         << s2 << "\t" << i << "\t"
         << s3 << endl;
if (cin.eof())
    cerr << "eof\n";
else
    cerr << "input error\n";
```

The second solution tests `cin` after each operation. The advantage is that when the error occurs, we pinpoint where it occurs. The disadvantage is that the code is not as readable as that of the first solution.

```
string s1, s2, s3;
int    i;
double d;

while (cin) {
    cin >> s1;
    if (cin.eof()) {
        cerr << "eof at 1st string\n";
        break;
    } else if (!cin) {
        cerr << "input error at 1st string\n";
        break;
    }
    cin >> d;
    if (cin.eof()) {
        cerr << "eof at double\n";
        break;
```

```
    } else if (!cin) {
        cerr << "input error at double\n";
        break;
    }
    cin >> s2;
    if (cin.eof()) {
        cerr << "eof at 2nd string\n";
        break;
    } else if (!cin) {
        cerr << "input error at 2nd string\n";
        break;
    }
    cin >> i;
    if (cin.eof()) {
        cerr << "eof at int\n";
        break;
    } else if (!cin) {
        cerr << "input error at int\n";
        break;
    }
    cin >> s3;
    if (cin.eof()) {
        cerr << "eof at 3rd string\n";
        break;
    } else if (!cin) {
        cerr << "input error at 3rd string\n";
        break;
    }
    cout << s1 << "\t" << d << "\t"
         << s2 << "\t" << i << "\t"
         << s3 << endl;
}
```

Exercise 20.3

Read from standard input an unknown number of strings. Store them in a list. Determine both the shortest and longest strings.

This solution is similar to the final program in L&L, Section 20.2. We use the same istream iterator to read all the strings and store them into the vector text:

```
istream_iterator<string> input(cin), eos;
vector<string> text;
copy(input, eos, back_inserter(text));
```

We also use the template filter `filter_string` (L&L, Section 20.2) to remove punctuation characters from each string:

```
template <class InputIterator>
void filter_string(InputIterator first, InputIterator last,
                   string filt_elems = string("\",?."))
{
    for ( ; first != last; first++) {
        string::size_type pos = 0;
        while ((pos = (*first).find_first_of(filt_elems, pos))
                                        != string::npos)
            (*first).erase(pos, 1);
    }
}
```

We invoke `filter_string` to remove punctuation characters that appear in `filt_elems`:

```
string filt_elems("\",.?;:");
filter_string(text.begin(), text.end(), filt_elems);
```

The generic algorithm `max_element()` returns the maximum element within a range. The algorithm expects two iterators (the starting and ending points of the data structure), uses `operator <` to perform the comparisons, and returns an iterator positioned at the maximum element in the range. Because we do not wish to use `operator <` to compare the lexical values of the strings, we provide the function `length_less`, which compares the length of two strings and returns `true` when the first string has a length that is less than the length of the second string:

```
bool length_less( const string &s1, const string &s2)
{
    return s1.size() < s2.size();
}
```

We use `max_element()` and `length_less()` to obtain the position of the longest string in the vector `text`:

```
vector<string>::iterator max =
    max_element(text.begin(), text.end(), length_less);
```

We use the same generic algorithm `max_element()` to obtain the shortest string in `text`. We use `length_greater()`, which performs the antisymmetric test:

```
bool length_greater( const string &s1, const string &s2)
{
    return s1.size() > s2.size();
}
```

We use `max_element()` and `length_greater()` to obtain the position of the shortest string in the vector text:

```
vector<string>::iterator min =
    max_element(text.begin(), text.end(), length_greater);
```

Here's the complete main() program:

```
int main()
{
    istream_iterator<string> input(cin), eos;
    vector<string> text;

    copy(input, eos, back_inserter(text));

    string filt_elems("\",.?;:");
    filter_string(text.begin(), text.end(), filt_elems);

    vector<string>::iterator max =
        max_element(text.begin(), text.end(), length_less);
    vector<string>::iterator min =
        max_element(text.begin(), text.end(), length_greater);

    cout << "The number of words read is " << text.size() << endl;
    cout << "The longest word has length of " << max->size() << endl;
    cout << "The longest word is " << *max << endl;
    cout << "The shortest word has length of " << min->size() << endl;
    cout << "The shortest word is " << *min << endl;

    return 0;
}
```

We used the following input:

```
Alice Emma has long flowing red hair. Her Daddy says
when the wind blows through her hair, it looks almost alive,
like a fiery bird in flight. A beautiful fiery bird, he tells her,
magical but untamed. "Daddy, shush, there is no such thing,"
she tells him, at the same time wanting him to tell her more.
Shyly, she asks, "I mean, Daddy, is there?"
```

We obtained the following results:

```
The number of words read is 65
The longest word has length of 9
The longest word is beautiful
The shortest word has length of 1
The shortest word is a
```

Exercise 20.4

Read in the following character sequence from standard input, including all white space, echoing each character in turn to standard output:

```
a   b c
d       e
f
```

Because we must read each character, including white space, we use get(). The function put() writes a character to an output stream.

```cpp
int main()
{
    char c;

    while (cin.get(c))
        cout.put(c);
    return 0;
}
```

Exercise 20.5

Read the sentence "riverrun, from bend of bay to swerve of shore" as (a) a sequence of nine strings and (b) a single string.

We can read each string into a string object. The delimiters are white space characters, so riverrun, is treated as a string. (See Exercise 20.3 and the template function filter_string() to remove the punctuation characters.)

```cpp
string s;
int     cnt = 0;
while (cin >> s)
    cout << ++cnt << "\t" << s << endl;
```

An easy way to read the sentence as a single string involves using the nonmember function getline():

```cpp
getline(istream &is, string &str, char delimiter);
```

Because getline() uses the '\n' as the default delimiter character, we supply the istream and the string objects:

```cpp
string s;

while (getline(cin, s))
    cout << s << endl;
```

Exercise 20.6

Using `getline()` and `gcount()`, read in a sequence of lines from standard input. Determine the largest line read (make sure a line requiring multiple applications of `getline()` is counted as one line).

We read one line at a time, and we concatenate each line into a string tmp. When `gcount()` returns a length less than `lineLength - 1`, it means we found a newline character. Otherwise, we read only part of the line and concatenate the current line with a blank and the existing string. We use `size()` to determine the size of the string, and we initialize max to zero (instead of −1) because `size()` returns an unsigned value. (If we had used −1, it would be converted to a large unsigned value before the comparison to the value returned by `size()`.)

```
const  int lineLength = 100;
char   line[lineLength];
string largestLine = "", tmp = "";
int    len, max = 0;

while (cin.getline(line, lineLength)) {
    len = cin.gcount();                // length of current line
    tmp += line;
    if (len < lineLength - 1) {    // found newline?
        if (tmp.size() > max) {
            max = tmp.size();
            largestLine = tmp;
        }
        tmp = "";                      // empty string
    }
}
cout << "largestLine: " << largestLine << endl;
cout << "has length  " << largestLine.size() << endl;
```

Note that reading in n - 1 characters causes the `istream` to be placed in a fail state. This does not necessarily preclude reading a larger line, but you would have to test `gcount()` to determine what caused the failbit to be set.

Exercise 20.7

Given the following class Date definition,

```
class Date {
  public:
    // ...
```

```
    private:
       int month, day, year;
};
```

provide an overloaded instance of the output operator
(a) generating the format

```
// spell the month out
September 8th, 1997
```

(b) generating the format

```
9 / 8 / 97
```

(c) Which, if either, is preferable? Why?
(d) Should the Date output operator be a friend function? Why? Why not?

(a)   generating the format

```
// spell the month out
September 8th, 1997
```

We add a constructor and a friend operator << to the class Date.

```
class Date {
    friend ostream &operator <<(ostream &, const Date &);
  public:
    Date(int m, int d, int y) : month(m), day(d), year(y) { }
  private:
    int month, day, year;
};
```

The overloaded instance of the operator << is straightforward. Because we must print the month name, we check for a valid month. If the month number is valid, we use it as an index into the array month_name and print its name. Otherwise, we display a question mark (?). We print the proper suffix for the day, follow it with a comma, and then print the year. Here's an overloaded operator << that prints an object of type Date:

```
ostream &operator <<(ostream &os, const Date &d)
{
    char *month_name[] = {
                "January",    "February", "March",     "April",
                "May",        "June",     "July",      "August",
                "September",  "October",  "November",  "December" };
    if (d.month < 1 || d.month > 12)
        os << "? ";
```

```
        else
            os << month_name[d.month - 1] << " ";
        os << d.day;
        if (d.day == 1 || d.day == 21 || d.day == 31)
            os << "st, ";
        else if (d.day == 2 || d.day == 22)
            os << "nd, ";
        else if (d.day == 3 || d.day == 23)
            os << "rd, ";
        else
            os << "th, ";
        os << d.year;
        return os;
    }
```

(b)   generating the format

9 / 8 / 97

This is a simpler implementation of `operator <<`. Because we are asked to display the last two digits of the year, we use the modulus operator (%). It is the "year 2000" problem, but we are conforming to the problem as it is described.

```
    ostream &operator <<(ostream &os, const Date &d)
    {
        if (d.month < 1 || d.month > 12)
            os << "?";
        else
            os << d.month;
        os << " / " << d.day;
        os << " / " << d.year % 100;
        return os;
    }
```

We could add a function to test the validity of day and also account for leap years. Our solution validates only the month.

(c)   Which, if either, is preferable? Why?

This is a question that is subject to different interpretations. For example, the second implementation of the `friend operator <<` uses only numbers and apparently is easier, but differences in interpretation of the numbers are well known. The first implementation spells out the name of the month, but it seems a bit more involved to implement the input to an `operator >>`. Take your pick.

(d)   Should the `Date` output operator be a `friend` function? Why? Why not?

In this case, inline access functions of the `int` data members provide sufficient performance that the output operator need only be a `friend`.

Exercise 20.8

Define the output operator for the following `CheckoutRecord` **class,**

```
class CheckoutRecord {
  public:
    // ...
  private:
    double  book_id;
    string  title;
    Date    date_borrowed;
    Date    date_due;
    pair<string, string> borrower;
    vector <pair<string, string> *> wait_list;
};
```

We add the declaration of the operator << to the class `CheckoutRecord`.

```
friend ostream &operator <<(ostream &os, const CheckoutRecord &c);
```

In the method for operator <<() we display `book_id` and `title`:

```
os << c.book_id << "\t'" << c.title << "'\n";
```

Because `Date` implements its own output operator, we can easily display `date_borrowed` and `date_due`:

```
os << "date borrowed: "  << c.date_borrowed << "\n";
os << "date due:      "  << c.date_due << "\n";
```

The borrower is made up of a pair of `string`s. A pair has two public data members: `first` and `second`. So we display the two strings:

```
os << "borrower:      "  << c.borrower.first << ", "
                         << c.borrower.second << "\n";
```

The last part involves displaying the vector `wait_list`. For each element in the `wait_list` we must display a pair of strings, so we iterate through the vector doing that. The incoming argument c is a const of type `CheckoutRecord`. Because it is a constant, we must use const iterators to traverse the vector:

```
os << "wait list:\n";
vector <pair<string, string> *>::const_iterator iter =
                               c.wait_list.begin();
vector <pair<string, string> *>::const_iterator iter_end =
                               c.wait_list.end();
for ( ; iter != iter_end; ++iter)
    os << "\t" << (*iter)->first << ", " << (*iter)->second << endl;
```

Here's the complete operator <<():

```
ostream &operator <<(ostream &os, const CheckoutRecord &c)
{
    os << c.book_id << "\t'" << c.title << "'\n";
    os << "date borrowed: "  << c.date_borrowed << "\n";
    os << "date due:      "  << c.date_due << "\n";
    os << "borrower:      "  << c.borrower.first << ", "
                             << c.borrower.second << "\n";
    os << "wait list:\n";
    vector <pair<string, string> *>::const_iterator iter =
                                    c.wait_list.begin();
    vector <pair<string, string> *>::const_iterator iter_end =
                                    c.wait_list.end();
    for ( ; iter != iter_end; ++iter)
        os << "\t" << (*iter)->first << ", "
           << (*iter)->second << endl;

    return os;
}
```

Exercise 20.9

The WordCount **input operator directly handles the input of individual** Location **items. Factor this code into a separate** Location **input operator.**

We modify the class Location to support the operator >>:

```
friend istream &operator >>(istream &, Location &);
```

The operator >> for Location is an implementation that comes from part of the input operator for WordCount in L&L:

```
istream &operator >>(istream &is, Location &lc)
{
    int ch;

    while (is && (ch = is.get()) != '<')
        ;
    is >> lc._line;
    while (is && (ch = is.get()) != ',')
        ;
    is >> lc._col;
    while (is && (ch = is.get()) != '>')
        ;
    return is;
}
```

Here's a modified version of operator >> for WordCount:

```
istream &operator >>(istream &is, WordCount &wd)
{
    int ch;

    if ((ch = is.get()) != '<') {
        is.setstate(ios_base::failbit);
        return is;
    }
    int occurs;
    is >> occurs;
    // grab >; not checking for error
    while (is && (ch = is.get()) != '>')
        ;
    is >> wd._word;
    // read each Location
    Location lc;
    for (int ix = 0; ix < occurs; ++ix) {
        is >> lc;
        wd._occurList.push_back(lc);
    }
    return is;
}
```

Exercise 20.10

Provide an input operator for the class Date defined in Exercise 20.7 of Section 20.4.

In Date we add the declaration for operator >>:

```
friend istream &operator >>(istream &, Date &);
```

The implementation looks for x / x / x, where an x represents an int. The last integer represents the last two digits of the year. After we read the number, we add 1900 to it. (This is a Y2K problem, but we are conforming to the problem as it is stated in Exercise 20.7.) The overloaded operator >> looks like this:

```
istream &operator >>(istream &is, Date &d)
{
    // format: x / x / x
    // x is an integer
    int ch;

    is >> d.month;
```

```
        if (!is)
            return is;
        while (is && (ch = is.get()) != '/')
            ;
        is >> d.day;
        while (is && (ch = is.get()) != '/')
            ;
        is >> d.year;
        d.year += 1900;

        return is;
    }
```

With this operator and operator <<, we can write code fragments such as this one:

```
    Date d1;
    cin >> d1;
    cout << d1 << endl;
```

Exercise 20.11

Provide an input operator for the class `CheckoutRecord` **defined in Exercise 20.8 of Section 20.4.**

We add a declaration for the `friend` operator >> in `CheckoutRecord`:

```
    friend istream &operator >>(istream &, CheckoutRecord &);
```

All the work goes into the details of operator >>. We read a `double` value into `book_id` and skip characters until we encounter a ' that marks the beginning of the title. We then use `getline()` to read the book title until the next ':

```
    getline(is, c.title, '\'');         // read the book title 'xxx'
```

The string `date borrowed:` appears on the next line. We discard the newline character and read the string:

```
    is.get();                           // get and ignore newline
    getline(is, tmp, ':');              // read string "date borrowed"
    if (tmp != "date borrowed") {
        is.setstate(ios_base::failbit);
        return is;
    }
```

If the string matches, we use `Date`'s input operator to read the `date_borrowed`:

```
    is >> c.date_borrowed;              // use Date's operator >>
```

We use similar steps to obtain the `date_due`:

```
is.get();                           // get and ignore newline
getline(is, tmp, ':');              // read string "date due"
if (tmp != "date due") {
    is.setstate(ios_base::failbit);
    return is;
}
is >> c.date_due;                   // use Date's operator >>
```

Next, we look for `borrower` and skip blanks until we get to the first character of the borrower's name:

```
is.get();                           // get and ignore newline
getline(is, tmp, ':');              // read string "borrower"
if (tmp != "borrower") {
    is.setstate(ios_base::failbit);
    return is;
}
while (is && (ch = is.get()) == ' ')
    ;                               // get and ignore blanks
is.unget();                         // went one character too far
```

Then we obtain the last name (up to the comma), skip the next blank character, and get the first name. We rebuild the `pair` of strings for the borrower's name:

```
getline(is, tmp, ',');              // read string Lastname
is.get();                           // get and ignore blank
getline(is, tmp2);                  // read string Firstname
c.borrower = make_pair(tmp, tmp2);
```

The final step involves getting the wait list, if one is present. The list is preceded by `wait list:` and a newline character. If there is a wait list, each entry is preceded by a tab character.

```
getline(is, tmp);                   // read string "wait list:"
if (tmp != "wait list:") {
    is.setstate(ios_base::failbit);
    return is;
}
while (is && (ch = is.get()) == '\t') {
    getline(is, tmp, ',');          // get Lastname
    is.get();                       // get and ignore blank
    getline(is, tmp2);              // get Firstname
    c.waitlist(make_pair(tmp, tmp2));
}
is.unget();                         // put back non-tab char
```

Here's the complete version of operator >> for CheckoutRecord:

```
istream &operator >>(istream &is, CheckoutRecord &c)
{
    int ch;
    string tmp, tmp2;
    is >> c.book_id;                        // get the book id
    while(is && (ch = is.get()) != '\'')
        ;
    getline(is, c.title, '\'');             // read the book title 'xxx'
    is.get();                               // get and ignore newline
    getline(is, tmp, ':');                  // read string "date borrowed"
    if (tmp != "date borrowed") {
        is.setstate(ios_base::failbit);
        return is;
    }
    is >> c.date_borrowed;                  // use Date's operator >>
    is.get();                               // get and ignore newline
    getline(is, tmp, ':');                  // read string "date due"
    if (tmp != "date due") {
        is.setstate(ios_base::failbit);
        return is;
    }
    is >> c.date_due;                       // use Date's operator >>
    is.get();                               // get and ignore newline
    getline(is, tmp, ':');                  // read string "borrower"
    if (tmp != "borrower") {
        is.setstate(ios_base::failbit);
        return is;
    }
    while (is && (ch = is.get()) == ' ')
        ;                                   // get and ignore blanks
    is.unget();                             // went one character too far
    getline(is, tmp, ',');                  // read string Lastname
    is.get();                               // get and ignore blank
    getline(is, tmp2);                      // read string Firstname
    c.borrower = make_pair(tmp, tmp2);
    getline(is, tmp);                       // read string "wait list:"
    if (tmp != "wait list:") {
        is.setstate(ios_base::failbit);
        return is;
    }
    while (is && (ch = is.get()) == '\t') {
        getline(is, tmp, ',');              // get Lastname
```

```
            is.get();                          // get and ignore blank
            getline(is, tmp2);                 // get Firstname
            c.waitlist(make_pair(tmp, tmp2));
        }
        is.unget();                            // put back non-tab char
        return is;
    }
```

Exercise 20.12

Using the output operation defined for the Date **class of Exercise 20.7 or** CheckoutRecord **class of Exercise 20.8 (both in Section 20.4), write a program to create and write to an output file.**

We must create a file for output and test whether the file was successfully opened:

```
ofstream out("out");
if (!out) {
    cerr << "cannot open 'out' for output\n";
    exit(-1);
}
```

We could have written

```
ofstream out("out", ios_base::out);
```

but that is redundant because we want to open the file in default output mode.
We create a few objects of type Date, such as

```
Date d1(1, 1, 1997);
```

In Section 20.6, page 1098, L&L state that "user-defined instances of the output operator can also be applied to an ofstream class object." Because Date has an overloaded implementation for the operator <<, we can write

```
out  << d1  << endl;
cout << d1  << endl;
```

The line with out << writes to the file named out. (Note that the output file name is "out" and the object of type ofstream is called out. We are using the object out.) The second line allows us to write the same information to the output screen.
When we complete our task, we close the output file:

```
out.close();
```

Every time we open a file, we use part of a finite resource pod on the system. When we complete our task involving the file, we should free up the resources we were using by explicitly closing the file.

Here's the complete program:
```
#include    <fstream>
#include    <iostream>
using namespace std;

int main()
{
    ofstream out("out");
    if (!out) {
        cerr << "cannot open 'out' for output\n";
        exit(-1);
    }

    Date d0(0, 1, 1997);
    Date d1(1, 1, 1997);
    Date d12(12, 12, 1997);
    Date d13(13, 13, 1997);
    cout << d0  << endl;
    out  << d0  << endl;
    cout << d1  << endl;
    out  << d1  << endl;
    cout << d12 << endl;
    out  << d12 << endl;
    cout << d13 << endl;
    out  << d13 << endl;
    out.close();

    return 0;
}
```

Exercise 20.13

Write a program to open and read the file created in Exercise 20.12. Display the contents of the file to standard output.

The necessary steps for this solution are similar to the steps we took in Exercise 20.12. We used the modified class Date in the solution for Exercise 20.10 because it implements both the operator << and the operator >>.

We must open a file for input and test whether the file was successfully opened:
```
ifstream in("out");
if (!in) {
    cerr << "cannot open file 'out' for input\n";
    exit(-1);
}
```

We create a few objects of type Date, such as

```
Date d1;
```

These objects will receive the information we are reading from the file out (produced by the solution to Exercise 20.12) using the object in of type ifstream.

From L&L, Section 20.6, page 1099, we learn that user-defined instances of the input operator can also be applied to an ifstream class object. Because Date has an overloaded implementation of the operator >>, we can write

```
in >> d1;
```

to read a Date object from in. To display the information we have just read, we use the overloaded operator << created for Date in the solution of Exercise 20.7:

```
cout << d1   << endl;
```

If this is the end of our program, we could skip the step of explicitly closing the file because all the files are properly closed upon the termination of the program. But remember that your program may evolve and open more files. Do the right thing, and explicitly close the file:

```
in.close();
```

Here's the complete program:

```
#include     <fstream>
#include     <iostream>
using namespace std;

int main()
{
    ifstream in("out");
    if (!in) {
        cerr << "cannot open file 'out' for input\n";
        exit(-1);
    }

    Date d1;
    Date d2;
    Date d3;
    Date d4;
    Date d5;
    Date d6;
    Date d7;
    Date d8;
    Date d9;
    Date d10;
    Date d11;
    Date d12;
    Date d13;
```

```
        in >> d1;
        in >> d2;
        in >> d3;
        in >> d4;
        in >> d5;
        in >> d6;
        in >> d7;
        in >> d8;
        in >> d9;
        in >> d10;
        in >> d11;
        in >> d12;
        in >> d13;

        cout << d1  << endl;
        cout << d2  << endl;
        cout << d3  << endl;
        cout << d4  << endl;
        cout << d5  << endl;
        cout << d6  << endl;
        cout << d7  << endl;
        cout << d8  << endl;
        cout << d9  << endl;
        cout << d10 << endl;
        cout << d11 << endl;
        cout << d12 << endl;
        cout << d13 << endl;

        in.close();

        return 0;
    }
```

Exercise 20.14

Write a program to open the file created in Exercise 20.12 for both input and output. Output an instance of either the Date **class or the** CheckoutRecord **class (a) at the beginning of the file, (b) after the second existing object, and (c) at the end of the file.**

To open a file for both input and output, we use the bitwise-OR (|) operator to "add" the two options and then test whether the file was successfully opened:

```
fstream file("out", ios_base::in | ios_base::out);
if (!file) {
    cerr << "cannot open file 'out' for input/output\n";
    exit(-1);
}
```

We create an object d of type Date

```
Date d(3, 4, 98);
```

and we output an instance of the Date class.

(a) at the beginning of the file

Because we will overwrite the first Date record at the beginning of the file, we position ourselves at zero bytes from the beginning of the file and write the object d:

```
file.seekp(0);              // move to the beginning of the file
file << d;                  // write d to the beginning of the file
```

(b) after the second existing object

After overwriting the first record we find ourselves at the beginning of the second record. To overwrite the third record, we move two bytes over (because of \r\n) and then read characters until the next \n:

```
char ch;
file.seekp(2, ios_base::cur);
while (file.get(ch)) {
    if (ch == '\n')         // find the end of next record
        break;
}
file << d;                  // write d after 2nd record
```

Note that if your system stores \n for a newline character (instead of \r\n, which occurs in DOS and Windows), you'll need to change the constant in seekp() from 2 to 1.

(c) at the end of the file

To output an instance of d of type Date at the end of the file, we move to the end of the file:

```
                            // move to the end of the file
file.seekp(0, ios_base::end);
file << d;                  // write d at the end of the file
```

To verify that we have written the appropriate records in the appropriate places of the file, we return to the beginning of the file and read and display each record:

```
                            // return to the beginning of the file
file.seekp(0, ios_base::beg);
while(file >> d)            // read and display the file
    cout << d << endl;
file.close();
```

Here's the complete program:

```
#include    <fstream>
#include    <iostream>
using namespace std;

int main()
{
    fstream file("out", ios_base::in | ios_base::out);
    if (!file) {
        cerr << "cannot open file 'out' for input/output\n";
        exit(-1);
    }

    Date d(3, 4, 98);
    file.seekp(0);             // move to the beginning of the file
    file << d;                 // write d to the beginning of the file

    char ch;
    file.seekp(2, ios_base::cur);
    while (file.get(ch)) {
        if (ch == '\n')        // find the end of next record
            break;
    }
    cout << endl;
    file << d;                 // write d after 2nd record
                               // move to the end of the file
    file.seekp(0, ios_base::end);
    file << d;                 // write d at the end of the file
                               // return to the beginning of the file
    file.seekp(0, ios_base::beg);
    while(file >> d)           // read and display the file
        cout << d << endl;
    file.close();

    return 0;
}
```

Exercise 20.15

**Revise either (or both) the input operator for the Date class of Exercise 20.7 and/or the
CheckoutRecord class of Exercise 20.8 (both in Section 20.4) to set the condition state of
the istream object. Modify the program(s) used to exercise the operator to check for**

the explicit set conditions and, once reported, to reset the condition state of the istream **object. Exercise the revised program by providing both good and bad formats.**

We revise the input operator for the Date class of Exercise 20.10 instead, because it is an improved version of the class in Exercise 20.7.

The input that operator >> handles looks like x / x / x, where x represents an int. The first x could be a question mark (?) generated by the output operator << when the month number is incorrect.

We attempt to read an int into month for the incoming reference argument d. We know that the first number could instead be a ? and that the operation could fail. If the operation fails, we restore is to a good state and skip the remaining characters in the input line (or until EOF):

```
is >> d.month;
if (is.fail()) {                    // invalid input?
    is.clear();                     // reset is
    while (is && ((ch = is.get()) != '\n' && ch != EOF))
        ;                           // skip the remaining of the line
    return is;
}
```

This modification allows us to skip bad input records while reading valid records.

Here's the complete implementation for the revised operator >>:

```
istream &operator >>(istream &is, Date &d)
{
    // format: x / x / x
    // x is an integer; first x could be a ?
    int ch;

    is >> d.month;
    if (is.fail()) {                // invalid input?
        is.clear();                 // reset is
        while (is && ((ch = is.get()) != '\n' && ch != EOF))
            ;                       // skip the remaining of the line
        return is;
    }
    while (is && (ch = is.get()) != '/')
        ;
    is >> d.day;
    while (is && (ch = is.get()) != '/')
        ;
    is >> d.year;
    d.year += 1900;

    return is;
}
```

Examples of good format are

```
1 / 1 / 97
2 / 2 / 97
3 / 3 / 97
```

Examples of bad format are

```
? / 3 / 97
? / 13 / 97
```

Exercise 20.16

In C, the formatting of an output message is accomplished using the standard C `printf()` family of routines. For example, the following program fragment,

```
int ival = 1024;
double dval = 3.14159;
char cval = 'a';
char *sval = "the end";

printf("ival: %d\tdval: %g\tcval: %c\tsval: %s",
        ival, dval, cval, sval);
```

generates

```
ival: 1024    dval: 3.14159    cval: a      sval: the end
```

The first argument to `printf()` is a format string. Each % character indicates that an argument value is to be substituted; the character following indicates its type. Here are some possible types of values supported:

```
%d    integer
%g    floating point
%c    char
%s    C-style string
```

(See [KERNIGHAN88] for a complete discussion.)

The additional arguments to `printf()` are matched positionally to each occurrence of the % format pair. The other characters of the format string are treated as literals and are written directly.

The two primary weaknesses of the `printf()` family of routines are (1) the format string is not extensible to recognize user-defined types and (2) if the type or number of arguments do not match the format string, the error is undetected and the output is badly malformed. The primary appeal of the `printf()` family of routines is the compactness of the format string strategy.

(a)   Generate the equivalent formatted output using an `ostringstream` object.

(b)   Contrast the benefits and drawbacks of the two approaches.

(a) Generate the equivalent formatted output using an `ostringstream` object.

We create an object of type `ostringstream` and send our formatted output to it. To display the formatted object we use the `str()` method.

```
#include     <iostream>
#include     <sstream>
using namespace std;

int main()
{
    int      ival = 1024;
    double   dval = 3.14159;
    char     cval = 'a';
    char    *sval = "the end";

    ostringstream format_string;
    format_string << "ival: "    << ival
                  << "\tdval: " << dval
                  << "\tcval: " << cval
                  << "\tsval: " << sval;
    cout << format_string.str() << endl;

    return 0;
}
```

(b) Contrast the benefits and drawbacks of the two approaches.

Using an `ostringstream` takes a bit more work when compared with the straightforward use of `printf()`. Because we are using the `operator <<`, which is overloaded to support all the built-in types, we know the output will be correct. Although `printf()` is simple, it allows for unpleasant results such as the ones produced by

```
printf("ival: %g\tdval: %d\tcval: %s\tsval: %c\n",
       ival, dval, cval, sval);
```

Here, we attempt to print

- An `int` with %g (instead of %d)

- A `double` with %d (instead of %g)

- A `char` with %s (instead of %c)

- A `char *` with %c (instead of %s)

The preceding statement compiles correctly but produces invalid results. The correct use should be

```
printf("ival: %d\tdval: %g\tcval: %c\tsval: %s\n",
        ival, dval, cval, sval);
```

Although ostringstream requires slightly more typing, the results will never be subject to the pitfalls of a printf() when an incorrect format specifier is used.

See *The C Answer Book,* second edition, by Clovis L. Tondo and Scott E. Gimpel, Prentice Hall, 1989, for solutions to all the exercises in [KERNIGHAN88].

Index

Addison-Wesley Computer and Engineering Publishing Group

How to Interact with Us

1. Visit our Web site

http://www.awl.com/cseng

When you think you've read enough, there's always more content for you at Addison-Wesley's web site. Our web site contains a directory of complete product information including:

- Chapters
- Exclusive author interviews
- Links to authors' pages
- Tables of contents
- Source code

You can also discover what tradeshows and conferences Addison-Wesley will be attending, read what others are saying about our titles, and find out where and when you can meet our authors and have them sign your book.

2. Subscribe to Our Email Mailing Lists

Subscribe to our electronic mailing lists and be the first to know when new books are publishing. Here's how it works: Sign up for our electronic mailing at **http://www.awl.com/cseng/mailinglists.html**. Just select the subject areas that interest you and you will receive notification via email when we publish a book in that area.

3. Contact Us via Email

cepubprof@awl.com
Ask general questions about our books
Sign up for our electronic mailing lists
Submit corrections for our web site

bexpress@awl.com
Request an Addison-Wesley catalog
Get answers to questions regarding your order or our products

innovations@awl.com
Request a current Innovations Newsletter

webmaster@awl.com
Send comments about our web site

mikeh@awl.com
Submit a book proposal
Send errata for an Addison-Wesley book

cepubpublicity@awl.com
Request a review copy for a member of the media interested in reviewing new Addison-Wesley titles

We encourage you to patronize the many fine retailers who stock Addison-Wesley titles. Visit our online directory to find stores near you or visit our online store: **http://store.awl.com/** or call **800-824-7799**.

Addison Wesley Longman
Computer and Engineering Publishing Group
One Jacob Way, Reading, Massachusetts 01867 USA
TEL 781-944-3700 • FAX 781-942-3076